motorcycles

motorcycles

*from the inside out
(and how to keep them
right side up)*

Michael M. Griffin

Prentice-Hall, Inc., Englewood Cliffs, N.J. 07632

Library of Congress Cataloging in Publication Data

GRIFFIN, MICHAEL M (date)
    Motorcycles from the inside out.

    Includes index.
    1. Motorcycles.   2. Motorcycling.   I. Title.
TL440.G697   629.28'4'75   77-12395
ISBN 0-13-604041-1
ISBN 0-13-604033-0 pbk.

© 1978 by Prentice-Hall, Inc.
Englewood Cliffs, New Jersey 07632

Printed in the United States of America

10   9   8   7   6   5   4

PRENTICE-HALL INTERNATIONAL, INC., *London*
PRENTICE-HALL OF AUSTRALIA PTY. LIMITED, *Sydney*
PRENTICE-HALL OF CANADA, LTD., *Toronto*
PRENTICE-HALL OF INDIA PRIVATE LIMITED, *New Delhi*
PRENTICE-HALL OF JAPAN, INC., *Tokyo*
PRENTICE-HALL OF SOUTHEAST ASIA PTE. LTD., *Singapore*
WHITEHALL BOOKS LIMITED, *Wellington, New Zealand*

To Sandra, Bebop, Holmes, Dain, Frank (and Cheryl),
Tony, the late Bob (who was very good to me),
my ear doctor, my back doctor,
and Rich (with whom I go riding a lot).

contents

preface

For many people—too many, really—the motorcycle presents an intimidating image. The bloody things are noisy, critics say, and they are dangerous. They rip up the environment. Furthermore, the sort of person attracted to these unstable projectiles is probably equally unstable. And so it goes.

But negative criticism has always come cheaply, particularly that employing sweeping generalities. Since when should a sport be characterized by its abusers or by its negative aspects? After all, does a sportsplayer's uncivilized conduct exemplify the highest ideals of that sport? No, I'm not saying that all antimotorcycle criticism is unjustified. We have in our ranks our own share of thoughtless, immature individuals just like any other sport. And they've caused problems . . . big ones. Current federal, state, and local laws concerning motorcycle design and application are the result of such behavior. Prospects for the sport's future look dim because of this legislative reaction to motorcycling misbehavior.

As motorcyclists, we should reconcile ourselves to the fact that much of the nonmotorcycling public is so prejudiced. But judicious pursuit of our sport can allay much of this prejudice. Of course, conscientious motorcyclists cannot undo harm done by other bikers in the past. But they can develop personal awareness of the effects their motorcycles have on the environment and other people. A motorcycle, used maturely and properly, poses no threat to life, limb, or environment.

The purpose of this book is to explain to the not-so-experienced motorcyclist what makes his motorcycle go and how to use it without falling off. If, in the process, it even indirectly helps de-fuse a little of the above mentioned prejudice, I would consider it successful.

acknowledgements

I would like to thank the following companies and individuals for permission to use the illustrations listed below:

American Honda Motors Company   Figures 1.13, 1.14, 2.8, 2.9, 2.10, 2.11, 2.12, 2.14, 4.1, 4.3, and 4.9

AMF Harley-Davidson Motor Company, Incorporated   Figures 1.5, 1.6, 1.7, 1.12, 1.18, 1.19, and 1.20

Bell Helmets, Incorporated   Figures 2.1, 2.2, 2.3, 2.4, and 2.5

Bill Walters Leathers, Incorporated   Figure 2.16

Champion Spark Plug Company   Figures 9.6, 9.11, 9.12(a) and (b), 9.13, 9.14, 9.15, 9.17, 9.18, and 9.19

Cycle World magazine   Figures 1.1, 1.2, 1.3, 1.4, 1.8, 1.9, 1.10, 1.11, 1.12, 1.15, 1.16, and 1.17

Tony Murphy   Figure 4.7

Petersen Publishing Company   Figures 6.2, 6.11 (left) and (right), and 6.12

Frank Scurria   Figures 2.7, 2.13, 3.1(a) and (b), 3.2(a), (b), and (c), 3.3, 3.4, 4.8, 4.10, 4.11, 4.12, 4.13, 4.15(a) and (b), 9.1, and 11.1

U.S. Suzuki Motor Corporation   Figures 2.6, 4.2, and 4.5

Yamaha International   Figures 2.15, and 4.4

Michael M. Griffin

motorcycles

1 the history of motorcycling

Innovation, Evolution . . . and Inspiration

Man's greatest invention, the wheel, was not an invention at all—it was a discovery. Prehistoric man probably found a flat, circular rock and began rolling it along as he walked in his apelike manner. The rotating rock, which rolled along as he walked, must have fascinated him. An inward satisfaction was fulfilled, a kind of entertainment. Just as the first wheel fascinated the inquisitive caveman, it also frustrated him. How could this piece of rock, with its flat sides and round diameter, roll so lazily next to him? Why did he have to push it to make it move? Well, as the pages of history began to turn, man did in fact learn to make good use of that fateful discovery—the wheel.

He began by hitching two wheels to a common axle, then affixing this assembly to a box. The cart was born. He could put heavy loads in it and could pull the cart, perhaps with the help of a neighbor friend. Soon, animals were domesticated by man, relieving him of some of the burden in pulling the cart. At this stage, man seemed to be satisfied with his inventive fortitude and conquest of beasts. The horsedrawn carriage, and various other modes of transportation, evolved. But when he got right down to it, man still relied on animals for power—or he had to do it himself, which put him back about three million years.

Suddenly, about the end of the eighteenth century, man began to awake, both spiritually and mentally. The age of revolutions arose. His destiny of self-government made him aware of his inner self, the rights of man. And the awareness he sought awoke an even more powerful force within him: the ability to create and invent. The Industrial Revolution began. That was in the early 1800s, and it hasn't stopped since.

Now, what does this have to do with the motorcycle? Plenty! For millions of years, man used his discovery of the wheel to his advantage, but he never really worked to improve it the way he has since the Industrial Revolution. Man's mechanical prowess led him to his invention of the motorcycle—but not without several flops, some peculiar machinery, and an undaunted willingness to succeed.

The motorcycle actually had its origins as a bicycle (Fig. 1.1). Through the ingenious resources of such men as Gottlieb Daimler, Sir H. C. L. Holden, and the Werner brothers of France, the motorcycle soon got its birth. These first machines were crude by today's standards. But you must remember, there was no precedent for design then as there is today. To compound the difficulty, components commonly had to be sought from existing manufacturers; that is to say, there were no engines intended for motorcycle use. The inventor either had to make one from scratch or adapt the desired part intended for industrial use to his two-wheeled contraption. Engineering a motorcycle in the early days was a rugged task, indeed.

FIGURE 1-1. Early motorcycles were typically little more than motorized bicycles, as exemplified by this 1899 Werner.

When discussing the history of the motorcycle, it would be wise for us to look back at what is accredited as having been the first true motorcycle. It was a very primitive machine compared to today's multicylinder, exotic luxury bikes such as the Kawasaki 1000 and the MV 750 four. The inventor was a German named Gottlieb Daimler, who would later go on to make history as one of the early automobile pioneers. In 1886, Daimler unveiled his two-wheeler (although, in fact, the machine had two side wheels as well, which we will also describe). The bike, including the ten-spoke rims, was made predominantly of wood. The small wheelbase of 40 inches made for a very short, squatty machine. A rounded pad atop the engine served as Herr Daimler's seat. The engine was a most unusual piece of equipment. Remember, the four-cycle engine was still being developed at this time, so Daimler had to make his own. This he did in 1885. The ignition was basic: a Bunsen burner-type flame, which shot into the combustion chamber. The only premix system for fuel and air was through the fuel line leading to the flame. (Fuel, incidently, was either coal, or whale oil, whichever was on hand.) Since there was no carburetor float bowl to keep fuel from spilling when the bike was leaned to either side during turns, two small wheels were positioned on either side of the bike. These side wheels helped keep the machine erect, thus preserving the fuel. They also served as side stands, alleviating another problem for Daimler, who was more concerned with operation than aesthetics.

With an engine speed of less than 1000 rpm, Daimler took his bike out for the trial run, which turned out less than encouraging when the bike's engine failed to come to life. The second time out, with all the bugs worked free, the bike ran for a total of 17 miles, an incredible distance when you consider that the roads of his day were rough dirt paths used by horse-drawn carriages, not the smooth, paved boulevards of today.

The year 1886, then, marked the first run of a true motor-driven cycle. Subsequent years would reveal machines much more sophisticated, but only after many attempts by their inventors. By the turn of the century, manufacturers of motorcycles were mounting some very reliable (for the time) engines into bicycle frames constructed of steel tubing. The result was a dependable piece of equipment that would not create too many problems for the rider.

While Daimler was busy designing his wooden motorcycle on the continent, across the English Channel another German, Siegfried Berrmann, began a bicycle shop that would one day produce some of the world's finest motorcycles. For about 15 years, he built and repaired bicycles in his London shop, all the time keeping in the back of his mind a motor-driven two-wheeler that he would one day build. Then, in 1902, another German, M. J. Shulte, joined Berrmann in his shop, and the two of them began constructing their first motorcycle. It had a single-cylinder engine, with a bore of 66 mm and a stroke of 70 mm. The engine featured an automatic inlet valve and battery-coil ignition. The engine was positioned below the front downtube of the bicycle frame, helping to set the precedent for future designs. It was a smashing success, and the two Germans decided to go into business manufacturing and servicing their machines. That was the start of the Triumph motorcycle company.

In the early years, the factory was concerned very much with racing their machines to help prove the speed and reliability for marketing purposes. But by the mid-1920s, racing had become such an expensive and time-consuming enterprise that the factory had to withdraw. It was during this era that race bikes began to look less and less like the ordinary street bikes that were sold. To race and win required a special motorcycle designed and developed for racing only. Triumph wanted to race their production models and so could not compete with the other factories without producing out-and-out racers. Not until after World War II did Triumph go back to racing, using their Tiger 100. It was one of the first postwar production racers, built and sold by Triumph. The bike offered the privateer a chance to buy a race-ready motorcycle capable of competing to some degree against the leading factory bikes of the time, including Norton, AJS, and Gilera. Triumph's most recent racing effort occurred in 1970, when the factory sported a complete team for the American Motorcyclist Association Grand National Championship circuit. Based on the Triumph Trident 750 roadster, the racers were fast machines. Dick Mann won the 1971 Daytona 200 aboard a BSA 750 three, which was basically the same machine as the Triumph, only under different marketing colors. This was the result of a merger between BSA and Triumph some years before, putting both factories, which had been hard hit by labor strikes and rising costs, under one roof. The merger, it was felt, would save both companies from insolvency, thus helping to keep England at the forefront of the world's motorcycle market. But the Japanese onslaught proved too much, and BSA was dropped entirely, while the Triumph name was put under Norton's guidance.

Besides Triumph and BSA (Fig. 1-2), another famous name to make its mark on the motorcycle scene at the turn of the century was Indian. From the very beginning, Indian was a success, almost a household word for people everywhere. The American company began, as so many of the early manufacturers did, by building bicycles. At the turn of the century, George Hendee made some of the best bicycles in New England. About the same time, Oscar Hedstrom was racing motorcycles on the rough, dusty tracks in New York. He was a rather good rider, his mounts

FIGURE 1-2. This early BSA motorcycle featured side valves, chain primary drive, and a leather belt final drive.

having competitive engines but lacking well-constructed frames. Hedstrom met Hendee at a bicycle show, and the two decided to build a motorcycle together, Hendee putting his knowledge about frames into the project, while Hedstrom would produce the engines.

In May, 1901, the first bike rolled out of the shop. It featured a bowl-type carburetor (a novelty for the day), allowing for easy starting (another novelty!). An interesting feature, one we take for granted today, was the chain drive. Most early motorcycles used a leather belt for rear-wheel drive, because there were not many small chains available for use. The bike proved so popular in the local community that production soared to three units by year's end. Indian now had a foundation on which to build; from that time on, they never looked back. By 1904, production had skyrocketed to 546 machines (Fig. 1.3). As the company grew, the owners had to expand facilities and divide some of the chores. It was decided that Hedstrom would take over the production and Hendee would take care of managerial chores. The decision proved most important, for Indian continued to grow under the guidance of these two men. In 1905, Indian introduced their first V-twin, a design that would

FIGURE 1-3. Single-cylinder 1903 Indian.

stay with them until the demise of the company at midcentury. Not to ignore innovations, they introduced the first magneto ignition to the motorcycle world in 1908. Three years later, a two-speed transmission was offered, again a first. This proved to be one of the greatest contributions made by Indian to the development of motorcycles. Proof of the variable-speed transmission over the old single-gear primary drive was evidenced as Indian walked away from the competition at the Isle of Man Tourist Trophy (TT) races of 1911.

Indian continued to make history with their bikes, either by introducing new technical advancements to their production models or by setting the racetracks afire with their speed and reliability. The year following their Isle of Man TT victory, Charles B. Franklin took one of the V-twin racers out and went 300 miles in 300 minutes, the first time that feat was ever accomplished on a motorcycle. Franklin would later join the Indian company after World War I, helping to continue Indian's technical dominance over the rest of the motorcycle fraternity.

Many riders raced Indians, but one who became a legend was Cannonball Baker. In 1919, Cannonball made his first three-flag run: from Canada through the United States and into Mexico, in record time. His bike was a new Indian. Six years later, he straddled the Indian V-twin on the smooth, hard-packed sandy beaches at Daytona Beach, Florida to clock 125 miles per hour. The following year he upped his record to an astronomical 132 mph.

Indian continued to play a major role in the motorcycle industry (Fig. 1-4). Like many of the large companies around the world, however, it was hard hit by the Great Depression. With sales on almost every continent before the Big Crash, Indian had to withdraw many of its employees for regrouping. When World War II began, the company was given an economic reprieve in the form of large government contracts to build motorcycles for the U.S. Army. After V-J Day, Indian once again went into the red. A hasty marketing survey revealed that the postwar American motorcyclist now preferred a new kind of machine. So, rather than stick to the rugged 1200-cc V-twin, Indian shifted their resources to building lighter, quicker vertical twin-cylinder machines, much like England's Triumph and Royal Enfield. This proved to be a disastrous step, however, for now Indian had to compete against the lower-priced machinery from Europe. Devaluation of the English pound helped decrease the price for their bikes even more, a move that all but extinguished the Indian Scout. Although it featured a four-speed transmission, telescopic forks, and magneto ignition, the bike unfortunately was mechanically troublesome for its owners. By 1953, production ceased. To keep the Indian name in motorcycle showrooms, the company made a deal with the English firm of Royal Enfield to import their bikes and

FIGURE 1-4. Some of Indian's most popular models in the 1920s and '30s were those powered by four-cylinder engines. The model shown also has leaf spring front suspension and a rigid rear axle.

sell them under the Indian brand name. Meanwhile, Harley-Davidson continued to provide a horsepower-hungry America with the big 1200 V-twin, which had become the figurehead of American motorcycle technology.

The history of Harley-Davidson closely parallels that of Indian in the early years. Again, the bicycle was the underlying factor leading to the design of the first Harley-Davidson motorcycle. The enterprise began when two young friends, Bill Harley and Arthur Davidson of Milwaukee, Wisconsin, got together to invent a bicycle that would utilize the energy of a small motor to help in climbing steep hills. Work was begun in the middle of 1901.

With the help of Arthur Davidson's two brothers, William and Walter, the four began preparations for the first bike in the Davidson's basement, usually late into the night and on Sundays. By year's end, the first bike was produced (Fig. 1-5). The engine had a bore of 2-1/8 inches and a stroke of 2-7/8 inches. It proved fairly reliable, generating three horsepower. The carburetor was made from a tomato can, typifying the resourcefulness needed at the time to make a motorcycle. Although three horsepower was a considerable amount they felt that still more power was needed. So it was back to the workshop for the quartet. The next engine had a bore and stroke measuring 3 by 3-1/2 inches. The flywheel was also enlarged from 5 to 11-1/2 inches in diameter. The

FIGURE 1-5.   The first Harley-Davidson motorcycle was this model made in 1903.

FIGURE 1-6.   This 12- by-15 foot shed was the first Harley-Davidson factory.

tomato-can carburetor was also replaced with a more satisfactory unit. The result was a very efficient machine.

A shed built in the backyard of the Davidson's home marked the beginning of a 75-year history for the Harley-Davidson factory (Fig. 1-6). The present site is in a different location and is much larger than the original 12-by-15-foot structure! The first year of production saw three bikes roll off the assembly line. Old records indicate that the first machine was sold to a man named Miller, who rode the bike for 6000 miles before turning it over to one George Lyon, who added another 15,000. The third owner, a Doctor Webster, wound it around for another 18,000 miles before selling it to Louis Fluke, who rode the bike for 12,000 miles. The last known owner was Stephen Sparrow, who put on a whopping 32,000 miles, making a total of 65,000 miles traveled on the very first Harley-Davidson sold!

Like Indian, Harley-Davidson preferred to race their motorcycles to prove their speed and reliability. Harleys were known for their great speed, often finishing one-two-three in races (Fig. 1-7). One of the most renowned showdowns between the two companies occurred in England. In 1921, at the fabled Brooklands banked track, three bikes were rolled out to trackside for an attempt at attaining the 100-mile-per-hour figure, a mark that had eluded competitors up to that time. Two Harleys

FIGURE 1-7. 1913 single-cylinder Harley-Davidson powerplant.

were entered, ridden by Englishmen Douglas Davidson and Claude Temple. The lone Indian, of 1911 vintage, was ridden by Bert Le Vack, also from England. The Indian was a very sophisticated racer for its day, sporting four valves per cylinder and twin cylinders. The Harleys were brand new from the factory and represented the first concerted effort since the war at producing a bike solely for competition use. The hard adder-gauge tires made for a rough ride on the steeply banked track. Nevertheless, the three were willing to risk life and limb at topping the "ton." First to try was Temple, aboard his Harley. A run of 97.26 mph told the other two that it was going to be a rough go. Le Vack rolled the Indian out and upped the speed to 98.98, close but still not enough. Temple made one more pass, this time just missing the mark at 99.96. His ante was high, but 0.04 second held Temple from being the first man ever to go 100 mph on a motorcycle. Then Douglas strapped his leather helmet on and buzzed his Harley V-twin around the track for several laps. After a final check, he was ready for the attempt. With his machine sounding very healthy and his vision blurred by the terrific bouncing by the bike, he set the record at 100.76! He did it, putting Harley-Davidson into the record books as the first motorcycle ever to go 100 mph. But Le Vack was sure his ten-year-old Indian could equal or top the speeds set by the brand new Harleys. The next day he proved it by whistling through at an incredible 106.52 mph. This showdown was to set the stage for American motorcycle supremacy over the rest of the world for the next few years.

Harley-Davidson hasn't quit racing since. In the process the company has accumulated over 250 AMA Grand National wins, more than any other brand. Moreover, more AMA Grand National Championships have been won on the big orange and black racers from Milwaukee than on any other bike. (Grand National races comprise the Grand National circuit for a given year; the Grand National Championship. Each race win is worth a certain amount of points, second place finish a few less points, third place fewer and so on down the line. The racer earning the most racing points becomes Grand National Champion for a year.) Riders such as Joe Leonard, Carroll Resweber, Bart Markel, Mert Lawwill, Mark Brelsford, and Gary Scott won the Number One plate riding for Harley.

While Indian and Harley-Davidson were fighting it out for supremacy in America and around the globe, other small manufacturers were trying to establish themselves in the budding industry. Most were located in England and continental Europe. One of these companies was Norton, based in England. The firm was started in 1898 by James Norton, a very successful engineer. Norton had been building four-cycle engines for other companies when he decided in 1898 to build his own motorcycle. By 1908, he had developed a large 633-cc engine that was to prove very successful. A smaller model, measuring 500 cc, was developed a short time later. Its bore and stroke of 79 mm × 100 mm were destined to become legendary, setting the style for almost all Norton 500-cc engines from then on. These early Nortons had side-valve heads, which were not as efficient as the overhead valve arrangements found on the more successful motorcycle engines of the day. So James Norton redesigned the head and came up with a very potent 500-cc single. In 1929, Norton entered his overhead valve 500-cc singles in competition, winning many races and establishing his motorcycles as leading contenders in all races entered. The year 1924 marked the first-ever Isle of Man TT win for Norton with an earlier bike (Fig. 1-8). Ridden by Alec Bennett, a Norton motorcycle won the 500-cc class; the first of many future successes. The last 500-cc class win for Norton at the rugged Isle of Man was in 1961. Two years later, Norton discontinued production of the fabled Manx racer, one of the most successful production racers in motorcycling history (Fig. 1-9). Intended as a low-cost production racer, the legendary Manx proved that the basic design can be reliable, fast, and reasonably economical. Today, however, like Triumph and BSA, Norton has undergone troubled times. Time and again in recent years, union labor prob-

FIGURE 1-8.   This Norton V-twin competed at the very first Isle of Man road race.

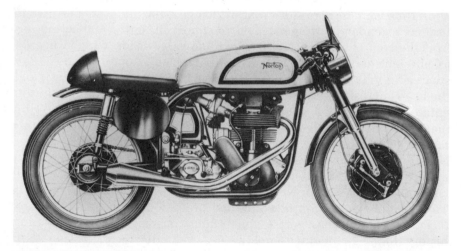

FIGURE 1-9.   The Norton Manx road racer, last produced in 1963, was one of the most successful production racers in the history of motorcycle competition.

lems have crippled production, and quality control has nose-dived. Regrettably, its future is shaky.

When discussing English motorcycles, some enthusiasts are impelled to wax lyrical over three other fabled brands: Brough Superior, Vincent, and Ariel. During their best times, these companies represented a level of development yet to be attained by other parts of the industry. Each made high claims—"the Luxury Motorcycle" (Ariel), "the World's Fastest Motorcycle" (Vincent), and "the Rolls Royce of Motorcycles" (Brough Superior). Interestingly, with regard to the last slogan, it is said that an emissary from Rolls Royce was sent to the Brough Superior factory; the R-R firm, it seems, had taken exception to Brough's use of their name in advertising. After inspection of the Brough Superior facilities, the Rolls Royce representative agreed with the claim and gave it his firm's corporate blessing!

Indeed, of the three brands, Brough Superior has the most colorful history. Designed by George Brough in 1920, the motorcycle was conceived in direct response to the dominance of the large-displacement motorcycle field by Indian and Harley-Davidson. George Brough, like so many other Englishmen, wanted to produce the "definitive" motorcycle. Within a ten-year span, his machines came to be regarded throughout the industry as the ultimate blend of civility, quality, and performance. One of the more notable Brough Superior owners was T. E. Lawrence, poet, scholar, gentleman, and motorcycle enthusiast, most famous for his feats as a soldier during World War I fighting in the deserts of Arabia. Lawrence of Arabia owned seven Brough Superiors. His eighth was on order when he crashed fatally while riding an English country road. So much did Colonel Lawrence love his Brough Superior SS 100 that he often wrote of what he felt while riding, the following being a fair example: "The burble of my exhaust unwound like a long cord behind me. Then my speed snapped it and I heard only the cry of the wind, which my battered head split and fended aside." Lawrence recorded almost 300,000 miles on his Broughs, a respectable figure even today.

The Ariel was famed for its somewhat unorthodox cylinder arrangement (Fig. 1-10). Its four cylinders were deployed in a square, which quickly earned the marque the nickname "Squariel." The first model was a 500-cc version. In later models, engine capacity was upped to 600 cc and then to a full 1000 cc. Excessive vibration was a common problem found in most motorcycles of that day, but not in the Ariel. It also incorporated a rear suspension, adding to smoothness of ride. This was significant because most motorcycles of the time had no rear suspension at all. For these reasons, the Ariel was regarded by many as the luxury motorcycle of the day.

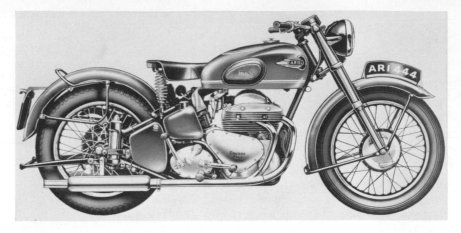

FIGURE 1-10. The Ariel Square four had a quartet of cylinders arranged in two pairs, one behind the other. Two crankshafts were used.

And, of course, there was the fabled Vincent. The first model, introduced in 1934, caused a stir from the beginning because of its performance. This initial model had a 500-cc single-cylinder engine; two years later, a larger, more powerful model was forthcoming. Singles notwithstanding, it was the awesome 1000-cc V-twins produced by Vincent which earned the most accolades. The Rapide, for example, predecessor to the famed Black Shadow, was, in all likelihood, the fastest stock motorcycle a man could buy (Fig. 1-11). Although some-

FIGURE 1-11.   The Vincent Rapide: a 1938 model. These machines were complex, innovative, and fast.

what hampered by mediocre handling and indifferent brakes, the rumbling Vincent twins commanded respect wherever they appeared. Black Shadow owners, however, often got caught up in the machine's legend, and it was not unusual for proud owners to boast of having motorcycles capable of attaining 150 mph! This claim was largely based on the Vincent speedometers, which struck fear in the hearts of competitors with its 150-mph upper limit. The speedometer register was more for psychological impact than anything else, though. In actuality, a crisply tuned Black Shadow could achieve 123–125 mph, somewhat short of the fabled 150-mph mark but still significantly faster than its competitors of that era.

The last Vincent was made in the mid-1950s; the company ceased production for a variety of corporate reasons. Nevertheless, the Vincent still represents to many motorcyclists the climax of British motorcycle engineering.

In the early days of the industry, not all motorcycle development was taking place in England and the United States. Italy, too, contributed to the rapidly expanding field of motorcycle technology. And today Italian motorcycles still represent a verve, a sensuality combined with style and performance, that has yet to be duplicated by other manufacturers. Italy is the land of the artisan, and its motorcycles reflect the ethic.

The story begins back in 1909, when a young Italian inventor named Giuseppe Gilera took up the challenge to make his first motorcycle. Within a very short time, the popularity of his machines exceeded his highest expectations. As business grew and grew, Gilera decided to join the fray and go racing, as many factories were. Gilera's first win came in 1912. Riding along the pounding dirt roads of Italy, he averaged a remarkable 28 mph. By 1931, his small Italian factory had established itself as a front-runner on international racing circuits, having won a trophy in the punishing competition of the International Six Days Trial.

But probably the most awesome machines produced by the Gilera factory were its dual-overhead camshaft, four-cylinder road racers of the 1950s. These machines were capable of awesome speed and, for a time, were technologically the ultimate motorcycles.

Another front-runner from Italy was the Benelli motorcycle. Typical of many companies of that time, Benelli entered the industry first as a repair and service company; looking after other makes before producing its own machines. The firm consisted of six mechanically inclined Benelli brothers. That was in 1923. One day, one of the brothers talked the other five into helping him build a racing motorcycle. This machine was completed in 1927. For the next nine years, the comparatively small motorcycle with its 175-cc overhead camshaft engine dominated racing in Italy. By the end of the '30s, Benelli had also successfully contested the 250-cc class with victory at the Isle of Man.

When the war broke out, Benelli, like the rest of Italian industry, was marshaled into producing military goods for the Italian government. Bombed by the Nazis in the later years of the war, the factory was also torn inside out by the evacuating German army, who were desperately searching for one of the intricate and highly advanced 250-cc four-cylinder racing engines that Benelli was developing when the war started. Although their search was unsuccessful, the Germans acquired much valuable data, and it is interesting to note that the very successful German 250-cc NSU racer of postwar years bore an uncanny resemblance to the 1939 Isle of Man winner.

Benelli resumed racing at war's end, but with the death of their top rider, Dario Ambrosini, in 1951, all efforts were stopped. It was not until 1964 that Benelli returned with the introduction of an air-cooled in-line four-cylinder bike, ridden by the famous Tarquino Provini, and later by the late Renzo Pasolini. In 1969, Kel Carruthers, an Australian, rode a much-modified version of this bike to the World Championship, marking the last time the Italian firm ever won this prestigious title.

Postwar Italy brought on two more dominating Italian motorcycle firms. One company got its start building airplane engines as far back as 1907. The founder was Giovanni Augusta, and for the next 38 years, the company he founded was manufacturing airplanes for Italy and the world. At war's end, however there was very little demand for this product in a war-torn state, so one of his sons, Domenico, decided to change production to motorcycles, specializing in small, inexpensive transportation vehicles. The company name was also changed to Meccanica Verhara Augusta, or, as it is more commonly known, MV Augusta. The first bike produced was a small 98-cc single-cylinder two-stroke. From that small beginning evolved some of the world's most sophisticated racers, including an air-cooled, four-cylinder, dual-overhead camshaft racer measuring 500 cc.

Throughout its history as a company, MV has been involved in world championship road racing and has won more titles than any other brand. Even in 1957, when the Italian motorcycle industry attempted a self-imposed ban on racing, MV alone said no and continued to dominate the flamboyant, fast-moving world of Grand Prix road racing. Their first world title came in 1952, when Cecil Sanford rode the 125-cc single to the world crown. Since that time, such notable racers as John Surtees, Mike Hailwood, Carlo Ubbiali, and the very distinguished Giacomo Agostini have ridden MVs to world championships (Fig. 1-12).

The other postwar Italian company is Ducati. Beginning in 1950, the small factory even had some of its shares of stock owned by the

FIGURE 1-12. In the history of road racing, rider Giacomo Agostini and MV Augusta motorcycles have won more championships than anyone else. Here, Agostini is on the 500-cc MV Augusta triple at Assen, Holland.

Italian government and the Vatican! Ducati by far has produced some of the most modern four-stroke engine designs ever seen. The most monumental piece of equipment to come from Ducati was the desmodromic valve arrangement, which eliminated valve float at high engine speeds. Ducati has always prided itself in producing some of the best single-cylinder four-cycle motorcycle engines ever, as well as a fast, fine-handling, stylish V-twin roadster, utilizing the desmodromic valve assembly.

Today the firm of Moto Guzzi, the last Italian company to be mentioned here, has confined its manufacturing efforts to large displacement touring and sporting motorcycles. These machines, powered by traversely mounted V-twin power plants, have proven themselves capable of high power output and superior reliability. As evidence of these traits, the touring Moto Guzzi has established itself in modified form among many police departments throughout the world as an excellent mount for patrol work. And in the competition arena, Moto Guzzi production racers have garnered an impressive string of speedway victories, with particular success at such ultrahigh-speed tracks as Daytona Beach, Florida and Imola, Italy.

However, most long-time motorcycle enthusiasts will agree that Moto Guzzi's best road-racing days were in the late 1930s and then in the 1950s. The prewar years saw the emergence of the Moto Guzzi 500-cc single-cylinder racer. This mount was respected both for its fine handling and excellent acceleration off the corners, traits which made it a short circuit favorite. The 1950s saw this basic configuration significantly refined for yet even more power and speed. Additionally, the street version of the machine, the Falcone, has survived these many years with mechanical updates into the 1970s. It is regarded as supremely quiet and reliable, although these models are somewhat difficult to obtain outside of the European continent because of limited exporting. Nonetheless, the Falcone is highly cherished by motorcycle purists everywhere.

But all continental motorcycle racing development was not confined to Italy. Germany, for example, had also blazed many a technological trial. BMW, an acronym for Bayerische Motoren Werke, or Bavarian Motor Works, was well established as an aircraft parts manufacturer when it became involved in motorcycle production. Although many different engine configurations were tried in those early days, the opposed twin-cylinder design was adopted in the early 1920s. Significantly, BMW motorcycles to this day still use this engine configuration. Ditto the famed BMW shaft drive, a design long on reliability and mechanical strength. What were probably BMW's greatest racing successes came at the hands of talented Georg Meier, a road racer and engine developer of remarkable abilities. Under Meier's guidance, many engines of different configurations and displacements were developed, probably the most dramatic of which was a 500-cc supercharged twin that established many international speed records in the years before World War II.

Today, BMW motorcycle racing is largely confined to production class competition. Machines of this category are required to maintain a close resemblance to showroom stock mounts, including mufflers, lights, and other road equipment. Even so, these 1000-cc opposed twins, although modified within the extent of the racing rules, are capable of producing about 100 horsepower and attaining 150 mph.

Perhaps BMW's most interesting competitive endeavor is its yearly participation in the International Six Days Trial, or ISDT. This is primarily an off-road event, hosted by a different country each year. It is regarded as the single most prestigious enduro contest in the world, where not just factories field their own teams but countries send their national teams as well, notably the Czechoslovakians, Russians, and Poles. A competitor's success here is predicated upon his acquiring as few penalty points as possible through a variety of contests encompassing six full days of riding. And while this primarily off-road fete would tend to favor lighter, nimbler two-stroke dirt motorcycles, the specially prepared 750-cc BMWs—easily the most massive machines in the contest—almost always seem to return home victorious in their class, certainly no mean feat for a 400-pounder competing with motorcycles weighing 150 pounds less.

Although most early technological motorcycle development occurred in America and Europe, it was not until the Japanese got involved shortly after World War II that the industry began to make headlong strides toward becoming a very sophisticated market. Shortly after the war's end, Japan was in dire need of inexpensive transportation for its people. This circumstance led many small firms to try and produce a worthwhile machine. Of the 100 or so companies that tried, only four really succeeded—Honda, Suzuki, Yamaha, and Kawasaki. All have unique histories, but none parallels that of the Honda firm.

Soichiro Honda, founder of Honda Motor Company, has sometimes been called the Henry Ford of the motorcycle industry, and for good reason. Just as Henry Ford was able to change the course of the automobile industry with his assembly-line tactics, so too did Soichiro Honda alter the course of the motorcycle industry with his methods of continual research and development, not to mention his unique marketing program that helped make Honda as synonomous with "motorcycle" as Frigidare is with "refrigerator."

Honda was born in Komyo, Japan in 1906, and from his earliest childhood loved mechanical things. His father's bicycle shop provided him with an exposure to two-wheel transportation that was to prove invaluable when he established his company in 1948. The first motorbike to roll out of the newly formed Honda company headquarters had a small two-cycle engine set within the confines of a bicycle frame. Five hundred of those were made until Honda ran out of engines. With a short supply of any usable motors in Japan, Honda decided to build his own motor. This proved to be one of the smartest moves he ever made. Ever since, the firm has been admirably independent of other companies, manufacturing itself what parts it needs.

As business picked up in the early '50s, Honda began to have a dream motorcycle he wished to sell to the Japanese public. In 1949, the first Dream machine was put into production. Power came from a small two-cycle engine putting out 2-1/2 horsepower. A chain drive was used, coupled to a two-speed transmission. The Dream became an instant success, so Honda decided to introduce a new model, the Benly, meaning "convenience" in Japanese. Both helped to establish Honda as one of the leading Japanese motorcycle manufacturers.

But Honda had even wilder dreams of becoming an international company. The only way he knew he could do that was to make Honda famous very quickly. As is often the case in motorcycling, the best way to become well known within the industry is to race on the international circuit. This Honda did. The first task was to design a machine capable of competing on an equal level with the well-proven European racers that had been on the world championship circuits from the very beginning. In 1959, Honda finally decided to butt heads with the rest of the world's motorcycle racing family. The setting was the Isle of Man TT, where a win or high finish would certainly make the presence of Honda known. There were three Honda 125-cc twin-cylinder four-cycle bikes entered. The suspension was archaic by European standards, featuring a leading link suspension on the front forks. Although the motors proved reliable, speed was definitely lacking. After placing sixth, seventh, and eighth and winning the team trophy, Honda rounded up his bikes and re-grouped to Japan, where much more R and D was needed . . . and done.

The mark of a new decade also marked the first full year of racing by Honda (Fig. 1-13). Along with new machinery, including a new 125-cc twin-cylinder and a 250-cc four-cylinder, top-notch riders were hired, captained by the Rhodesian, Jim Redman. Although no championships were won, it became very apparent that Honda would soon dominate the small-bore classes with their high-revving multicylinder machines. The following year, Honda won both the 125-cc and 250-cc class champion-ships, and hired the talents of Mike Hailwood, who was on his way to becoming probably the greatest motorcycle road racer ever.

As the decade progressed, so did the number of Honda wins and world championships. Before the factory pulled out of racing at the

The 1959 'double-knocker' Honda twin, '125'

FIGURE 1-13.   This was Honda's first road race machine. Made in 1959, it featured a 125-cc, dual-overhead camshaft engine.

conclusion of the 1967 season, they had captured 18 world titles, with at least one title in each of the five major solo classes. The high water mark of Honda's dominance in world championship road racing was in 1966, when all five solo classes—50-cc, 125-cc, 250-cc, 350-cc, and 500-cc—were claimed. This marked the first time in history that any one manufacturer had won every class in a single season.

But Honda's road-racing successes were not without challenge and setback. Indeed, some of the very machines that Hailwood rode to world championships—namely, the 250-cc, 350-cc and 500-cc multicylinder machines—were known to be less than ideally stable at high speed. Hailwood himself was seen on more than one occasion gesticulating furiously to semicomprehending mechanics, describing the dreadful slides and wobbles the Hondas would so often display. Honda engineers seemingly found it easier to extract great amounts of horsepower from the engines than to design stability into the chassis. In the opinion of many professional racers and designers, it was Hailwood's courage and racing virtuosity that earned certain championships despite Honda's inadequate chassis design.

Other challenges came from Yamaha, whose mastery of two-stroke engineering in the 1960s was unchallenged. Where Honda racing machinery was predicated upon comparatively complex powerplants, the Yamahas were very simple by contrast. The RD-56 model, for example, was a 250-cc twin, utilizing rotary valve induction and a seven-speed gearbox. In many respects, this mount was every bit as fast as the highly touted Hondas. Furthermore, its rather light weight gave the Yamaha a decided edge in cornering and braking. To be sure, there were other more complex motorcycles from the Yamaha racing stable, such as the 125-cc and 250-cc V-4s, but these dreadfully fast motorcycles went largely unappreciated by the racing public because Honda was by then quitting road racing, thus avoiding a once-and-for all competition slugfest. In the hands of such racing luminaries as Phil Read and the late Bill Ivy, these motorcycles equaled or bettered most of Honda's track records throughout the world.

The last major race victory by Honda happened in the 1970 Daytona 200. Honda made a one-race effort to return to racing, once again to prove a new design. The bike was the new four-cylinder 750, ridden by Dick Mann. After the race, Honda packed up its equipment and headed back to Japan, its goal once again attained.

But this contest was not won without question, for the Honda team motorcycles were of questionable legality under AMA rules. It was suspected early in prerace practice that nonstandard materials were used in engine construction. Specifically, it was alleged that the crankcases were made of nonstock, unapproved magnesium rather than the

legally acceptable aluminum. Despite complaints from other competitors, the AMA showed no interest in the controversy. Ironically,
these suspicions were proven true when one of the team racing
machines crashed during a practice session. The motorcycle caught fire.
And while the rider escaped with minor injuries, the exotic mul-
tithousand-dollar motorcycle made of magnesium burned with such
intensity that trackside fire extinguishers could not put out the flames.
Within minutes it was reduced to a puddle of alloy.

Nonetheless, Dick Mann's accomplishment is not diminished, for
the reliability of these machines proved marginal at best. All the other
team Hondas had dropped out of the race except for Mann's, and his was
sputtering badly during the last laps. It was an incredibly hard-fought
battle for this seasoned veteran. Ironically, just a few months after Mann
gave Honda its greatest U.S. racing victory, he was unceremoniously
dropped from their racing program.

Throughout its racing career, Honda never failed to continue developing new and better machines for the consumer. The bike that can
take credit for helping to change the course of motorcycling in America,
and probably the world, was the little 50-cc Cub. Featuring an automatic
transmission and a reasonably trouble-free engine, the Cub's impact on a
prosperous market eager for fun transportation was understandably
awesome.

Later years brought the Super Hawk, a 305-cc twin-cylinder
overhead-camshaft mount that established once and for all that large-
displacement engines are not the only method to achieve high performance (Fig. 1-14).

FIGURE 1-14.   The Honda Hawks were to capture the hearts of
thousands of motorcycle enthusiasts in mid-1960 America.

A year and a half after Honda's withdrawal from international road racing, the four-cylinder CB-750 roadster was introduced. Lessons gleaned from racing experience were put to use in developing this machine, which, for a while, put Honda at the technological forefront of the motorcycle industry.

the men who raced

However interesting the machines of the motorcycle world may be, it is still the men who ride them that make the difference between success or failure. It is the people that add essential color to the sport. Men have accepted challenges since the earliest days of our sport, some conquering, others being conquered. The lust for excitement drives them on. There is no record of the very first race, but you can bet it happened when two motorcyclists met each other on the road and, sizing up each other's equipment, decided to have a go and see whose was faster.

On a more organized scale, the factories began racing their bikes to prove to the doubting public that their equipment was both rugged and fast. To go at the speeds needed to win was a punishing proposition for any bike at the time, considering the conditions of the roads and the quality of the metal used in the motorcycles.

Although road racing was permitted on the continent, speed limits prevailed in England, prohibiting racing on streets. As a result, a speedway was constructed at Brooklands. It had a smooth track surface, with banked turns for maximum speeds. Brooklands became the premier site for absolute speed trials, as in the case of the big showdown between the two Harley-Davidsons and the lone Indian back in 1921.

Another famous race circuit to arise from the early days of motorcycle road racing was the Isle of Man. A tiny island just to the west of England, the Isle of Man is exempt from some English laws, including those that govern speeds on public roads. The very first Isle of Man race, called a Tourist Trophy, or TT for short, was held back in 1907. The circuit meandered around the island, covering a distance of just over 15 miles. In 1911, the course was altered. The new distance measured 37-3/4 miles and is the course used today. Initially there were two classes, the Senior and Junior Tourist Trophies. The Senior class represented machines from 351 to 500 cc. The Junior class was for 350 cc and under. In 1922, the 250-cc class was added, called the Lightweight TT. Not until 1951 did the Ultra-Lightweight, or 125-cc class, make the scene. For a short time, from 1962 to 1968, the 50-cc TT class (Fig. 1-15) was run, but lack of interest led to its demise.

The top three finishers in each class are given a gold, silver, and bronze Isle of Man TT replica medal for their efforts. To win this medal is

FIGURE 1-15. 50-cc road racers represent some of the most sophisticated internal combustion engineering today. Some of these machines produce nearly eight horsepower per cubic inch. Shown here is the start of the Dutch TT at Assen.

considered an honor; even to finish the grueling race is a feat for many. Such names as Bray Hill, Ramsey Ballaugh, Sulby, and Kirk-Michael mark various points on the twisty circuit, that reaches an elevation of 1640 feet from its near-sea-level starting point (Fig. 1-16). These places also have spelled death to many competitors who crashed and had the misfortune of hitting a stone wall or the hard curbing that lines the track.

The most notable rider to compete at the Isle of Man is Mike "The Bike" Hailwood. Hailwood has won 12 TTs, more than any other rider. Included in his feats are several triples: three race wins at a single TT. The only other man to attain ten TTs was Stanley Woods, who won ten during his brilliant riding career in the '20s and '30s.

Although not many Americans have competed at the Isle of Man, some colorful personalities from across the Atlantic participated in many other events during the early heyday of the sport. Best remembered of all these was the incredible Cannonball Baker, mentioned earlier. Dubbed Cannonball by a reporter writing about one Irwin G. Baker and his exploits on motorcycles in 1914, Baker was a man of the saddle, always in search of a record he could set while riding on two wheels. History counts 143 endurance records of sorts held by Cannonball, most of them on two wheels, although he did do time behind the steering wheel for some of his records.

Cannonball set his first coast-to-coast mark in 1914. While the rest of the world was at war, Cannonball could be seen streaking across the deserts of California, heading for the plains of Kansas aboard his Indian V-twin. Cannonball set that first transcontinental record in 11 days, 12 hours, and 10 minutes. This was to be one of almost 50 transcontinental runs for him. Later he would call himself a "trans-continentalist," a title which he used proudly.

Cannonball once rode an Ace four-cylinder to a shattering time of 6 days and 22 hours (Fig. 1-17), then turned around in New York to ride a

FIGURE 1-16. The Isle of Man road race, using a course 37-3/4 miles long, has long been regarded as the world's most prestigious road racing event. Shown here is Hans-Georg Anschiedt soaring at Ballaugh Bridge on a 50-cc Kriedler.

FIGURE 1-17. The late Irwin G. "Cannonball" Baker set dozens of transcontinental motorcycle riding records on machines such as this Ace four.

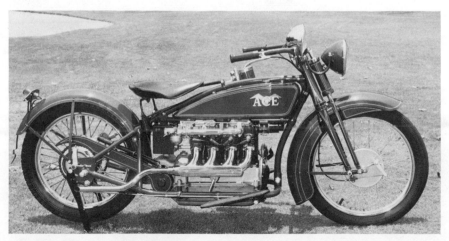

Ner-A-Car, a motorcycle resembling an automobile since the rider sat down as in a car, to test its fuel economy. Through the course of his trip, the Ner-A-Car consumed just 40 gallons of gasoline! Cannonball Baker set his last transcontinental record for Indian in 1941. Although most of the roads he followed were paved by then, with many roadside rests, he still enjoyed trying to better the old mark. Cannonball died in his Indianapolis home May 10, 1960. A golden era of record attempts died with him.

Motorcycle racing in America during the early part of the century was usually done on oval board tracks. Racing motorcycles had very poor suspension coupled with hard rubber tires. Only the best riders could win on them, let alone ride them fast! This was also the era that Harley-Davidson and Indian riders were at odds with each other. From this period dates the Harley-Davidson "Wrecking Crew." The name explains the success of this group of riders, who dominated racing at the conclusion of World War I. Four famous riders comprised the "Wrecking Crew": Fred Ludlow, Ralph Hepburn, Shrimp Burns, and Otto Walker (Fig. 1-18). Two of these riders, Walker and Hepburn, were destined to make their mark in motorcycle racing history.

Walker was considered by many to be the all-time great at board racing during the flamboyant era of 1914 to the middle of the '20s. He was always capable of running the opposition ragged in a sprint race on the boards, or knew how to pace himself and his machine in a rugged 300-miler. He probably acquired this asset from his early days as a trained mechanic, as so many of the successful racers were back then.

FIGURE 1-18. The Harley-Davidson "Wrecking Crew," which dominated board and dirt track motorcycle racing at the end of World War I.

FIGURE 1-19. Ralph Hepburn was a racing prodigy of great mechanical skill whose career encompassed both motorcycle and automobile racing.

Ralph Hepburn was a man who knew and loved racing for most of his 52-year life (Fig. 1-19). In fact, 35 years were devoted to racing, and it was the love of the sport that ended his life in 1948. But not without a very colorful and illustrious career that saw him rise to fame on the board tracks aboard his Harley-Davidson motorcycle, only to switch to automobile racing later on.

Hepburn got his start by running his own equipment against the formidable factory teams. Outclassed, he had only his wits and talent to help keep him in the running of a race. His perseverance earned him a place on the Harley-Davidson racing team and, consequently, membership in the fabled "Wrecking Crew." When Harley temporarily withdrew from racing, he was quickly signed with Indian, where he raced until 1925. Then he set sights on the Indianapolis 500 auto race. His versatility was quickly displayed as the fabulous Hepburn led the field until his car failed him. He had his best finish at the Brickyard in 1937, when the legendary Wilbur Shaw nosed him out at the finish line by only 2.16 seconds. Hepburn continued to race at Indy after World War II, although he was considered by many to be too old. He was the only man ever to master the brutal Novi racers and did extremely well with them until, time after time, the car failed in the course of the 500-mile race. It was in the monstrous Novi that Hepburn finally met his death, ending one of the longest racing careers ever.

One of the most heroic road racers in Europe was Geoff Duke. Duke got his start in racing by riding for the Norton factory team. At a time when the Italian Gilera fours were making their presence known shortly after World War II, Duke continued to place his single-cylinder Norton in first place ahead of the sophisticated multis and won many world titles. When Norton pulled out of racing, Duke switched to his adversary's bikes, riding them to victory as well. His style of tucking his knees close to the tank was quickly copied by many, setting the style for the classic road racers for the next fifteen or twenty years, until Mike Hailwood perfected the "knees out" technique.

Shortly after Duke left the European scene, another Englishman, John Surtees, took over as the master of the road race courses. Surtees rode for MV Augusta, and could do things on two wheels that many people considered impossible. By 1962, Surtees had decided to go Formula I automobile racing, and since has been the only champion on both two and four wheels.

Mike Hailwood followed Surtees's footsteps, riding for MV and later for Honda. Hailwood, long since been considered the master of road race motorcycles, earned the title of "Mike the Bike." Among other feats, he has won Isle of Man TTs in the 125-cc, 250-cc, 350-cc, and 500-cc classes. Hailwood, like Surtees, decided to switch to automobile racing at the conclusion of Honda's factory racing efforts. His new employer was John Surtees, who by now had acquired his own racing team.

In any discussion of road racing greats, Giacomo Agostini has to be mentioned. Agostini raced exclusively for MV until Yamaha signed him for the 1974 and 1975 seasons. "Ago," as he is affectionately called by his many fans and the press, has over 100 Grand Prix wins, more than any other rider in history. His 14 World Championships are also a first. At the start of the 1976 season, Ago made his return to MV, but will probably race in the following years as a privateer until he retires.

Not until the last ten years have Americans begun producing road racers of the European caliber. Three very notable riders to make their presence known on pavement courses are Kenny Roberts, Gary Nixon, Steve Baker, and the late Calvin Rayborn (Fig. 1-20). Both Roberts and Nixon are former two-time AMA Grand National Champs. When matched against some of the best of the rest of the world, all four have

FIGURE 1-20.   Probably America's finest road racer of recent years was the late Cal Rayborn, whose consummate skill awed Europeans as well as Americans. He was killed in a racing accident in New Zealand, 1973.

demonstrated skill worthy of being world champions. Roberts has made it publicly known that he would like one day to race in Europe to contest a world championship. He has already won international events in Italy, England, and several other countries. Also, road-race-specialist Baker has garnered an international championship. The feat of these men marks the comeback by the nation that once dominated motorcycle racing throughout the world.

2 fitting apparel: what to wear where

Hard facts for soft heads and thin skins

Chapters elsewhere in this book discuss the various perils of motorcycle riding and how to ride safely: motorcycle accident prevention, in other words.

But that's not the whole story. What about after the accident has happened? All the book learnin' and experience in the world won't help you now, as you slide nightmarishly across the ground. The only thing that's working for you at this point is what you're wearing, for the more insulation you have between yourself and the ground (or rocks or other cars or . . .) the better your chances of survival.

Don't lapse into the it-can't-happen-to-me syndrome. It can.

The proper rider apparel for motorcycling can mean the difference between life and death. Not only that, but well chosen riding clothes can add immensely to your enjoyment. You don't have to be on the brink of death to appreciate fully the value of proper riding gear. For example, a blister or a painful insect sting on your throttle hand can be extremely annoying, even though they sound minor. Yet niggling problems like these can be avoided by wearing gloves.

Simple precautions—that is, wearing the correct gear—can prevent major problems.

choosing your helmet

The importance of making a good choice of helmet is crucial to the motorcyclist, yet is often not fully understood. There are fallacies that deserve clearing up.

Heavy impact on an improperly fitted helmet can conceivably cause worse damage than that sustained by an unprotected head. If you're buying a helmet for physical protection, it is mandatory that you choose one that fits as closely to your head as possible. Only if you're seeking comfortable shelter from the elements should you consider anything other than a snug-fitting helmet. Unnecessary slack between helmet lining and head is dangerous. This is because the impact of a blow is not ideally spread throughout the helmet. The slack inside a loosely fitting helmet allows a secondary impact to happen, one occurring between your head and the helmet's lining. In this way force is allowed to concentrate on a relatively small area of your head. Initial impact occurs when the helmet hits an obstacle. Secondary impact occurs when your head travels across the slack area of the helmet with comparative freedom and then comes to a sudden stop against the lining. It all takes place in milliseconds.

The correctly fitted helmet does not allow this to happen. The initial impact is spread over maximum area, transferring the blow to the head in a more gradual manner. The skull is not struck a sudden, traumatic blow. Instead, it sustains a less violent deceleration, which maximizes its chances of coming through the whole affair unscathed.

By all means, try on helmets. Don't assume that "a medium will do." As a matter of fact, in the long run heads cannot be well fit within a small-medium-large spectrum; it's too indefinite, too difficult to achieve an ideal fit. Every individual has a specific head size and shape. You can achieve a more precise fit from helmets designed with smaller size increments. Bell helmets, for example, are made according to hat sizes—6-7/8, 7, 7-1/8, and so on. In this way you are much more likely to attain the best fit. A helmet should fit like a pair of shoes, and this means that it should also be tight when new. Helmets wear in. With time, the hard foam shock absorbing liner does conform to the contours of your head. A helmet does not get tighter with time, it gets looser. Here you should be careful, for when you try on a new helmet, it may feel snug and secure initially, but within a half-dozen or so riding hours, what was originally, say, a 7-1/8 can become a 7-1/4 helmet. Most auto and motorcycle racers are well aware of this situation and the hazards it poses. Drag racers, for example, typically wear the tightest helmets they can fit on their heads. Because drag races last but a few seconds, the helmet is on for a relatively short period of time, so discomfort is rather brief while safety is maximized.

A tight helmet commonly causes headaches. But if you've made a careful choice, the helmet will adjust to your head within four or six riding hours. Of course, if the helmet's internal dimensions are too small, it will never conform, and besides being uncomfortable you will have wasted hard-earned money. Rule of thumb: Determine the size of helmet that seems to fit you ideally right out of the box. This done, then choose the same make and model of helmet in a 1/8 smaller size.

When trying on helmets, be aware of major pressure points bearing on your head. These can cause pain and even alter vision if the helmet is worn too long. If the helmet is well made, however, minor pressure points will disappear in time.

The helmet you choose, whatever its size, should have three specific approval stickers inside it: Z90.1, SHCA, and Snell Memorial Foundation approval tags.

The Z90.1 sticker tells us that the helmet conforms to standards first formulated by the American National Standards Institute of the 1960s, amended in 1973. The Z90.1 specifications ensure at least minimal protection in case of impact. Unfortunately, these standards have no provision for continuing inspection of the manufacturing of the approved design. What this means is that while the helmets used in testing may be approved, the quality of production-line helmets may vary significantly.

The Snell Memorial Foundation came about in the early 1960s as a result of the death of auto racer Peter Snell. The foundation was formed to set up a more exacting set of safety standards for racing helmets as well as everyday consumer items—the Z90 rules did not apply to racing products. The Snell Foundation standards are regarded as the most stringent in the helment manufacturing industry. Approval by this group additionally requires ongoing inspection of production-line helmets.

The SHCA is the Safety Helmet Council of America. It is a group composed of members of the safety helmet industry. It is charged with policing its own members through inspections of manufacturing, quality control, and testing procedures.

A helmet bearing these three stickers is not guaranteed to save your life no matter what. Nothing can do that, much less a helmet. What they do tell you is that the helmet will sustain a fairly hard impact without shattering like an unlucky mirror. Do not buy a helmet not so approved.

There are three basic helmet configurations commonly seen in showrooms today. The lightest and smallest type is called the *half-helmet* or "shorty" (Fig. 2-1). It offers protection around the crown

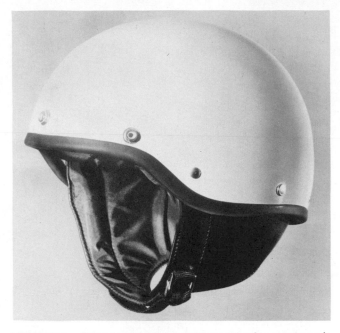

FIGURE 2-1. The "shorty" helmet is not recognized as a motorcycle crash helmet in some states.

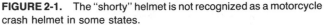

of the skull but does not extend down lower than the ears in most models. In shape it is not unlike a large, hard baseball cap with a padded interior. These are favored by some motorcyclists because they afford at least minimal protection, if not from impact, at least from the wind. The shorty-type helmets are relatively lightweight and, because the ears are not totally concealed, hearing is not seriously impaired. Shorty helmets are standard issue for many police departments for these reasons. However, this configuration generally offers the least cranial protection of the three predominant helmet shapes. It is interesting to note that despite the widespread use by motorcycle officers in some states, the shorty is not recognized as a legitimate motorcycle safety helmet in other states. If you are riding through those areas where helmets are required by law, we suggest you determine which helmets are legally approved. In Texas, for example, the shorty is not recognized as a motorcycle safety helmet but as a "riot control" helmet; thus, it's not a legitimate helmet for highway use.

The *standard* helmet probably enjoys the greatest popularity among motorcyclists (Fig. 2-2). This configuration extends down below the ears on each side and as far down the second cervical vertebra to the

FIGURE 2-2.   The standard helmet configuration enjoys the greatest
popularity in the United States for reasons of comfort and lightness.

rear in some models. The closer a helmet can be to a full sphere, the
greater its potential strength. The standard helmet has inherently better
structural integrity than a shorty for this reason. The standard can be
relatively light as well, weighing perhaps 4 pounds.

Probably the safest, certainly the strongest structurally, is the
full-coverage helmet (Fig. 2-3). This type encases the head completely.
An oblong port is molded into the front of the helmet to see through. Not
only are the skull, skull base, and ears protected, but the face and jaw as
well. This type of helmet is relatively new and did not achieve its present
popularity until the late 1960s. The Bell Star helmet epitomizes this type
and historically was one of the first on the scene. In terms of sheer impact
safety, this type of helmet is unexcelled. Full-coverage helmets tend to
weigh a pound or so more than the standard types. Some riders have also
complained about restricted visibility from within. The concern of
weight, however, tends to fade with time as the rider gets used to the
helmet. Moreover, recent years have spawned a new generation of full-
coverage helmets offering increased peripheral vision. These helmets
are generally called "120s," because they offer 120 degrees of visual
scope (Fig. 2-4). The 120 helmets, because of their larger window, are not
thought to be as strong as their smaller-windowed predecessors, and for

FIGURE 2-3. The Bell Star full-coverage helmet is regarded by many as offering the greatest skull protection.

FIGURE 2-4. Recent legislation has set standards for peripheral vision for helmet wearers; thus the 120 helmet, which offers 120 degrees of peripheral view.

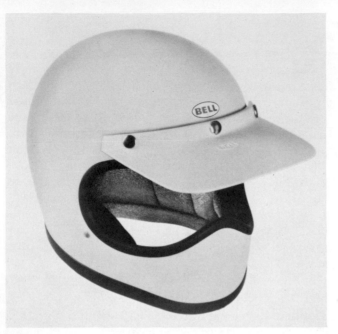

FIGURE 2-5.   The Bell Motostar helmet is made specifically for off-road motorcyclists. It offers full-coverage protection, yet allows the use of goggles.

this reason most racers still favor the older design. However, the 120 helmets do offer an excellent combination of facial protection and vision. Also, the laws of some states prohibit sale of small-window full-coverage helmets for street use.

In 1975, a variation on the full-coverage configuration was developed by Bell helmets (Fig. 2-5). The impetus for this latest style came from international motocross racers who desired a helmet offering full-coverage face protection plus a window large enough to accept goggles. Up to this point, full-coverage helmets typically used a sheet Plexiglas face-shield, which tended to fog up with the rider's breath. As a result, racers commonly used an open-face standard helmet with a football-type mouthguard. These mouthguards sometimes caused injuries when they came off on impact, or worse, pushed inward to lacerate the face.

This latest helmet configuration is similar to that of a 120-degree windowed helmet but has enlarged eye orbs and a high point directly in front of the nose. In this way vision remains uncompromised while facial protection is at a maximum. The helmet is known as the Bell Motostar.

eye protection

It is crucial for you to have some sort of eye protection. Full-coverage helmets are generally sold with face shields but the standard and shorty most often are not, leaving you the option of choosing goggles or face shield. Face shields are available for most helmets in clear and tinted styles. Tint colors are most often blue, yellow, and neutral. While the yellow and blue shields can alter color perception, neutral does not, and for this reason it is favored by most experts. Of course, nothing other than clear should be used for night riding.

At high speeds, the bubble-type face shield often has a tendency to lift due to aerodynamic forces. This can be unnerving, or at least distracting, as your helmet tends to float and turn your head. Flat face shields rarely do this.

There are many excellent types of goggles available today (Fig. 2-6). No longer does the motorcyclist have to put up with cumbersome war surplus tank corps goggles. Lightweight plastic-framed goggles which will last for years, barring mishap, can be purchased for less than $10. You will find that hard plastic lenses will resist scratching better than Plexiglas, which can be marred even by wiping with paper. Excellent goggles are also available with distortion-free, two-piece tem-

FIGURE 2-6.   If you don't wear a full-coverage helmet, good goggles are a must.

pered-glass lenses. Goggles that fit over eyeglasses are made by many manufacturers, as well. If you wear glasses and find goggles that fit over your spectacles unsatisfactory, there is one alternative: prescription goggles. A few goggle manufacturers offer prescription-ground lenses. Of course, your investment here is significantly more than for regular goggles, and if you take a spill and damage them, well, you're out that much more money. Local dealers and motorcycle accessory distributors should be able to direct you to manufacturers of such goggles.

It is important, particularly if you do significant off-road riding, that your goggles be vented to prevent lens fogging while not allowing dust to enter and irritate your eyes. If you're still having trouble finding suitable goggles, or if a motorcycle accessory shop is not nearby, try a sporting goods store or a ski shop, for many ski goggles are very similar to motorcycle goggles.

Of course, the reasons for wearing goggles off-road are self-evident, particularly when you are following other riders. But it is equally important to wear them when street riding. If not, your first encounter with a bug at 40 mph will surely change your mind . . . it's like being struck in the face with a hard-thrown mud pie.

protective footwear

Wearing the proper boots is a motorcycling must. Street riders as well as dirt enthusiasts should choose protective footwear suitable for fending off injury in case of a mishap. Long-time motorcyclists will attest that motorcycles are hard on ankles and shins. Also, you only need to have an obstinate engine kick back once through the start pedal to convince you of the importance of good arch protection. Granted, many motorcycles today are fitted with electric starters, but many others aren't. Starting kickback from an engine of moderate size can break an unprotected foot, and sometimes street shoes are inadequate to prevent a painfully bruised foot.

For street riding, there are several good makes of boot on the market costing about $40 and up (Fig. 2-7). If this seems a little expensive, bear in mind that such boots are made to last much longer than street shoes. They are characteristically made of heavier leather, stitching, soles, and padding in the right places. A good boot is relatively impervious to weather, too. Moreover, many of these boots are suitable for office wear, so officegoers needn't have to worry about keeping a change of shoes under the desk. Look for boots with double-stitched seams, particularly around the toe area, where abrasion from the shift

FIGURE 2-7. Hefty yet stylish boots made specifically for street riding can last years.

lever will occur. If the leather is smooth in that area, look for a tough abrasion-resistant leather finish that is not easily scuffed or worn. A good street boot should also have extra padding around the shin and ankle. It seems that no matter what bike you're on or how careful you are, footpegs, ankles, and shins will sooner or later collide. A zipper on the side makes their use that much easier; buckles tend to snag on slacks and just generally get in the way. Further, you want a boot that covers the ankle—preferably reinforced with extra leather or thermoplast here —and lower calf; a charley horse in the Achilles tendon, located at the lower part of the calf, is very painful, and a boot of adequate height obviates this. It is suggested that you get a boot with at least an 8-inch and preferably a 9-inch top. Finally, boots with soft, crepe-type soles may lessen vibration from the footpegs, but make sure the sole is not easily worn and won't delaminate under motorcycle usage.

In choosing boots for off-road use, style is not an important consideration. What you need here is something that will withstand intense exposure to the elements, offer maximum foot and leg protection, and last a long, long time. Good boots designed specifically for dirt riding can cost anywhere from $60 upward—a hefty investment—so plan on buying a pair that will stand at least two years of use.

FIGURE 2-8. The choice between lace-up and buckled boots is a matter of personal preference. The lace-ups shown are fitted with lugged enduro soles. The buckled boots have the smooth motocross sole.

Regulation off-road racing boots are not a "must" item, for there are some less expensive types of general-purpose boots available. Hiking and telephone linesman boots are popular, and they cost about $25 and up. Additionally, if you plan to do much walking in the wilderness, the hiking and linesman boots allow much greater flexibility. The linesman boots also commonly have steel arch reinforcements, which will easily bear a rider's weight as he stands on the footpegs.

There has been some debate about whether one should wear boots that have metal-reinforced toes. The objection to this type of boot is that the metal can painfully, maybe dangerously, clamp the toe like a vise if you inadvertently strike it against a fixed object. Other motorcyclists, however, including the author, can attest to toes being saved by metal reinforcement.

The choice between lace-ups and buckles is also a matter of taste (Fig. 2-8). Neither type is inherently better than the other, even though the buckle boots are much easier to put on and take off. It is important, though, that you get boots that extend well up the leg. Motorcycle boots that reach up to the knee are not terribly easy to walk in, but for riding only they cannot be faulted. Adult riders will be likely to require a boot with 16- to 18-inch tops for maximum leg protection.

Most boots made for off-roading have either no heel or a gently tapered one; heels tend to snag on rocks and such when sliding along the ground, often with painful results. However, boots made for other purposes often do have heels. Many motorcyclists take these boots to the local cobbler and have a wedge fitted to the sole just ahead of the heel, eliminating the snagging square edge of the heel. Other motorcyclists simply hacksaw the heel's forward edge off, leaving a beveled ramp.

Motorcycle boots commonly come in two sole types: motocross and enduro. The *motocross* sole is generally smoother than the enduro sole because its purpose is to slide along the ground when the motocross racer uses his foot as an outrigger. The *enduro* sole is heavily lugged to allow the rider's feet traction, because he is often forced to push his bike through gravel, muck, and mire. Once again, the choice is yours.

gloves for motorcycling

There is no substitute for good leather gloves, whatever your type of riding. Warm, flexible, and strong, leather gloves protect your hands from the weather and blisters as well as keeping your skin intact as you slide along the ground. A few motorcyclists are of the opinion that double-layered cotton flannel gloves, usually sold as around-the-house work gloves, are a better choice, because leather gloves get stiff, can't be washed, and so on. But look at it this way: surgeons tell us that the area of the human body hardest to reconstruct after injury is the hand. Take no chances.

There are two basic types of leather gloves for street motorcycle use. The *gauntlet* glove extends well up the forearm for maximum comfort and protection (Fig. 2-9). This type is favored by many long-

FIGURE 2-9. The gauntlet glove for street motorcycling extends well up the forearm.

distance touring riders. The cuff of the glove is often made to fit over your jacket sleeve so that wind cannot penetrate. The gauntlet is usually zippered to allow for snug fit over the sleeves.

The *standard* motorcycle glove is much like the gauntlet except that it doesn't extend as far up the arm (Fig. 2-10). Understandably, the gauntlet can get pretty warm in hot weather, so you might find the standard style more to your liking for summer riding. In both gauntlet and standard gloves, drawstrings or elastic are often found at the wrists. Look also for nylon lining and foam insulation in both styles of glove.

Gloves are very important for off-road motorcycling. The often strenuous nature of off-road riding places great importance on personal comfort. Your hands get a real workout even during leisurely riding. Not only do gloves work for you when you fall off your bike, but correctly fitting gloves will prevent your getting painful blisters. As a result, all seams on your glove should be external. If not, you'll be well aware of it within your first half hour in the saddle. Try on various kinds of gloves. There should be no rough surfaces or ridges to chafe against your hands.

Motocross gloves are generally well suited to trail riding (Fig. 2-11). Cowhide allows excellent flexibility and absorption of your hands' perspiration, which will occur even on cold days. Look for these features as well: reinforcement at the web between the thumb and index finger (this is a highly stressed area and the reinforcement should be sewn into the glove) and backhand ridges, also very important. Thick rubber strips sewn or glued onto the back of each glove, these ridges add an extra degree of protection because they prevent direct contact of the

FIGURE 2-10.   The standard street motorcycle glove does not extend as far up the arm and is cooler, for warm-weather riding.

FIGURE 2-11. Motocross gloves are generally heavily stitched and reinforced at various points. They also feature external seams and protective rubber ridges on the backhand.

hand with branches, rocks, and such. They make a rap on the knuckles much less painful.

Often gloves of exotic leathers will usually offer an increased degree of comfort . . . at an increased rate of wear and increased cost. Dress gloves also wear rapidly. A good pair of motocross gloves, however, can be purchased for $8 to $15 and will last indefinitely.

riding suits and leathers

Motorcycling's greatest asset can also be its greatest drawback: exposure to the elements. There is no disputing that the gentle buffeting of the wind against your body is indeed often a pleasant sensation. For example, the bracing chill of an early morning ride on a country road can make an otherwise humdrum day a unique experience. But if the weather turns sour—well, that's quite another matter. Not only can riding in a surprise rain shower be soakingly miserable, it also can be dangerous, for being preoccupied with your own discomfort might distract your mind from the duties of keeping your bike upright and on the road.

There also is the consideration of safety, no matter what the weather. If you fall down on your bike, how much protection does your clothing offer? Light clothing that shreds upon first contact with the ground will probably leave you with more than a few raspberries.

Choosing good clothing for street riding can be a little more complicated than garments for the dirt. This is because the only real factor in buying the latter is functionality. Handsome off-road clothing is fine, but the true measure of clothes for dirt riding is comfort and protection. As a rule, the motorcyclist away from the road will only be meeting hikers, campers, or other motorcyclists. Additionally, the dirt motorcycle is almost never used as a utilitarian means of transportation; you don't ride one back and forth to work. On the other hand, the street motorcycle is often used for day-to-day transportation. Not only is it often ridden back and forth to work but for errands and sport as well. Many of us would feel a little silly wearing dirt leathers just for a Saturday morning jaunt to the hardware store.

The street motorcyclist must choose clothing that not only offers protection from the elements but also easy on-off versatility and good visibility without the flamboyance of off-road leathers.

Riding suits are available for on- and off-road motorcycling. Some of these suits are one-piece and others are two-piece. Some are bulky, padded, and thoroughly waterproof while others are lightweight and water-resistant.

The British can be credited with developing the first all-weather motorcycle riding suits. Of course, weather in the Isles is known to be less than ideal, while English enthusiasm for motorcycling has always been high. It is second nature for them to ride in weather conditions we would consider appalling. So along with being singularly hardy bikers, they have produced suits that are weatherproof, brushproof, and offer excellent abrasion protection. The two most popular kinds of English riding suit are made by Barbour and Belstaff. Made of waxed cotton, the suits are traditionally dark blue in color and have lots of pockets, snaps, and adjustments to adapt them to almost any riding condition.

There are disadvantages to these suits, however, particularly when compared to contemporary nylon garments. The waxed cotton items tend to be rather stiff. This is understandable, as they are based upon heavy, waterproofed canvas. Also, in terms of water repellency, this material does not compare well to modern synthetic fibers. Waxed cotton starts at 65 percent water repellency and drops drastically after just two or three washings. On the other hand, some synthetics—Full Bore's Trailex suit, for example—starts at 100 percent and drops to 65 percent after three washings. Additionally, many such fibers are brought back to full water repellency by a single Scotchgard treatment. Complete waxed cotton riding suits generally cost $65 and upward, with pants and jackets available separately. Among extras are snap-in liners and over-mitts for added warmth. Although such suits are popular with off-roaders, they are likely to prove too bulky for daily street use.

Heavy-duty nylon is one of the least expensive materials available that still yields good protection. Prices for nylon riding suits range from

FIGURE 2-12. Heavy-duty nylon riding suits offer excellent protection from the weather for street and touring motorcyclists.

about $35 to $70 (Fig. 2-12). Many motorcyclists now favor high-visibility colors, which are desirable for both street and off-road use. Look for suits that have the material treated for extra wind and moisture protection. Also, some suits feature a Scotchlite or similarly reflective strip on each sleeve for nighttime visibility. Many suits have insulated linings to preserve body heat, plus protective pads, or at least reinforcements, sewn into the elbows. Several manufacturers also have extra layers of quilting from knee to cuff, which allows your shins protection from wind and flying rocks. Velcro fasteners at ankles, calves, wrists, and collar are seen on some suits, but the type of fastener is not as important as the fact that there are fasteners of some sort at these points.

Wind has a way of penetrating wherever it can; the colder the weather is, it seems, the greater its penetration. Also, if there is slack in certain parts of the suit, the wind will make it flap and billow. Besides affecting your comfort, this also makes some fabrics wear faster. Street and dirt riding suits can also have zippers at the lower part of each leg. These allow you to put on and remove the coverall without having to remove your boots.

Some street riders will appreciate the lighter coverall-type nylon suits because these can easily be worn over a business suit. Your tie is kept from trailing in the breeze behind you like a World War I fighter pilot's scarf. It also keeps road grime from spattering your clothes.

Naturally, the ubiquitous Levi's and other types of denim work pants are most popular with leisure motorcyclists—street or dirt—for reasons of economy, if not any other. This fabric, however, does tear easier than nylon or leather, and the protection you receive is relatively meager. Most jeans are made of a material which gets stronger when wet, but the absorptive power of Levi's is terrific, and water that just soaked your ankles will soon have your whole pants leg damp. This dampness does two things: It attracts and retains dirt, and it makes you cold.

However, if you insist on wearing jeans, wear two pairs. They will give you better protection from road rash if you do fall.

Of course, serious off-road riders for years have used leather trousers (Fig. 2-13). Originally, they were cut much the same as conventional street trousers. They were relatively loose and straight-legged, and only occasionally did they have integral padding; you used what nature gave you. Since the mid-1960s, however, with the growing influence of European motocross, our leather pants are now made to fit snugly around hips and thighs and tightly around the calves. Boots now go on over the pants legs. Not too many years ago, the popular way was for the pants leg to fit over the boot. Almost all leathers today have generous pads sewn in at hips and knees. Also, areas of knees and thighs are stoutly reinforced. When you buy your leather pants, it is also suggested that you do yourself a nice favor and specify those with nylon linings. Leathers without linings cost maybe $15 less yet can be hot and uncomfortable. They are also often difficult to put on and take off.

A relatively interesting departure in this field involves a combination of leather and nylon in trouser construction. Bill Walters Leathers makes pants using the heaviest grade of nylon available for the main portion of the pants. However, the crotch, seat, and inseam are made of cowhide. In this way the main complaint against leather pants—that they are excessively hot in warm weather—is obviated. The Walters pants are also a couple of pounds lighter than full leather trousers.

But regardless of what style of pants you get for off-roading, make sure that they fit correctly; that all the padding is in the right places and that they aren't so tight you can't move or so loose they get snagged on footpegs and other parts of your bike.

Common sense tells us that Bermuda shorts should never be worn for riding, no matter how inviting the weather may be. Not only do they leave your legs totally unprotected from the ground in case of a spill, they also expose you to bugs and burns from exhaust pipes.

Experienced street riders strongly favor wearing at least a light jacket for protection, even though the weather may be sweltering hot. Such a jacket offers minimal protection in case of a mishap. Don't forget that such weather also invites painful windburn and sunburn, if you're not careful.

Cooler weather will require heavier clothing. There are many suitable jackets available that provide superb insulation. In many parts of

FIGURE 2-13.   Leather trousers for off-road riding are relatively comfortable and offer excellent protection in case of a mishap.

the United States, this is very important. The unwary motorcyclist is at the mercy of the prevailing wind-chill factor. Air Force studies tell us that if the body's internal temperature drops just 2 degrees, our physical ability to perform complex tasks is seriously decreased. And if we lose only 2 more degrees, we experience difficulty in speaking, sluggish thinking, even amnesia.

There are some things to look for when shopping for a jacket. A bright color may save your life. As we will indicate elsewhere in this book, auto drivers often do not see motorcyclists even though they may be looking directly at you. A brightly colored jacket just might provide that extra bit of recognition. (Nighttime riders, take note.)

Specify a mandarin-type collar. Other collars tend to flap annoyingly in the wind and chafe your neck and face. No open pockets; make sure they are zippered or otherwise securable. Having to worry about possessions falling from pockets is not only bothersome but distracts your mind from the job at hand.

To prevent billowing and wind penetration, make sure the jacket you buy has snug sleeves and waist. Some are elasticized and some have drawstrings. Either will do.

Many windbreakers have a zip-in liner for extra warmth (Fig. 2-14). This is good because it allows versatility in hot and cold weather. In this type of jacket, it is best to have buttonholes at the liner's sleeve ends mate with buttons inside the jacket to secure the liner. Overlapping zipper flaps are desirable because they prevent cold wind from penetrating.

Off-road riding is understandably hard on conventional clothing. Often the strenuous nature of this recreation will frazzle a conventional shirt in a relatively short time. Motocross racers wear expanded-mesh synthetic-fiber jerseys almost exclusively (Fig. 2-15). This material is similar to that used in football jerseys. It allows excellent ventilation, yet is very strong for its weight. These jerseys are available in varying weights for hot and cold weather riding. The jersey's stress points

FIGURE 2-14. A windbreaker with a zip-in liner provides extra warmth.

FIGURE 2-15. Expanded-mesh, synthetic fiber jerseys are popular
with off-roaders because of their durability and coolness.

should be reinforced, so look for double-thickness shoulder cowl and
elbow patches. Prices range from $8 to $15.

The kidney belt (Fig. 2-16) is a useful item for long-distance street
riders and off-road motorcyclists. These belts are broad, snug-fitting,
and usually made of leather or reinforced elastic. They are generally
secured by zipper, buckles, or Velcro fasteners. While some motorcyclists can ride hours, even days, on end without this supportive garment,
others swear by their use religiously, indicating that the orthopedic
support offered by the belts avoids fatigue and discomfort. This is
achieved by supporting the kidneys, upper lumbar and lower thoracic
vertebrae and protecting these parts from vehicle vibration. Generally
good kidney belts can be purchased for between $10 and $20.

FIGURE 2-16.   The large, wide kidney belt is worn by many motorcyclists for lower back support.

Proper care for motorcyle gloves, leathers, helmets, and boots is simple. There are just a few things to remember. All your leather, plastic, and vinyl products require minimal maintenance. Do your leather gloves get hard, dry, and brittle from exposure to weather and perspiration? Treat them with saddle soap or leather conditioners such as Armor All or RVL. These two products are simply sprayed on and rubbed into the material. They allow the leather to become more flexible, enhance its water repellency, and also remove dirt. One of the best forms of therapy for dried, brittle gloves is to treat them with saddle soap or other commercial preparations.

Riding boots, be they for street or dirt use, respond very well to the aforementioned commercial preparations. Just remove mud with a stiff brush; otherwise, all you have to do is dust them off with a light brush or a cloth. After this, apply the preparations. Of course, the frequency of this kind of maintenance is up to you: how much you ride, how dirty your boots get, and how dirty you can tolerate them to be.

Leather pants are cared for in much the same way, with one slight difference. To be sure, you don't want to run your leathers through a washing machine, for this will wreak havoc on stitching as well as leather. So, after a hard day's ride, or when the leathers have taken on a decidedly rural pungency, simply hose them off in the driveway or back yard. Give them a good rinsing inside and out. Next, let them hang dry. This done, the final step is to give them a good rubdown with leather conditioner when they are dry. Besides increasing the lifespan of the leathers, you'll also find that this treatment will make the trousers easier to clean the next time.

Helmet care is fundamental, providing, of course, that the unit is structurally sound to begin with. If there is serious question about the helmet's integrity, there is little point entrusting your life to it. So, let's say you just bought a used bike from your buddy down the street, and he tossed his old helmet in the deal out of generosity. Is that helmet knicked? Does it look as if it's been struck? Has your buddy fallen down while wearing the helmet? In other words, is there any evidence suggesting that the helmet has suffered a significant impact? If it has, there is a reasonable chance that the helmet's strength is compromised.

Why? Because contemporary helmet design is based upon use of an internal, crushable foam liner to absorb impacts. This foam, commonly polystyrene or polyurethane, absorbs energy by collapsing. Once it has collapsed, it absorbs no more energy. It's that simple. And don't confuse this hard foam with the softer, spongelike plastic foam used for comfort padding, which is easily replaced.

Only a few helmet manufacturers will even bother replacing the hard foam liner in an older helmet shell; it's just too much bother to be cost effective, and the legal liabilities are not insignificant—the manufacturer would rather sell you a helmet he *knows* is good, rather than refurbish a used one that's been through Lord knows what. Some manufacturers, however, do sell replacement kits for the soft padding foam.

The outer helmet shells are generally of two materials: fiberglass and polycarbonate plastic. There are excellent and poor brands of each. It is important to know, however, that polycarbonate, while being a superbly resilient plastic with excellent impact characteristics, is chemically sensitive to certain types of paint and cleaners, particularly those containing members of the ketone family. Exposed to these, polycarbonate wants to crack and dissolve. When you buy a new helmet, its accompanying literature will tell you what it's made of. But when acquiring a used helmet, you don't always know. If you buy one, make it a point to find out.

Helmet face shields are often made of softer plastics—Plexiglas, for example. Now this is just fine, because the material is lightweight and won't shatter. There is one hitch, though: It scratches easily. What to do? Well, one of the best ways to eliminate face shield scratches is to use a fine, fine abrasive as a rubbing compound and a soft, clean cloth. Interestingly, it so happens that toothpaste performs excellently here as an abrasive. Just squeeze a dollop of the paste on the shield's surface and rub, rub, rub with a very soft cloth. The stuff works wonders. But if you really want to splurge, jeweler's rouge also works well.

Otherwise, there is not much to remember in terms of helmet maintenance. If it gets dirty or slightly scuffed, a little soap, water, and wax will usually bring back its luster.

Without the proper clothing, motorcycling can be a miserable experience. There is little good to be said for being cold, blistered, scraped, and/or wet . . . or worse.

After the initial expenditure of buying a motorcycle, many of us find it hard to be enthusiastic about spending yet more money on accessories. After all, a good helmet and pair of boots can easily cost $150 or so. Seen in the long run, however, these purchases can be invaluable, particularly when they save your life or prevent serious injury, not to mention the comfort they provide.

Nor should you forget that the more expensive items, such as helmet, leathers, and boots, are made to last years, if properly cared for. Resist the temptation to cut corners when buying your safety equipment. In other words, if you have a $10 head, buy a $10 helmet—otherwise, look for the best.

3 the finer points of pavement safety

It's not a matter of surviving accidents—it's preventing them in the first place

All too often, the motorcycle has been characterized as a perilous, foolhardy means of transportation. And in many cases this has proven unfortunately true, for here is a vehicle whose stability is predicated on balance—which seems chancy enough—and offers little or no protection for its rider in case of a collision. Admittedly, the deck indeed appears stacked against the motorcycle rider. The fact that the vast majority of auto-motorcycle collisions are the fault of the car driver (68 to 78 percent, depending upon where you are and whose figures you use) offers little comfort. It will not make broken bones heal any quicker.

So, the motorcyclist must watch out for himself. On the road he is a mere individual amidst a swarm of four-wheeled behemoths. Surrounded by sheet steel, padded by foam and upholstery, and cinched in (sometimes) by shoulder harnesses, the big boys can often play bumper tag with relative immunity. You, the motorcyclist, cannot. What may be just a slight tap to an insulated Detroit heavyweight might as well be a nuclear shock to you and your mount, sending both into instantaneous oblivion.

The stakes are high, but with the proper attitudes and skills the motorcyclist can successfully live in this wandering jungle of concrete, steel, and rubber. Throughout the years, much knowledge and experience has been gleaned from professionals in the field—motorcycle patrolmen, bike clubs, racers, enthusiasts, and so on. Applied correctly, this experience and knowledge is clearly your best friend on the road. It will serve to keep you unscathed while allowing a fuller enjoyment of motorcycling.

when you begin . . .

In terms of behavior and response, the motorcycle has very little in common with the automobile. This statement may seem absurdly obvious to some motorcyclists, but there are an uncomfortable number of motorcycle enthusiasts who ride their bikes in the same manner they drive their cars. This is unfortunate, for the motorcycle demands a great deal more from its rider than an auto does from its driver. In many cases cars are driven by unthinking, unplanned response. Indeed, it seems that much of today's traffic enforcement is designed to encourage such driving. The harried family man turned leisure-time biker will likely see the riding experience in an entirely different light than does the "shagger," a motorcycle-mounted blueprint delivery man common to most big cities. Yet even though the shagger might tote up more than 100,000 miles each year on city streets, his chances for avoiding disaster are much better than Mr. Familyman's. Most often, it is the casual motorcyclist who comes to grief, not the professional. Studies also indicate that the likelihood of a motorcyclist's becoming involved in an accident is greatest during the first six months of riding, or in the 16- to 20-year-old age group. Other researchers have found that this same age group with less than six months riding experience suffered twice the accident rate of those of the same age but with greater experience. A 1968 California study shows that the accident rate for inexperienced young riders is significantly higher for motorcycles in comparison to other vehicles. And probably the most telling statistic indicates that about 20 percent of the persons involved in motorcycle accidents were riding for the first or second time.

In many cases the novice motorcyclist has had significant experience as an automobile driver. In teaching the basics of motorcycle riding, this can be a disadvantage. Because motorcycle riding requires somewhat different skills and attitudes, some undesirable habits must be unlearned. The laxity common to many auto drivers can have disastrous consequences if transferred to a motorcycle. It is essential that riders think two wheels, not four.

the intersection

More statistics: almost 40 percent of motorcycle accidents involving another vehicle occur at intersections. Automobile drivers are to blame in almost 70 percent of these accidents, motorcyclists are at fault almost 30 percent of these, and both share the fault in about 2 percent of the accidents.

The most common shortcoming of auto drivers at intersections is failure to yield right of way to the motorcyclist (89 percent). Motorcyclists also most commonly fail to yield right of way (49 percent).

When riding on the open road, the motorcyclist will encounter several different types of intersections: four-way, three-way, signal controlled, uncontrolled, and simple driveways, among others.

The motorcyclist should approach all intersections with great caution. Identify traffic approaching from all directions. Be aware of how fast traffic is approaching. Besides checking traffic from the right and left, pay extra attention to oncoming traffic for vehicles which might be turning left in front of you.

In turn, the motorcyclist should be aware of three things: (1) The motorcycle's relatively small size makes it not so obviously apparent to some motorists as another automobile is. (2) Determining the speed of a motorcycle is not always easy for the car driver. Whatever you do, don't make things harder for the driver by varying your approaching speed. You'll just make matters worse. (3) The vast majority of automobile drivers are looking for other cars at intersections, not motorcycles. The unconscious mind plays tricks on these individuals. As you approach an intersection, just because a motorist looks at you does not necessarily mean he sees you. Proceed with caution, but always expect the unexpected.

Many intersections are made more dangerous by limited vision. Parked trucks, autos, buildings, and shrubbery all contribute to a potentially hazardous scene. Watch out for last-minute surprises. If you are unsure about what lies beyond, don't be reluctant to slow down and double check (Fig. 3-1).

Driveways offer more than their share of thrills, particularly in residential neighborhoods. Very often when a car is coming out of a driveway, it is backing out. The driver's vision and control are significantly hindered. As you approach the driveway entrance, make sure the driver sees you. If necessary, slow down, toot your horn. Once again, the motorist is looking for other cars. Whether he sees you and your motorcycle is yet another matter. Make sure the driver sees you before you reach the driveway entrance.

FIGURE 3-1(a). The street rider should always be aware of how his motorcycle relates to the mainstream of traffic.

FIGURE 3-1(b). Driveways always pose potential hazard to the motorcyclist. Statistics show additionally that, contrary to belief, daylight use of the headlight does not increase rider visibility.

lane position

Throughout our land, lane width is generally between 12 to 14 feet. An auto may fill 7 feet of that, a motorcycle will take up 3 feet or so. To the beginning motorcyclist, it is only logical that he should ride in the center of that lane, leaving comfortable margins on each side.

Don't . . . for several reasons.

The center strip of a lane is usually coated with a layer of dirt and oil. The oil comes from automobile crankcase breathers, drippy transmission seals, and other such sources. This thin layer retains dust, some rubber powder, and fine bits of dirt. It all adds up to a less than ideal tractive surface. If you have to hit the brakes hard, you'll find this out in a hurry. This hazard is most common on the uphill side of a grade, where engines labor harder, forcing out more oily crankcase fumes. The center portion becomes much more hazardous in the rain, when the oil coating combines with water for an extremely slippery surface (Fig. 3-2).

The motorcyclist should also be aware that riding straight behind some automobiles is dangerous because is is not always easily seen there through the rearview mirror. It is suggested that you ride to either side of the lane's center strip. There is some debate about which side of the lane a rider should travel in. But one thing the motorcyclist should be sure of is that he is visible to the driver in front of him. This can be determined easily. You can tell from a safe distance—even at freeway speeds—if a driver can see you by looking through his rear window. Can you see the driver's face in his rear view mirror? If you can see his eyes, he can see you. This is difficult to do at night, however, so it is suggested that you ride in the left third of the lane and follow at a safe distance.

The automobile driver *should* respect the vehicle space of a motorcycle and its relation to the traffic pattern. Auto drivers should avoid crowding or passing a motorcycle in the same lane. Of course, common sense tells drivers not to do this, but after all, the motorcycle is so small, and it doesn't need the whole lane, does it? Many motorists cannot resist the temptation here and allow precious little space for the motorcyclist. The motorcycle should be allowed as much space when being passed as a full-size sedan.

In turn, the motorcyclist, when passing another vehicle, should abide by the same rules. Before he makes a move he should first determine that the other drivers see him. Before passing, he should be in the left third of the lane. In this position, oncoming and following traffic can be checked. When you do pass, do not try to assert your territory by crowding close to the car you are passing. Before returning to your lane, make a backward check to make sure you have left sufficient room for the car behind you.

FIGURE 3-2(a). Because auto and truck engines labor harder while ascending hills, the motorcyclist should expect to encounter an oilier, sootier road surface than on a downgrade.

FIGURE 3-2(b). Don't play games with automobile drivers who follow you too closely. Pull over as soon as it is safe and let them pass.

FIGURE 3-2(c). The motorcyclist should use his rearview mirror frequently to be aware of constantly changing traffic patterns.

Be extra careful if you are riding in a passing lane, for situations can arise which might encourage drivers to enter your lane from the right. For example, a four-lane road narrowing into two lanes or a parked car with its door half open: be vigilant here.

be thick-skinned

Something strange happens to many automobile drivers when a motorcycle comes into view. It seems that they refuse to believe that a human being is on that motorcycle; a warm, breathing, vibrant system of organs, bones, and blood. These drivers will not take you seriously, either as a fellow tax-paying motorist or even as another *Homo sapiens*, encumbered by the same concerns of mortgages, children, and so on.

For example, whereas another automobile driver would be unwaveringly afforded the courtesies of a safe following distance and full stops where the red octagonal sign says to, the motorcyclist is not a real, legitimate motorist, so it's okay to tailgate him and taunt him with rolling stops at the intersection.

Nothing personal, of course. It's just that you're not really there.

There is something highly personal, however, about being ground into the pavement by these automatons. And when confronted with an oblivious tailgater, stopsign-runner, or lane-changer, it is only natural that adrenalin starts to flow, telling our bodies to survive! survive! And, in a split second, we become angry, indeed.

The tendency of the motorcyclist is to make that drowsy four-wheeled peril aware of his incredible lack of judgment, questionable pedigree, and overall lack of driving skill. This is most commonly done through steely stare, word of mouth, or gesture.

At this point, however, the motorcyclist must show great restraint.

Four-hundred-pound motorcycles seldom win physical battles with 4000-pound cars. The auto driver is aware of this, of course, but, in your self-righteous rage, are you? Don't be vindictive, trying to *get back* at that person who just cut you off. You're not going to win. Fancy braking games in front of that driver or swooping lane changes to show your displeasure are both self-defeating and illegal, and one way or another they will bring you grief.

Moreover, motorcycle riding requires your full and constant attention all the time. Reproving anger directed at other motorists will only distract you, increasing your personal risk. The traffic pattern can change drastically in those brief seconds that you are mentally tweaking the other guy's nose. Interestingly, rear-end collisions very often result from this type of lapse in attention.

Granted, these pitfalls are rather obvious and commonsensical, but one natural purpose of adrenalin flow is to override what otherwise may be common sense and prepare the body for "fight or flight."

The motorcyclist should be able virtually to ignore the short-comings of other motorists, no matter how threatening they may be. He should concentrate instead on maintaining an upright stature at a hope-fully safe distance.

can you see me? the danger of daytime headlights

Time and again it has been established that the motorcycle is not inher-ently difficult to see on the road. After all, the machine-rider package presents an image maybe 7 feet long, 5 feet tall, often sparkling with chrome, bright colors, and other high-visibility features. No, as we mentioned before, the visibility problem most often rests with the motorist, who is looking for other cars, not motorcycles. To counter this, some well-meaning individuals and organizations have been encourag-ing motorcyclists to ride with headlights burning during daylight hours as well. Indeed, in some cases their pressure was so intense that laws were enacted by some states to require full-time headlights on motorcy-clists, despite testimony to the contrary by many legitimate experts in the field of motorcycle safety.

There is no conclusive proof, however, that daytime headlights have aided motorcycle safety. As a matter of fact, of the eight states that have had such laws for more than two years, seven experienced in-creases in motorcycle accident rates.

The accident figures are compiled on a per-1000-registrations basis over a two-year minimum span. The increases per state are as follows:

Arkansas	+26.71%
Florida	+ 1.75%
Illinois	+16.43%
Indiana	+13.69%
Montana	+ 0.46%
New York	+ 5.75%
Wisconsin	+ 4.61%

The one state among the eight that had experienced a decrease, Wyoming, also experienced the smallest growth in motorcycle registra-tions.

By comparison, of the states that have not implemented daytime headlight laws and for which complete registration and accident data are available, sixteen have experienced an overall decrease in the number of accidents per 1000 registrations, nine have had an increase, and three remained constant.

Why is riding with a headlight on in the daytime more dangerous? There are two primary reasons.

The motorcycle typically has one headlight, centrally mounted on the front of the machine. A glowing headlight serves to obscure the motorcycle in daylight by causing it to blend with ambient light surroundings. In this way the motorcycle's rate of approach becomes very hard for other motorists to judge. This can lead to particularly perilous situations at intersections, where clear-cut hazards already exist.

With full-time headlight and taillight operation, the motorcyclist is also imperiled because headlights and brakelights lose their effectiveness. There is rarely enough difference in intensity and contrast between taillight and brakelight operations. Following motorists experience difficulty in recognizing that a motorcycle is slowing. In this respect, the motorcyclist has a greater chance of being struck from the rear.

There is a natural light-related hazard the motorcyclist should also be aware of. When the sun is low in the sky and you are traveling away from it, you and your vehicle are difficult to see. For example, an eastbound motorcyclist at sunset can be just barely discernable from his surroundings when approached by a westbound driver. Shadows are low and long, and light-dark contrasts are severe. And the fact that the sun is glaring into the westbound driver's eyes does nothing to help matters. What to do? Well, not much. Just use your head . . . ride cool and easy. Ride as if you were invisible, although still a frangible flesh-and-blood mortal.

following distance

Given adequate traction, the street motorcycle is capable of fair-to-excellent stopping performance. This is good. The majority of automobile drivers, however, are unaware of such potential. This is bad. An automobile following a motorcycle too closely presents a frightening specter to motorcyclists, for the automobile can sweep bike and biker off the road in less time than it takes to think about it. The rider knows this while the driver probably doesn't. Also, the motorcyclist, being relatively exposed to the elements, is far less likely to fall prey to hazardous lapses in concentration. The automobile driver, however, sealed in his airtight, soundtight cocoon, is much more likely to let his mind wander from the tasks at hand. The motorcyclist's peril under these circumstances is considerable.

Your rearview mirrors should be consulted frequently. Make it a point—force yourself—to check the mirrors at regular intervals; at least three times per city block, for example, or ten times each freeway mile. If you don't know who and what is behind and alongside you, your ability to take sudden, life-saving evasive action is jeopardized.

Tailgaters are sometimes discouraged by tapping your brake pedal to flash your stoplight. Don't expect miracles, though. The person oblivious enough to tailgate you can't be expected to respond to the flickering of a motorcycle's taillight. The same goes for motioning the following driver back with your hand. Moreover, the car driver sometimes sees your hand-waving as a personal challenge or insult—people do act peculiar when they get behind the wheel of a car. Don't aggravate tailgaters; they hold all the cards. If you're dawdling, speed up to get clear. Otherwise, move over and let them pass.

And if you're the one who's following? That old rule of thumb about allowing one car length for each 10 mph is still valid. After all, a mediocre street motorcycle can stop from 60 mph in 160 feet or so. You can figure an auto's length to be 18 or 20 feet, so if a rider is alert, he can stop with yards to spare.

Do not concentrate solely on the car immediately in front of you. Be concerned with those several cars ahead of the one you're behind. Nor should you be dependent on the brakelights of that car ahead of you. Use them as general indicators rather than gospel truth. Brakelights don't always work. Also, they do not relate the degree of stopping power being used.

Motorcycle riders and auto drivers should both be aware of safe following distances under different traffic conditions. Another method of determining a safe following distance is rapidly finding favor among experienced riders and drivers alike. It is the "count" method. Here the following rider selects a fixed point ahead of the leading vehicle—a telephone pole, traffic sign, or fire hydrant, for example. When the vehicle ahead passes that point, the motorcyclist or driver counts "one thousand one, one thousand two." If the following vehicle passes the fixed point before the count is completed, the distance between the two is insufficient. This method is good because it works at any speed. As speed increases, the 2-second interval will result in increased distance between the lead and following vehicles. The method is also good because it requires less time to calculate safe following distances and so minimizes rider distraction. Being able to judge distance accurately will prove one of the most valuable abilities you, the motorcyclist, can have.

A motorcyclist approaching another rider in the same lane from the rear is sometimes tempted to pass on the right side. This is not advised. Moreover, some states have laws prohibiting this. It can prove a great mistake to assume that the other rider even knows you're there. A good rider, of course, will be aware of your approach and will pull over to permit you to pass within the lane. But the risk of tangling handlebars requires discretion, even though your locale may allow passing within the lane.

braking technique

Generally speaking, the stopping potential of street motorcycles is much greater than that of automobiles. And at higher speeds, the differences in stopping power become even more startling. The reason for this is simple. It's a lot easier to stop, say, a 500-pound vehicle than it is to stop a 4000-pounder. But don't get overconfident, because there's a hitch. You see, statistically speaking, it's easier for the *average* motorist to realize maximum stopping power from his car than it is for the *average* motorcyclist to achieve best stopping power from his mount. In other words, the auto offers less than a motorcycle, but it's easier to use all it has. The motorcycle's stopping potential is greater but requires more skill to achieve. This is because the auto driver does not have to worry about such things as balance and separate front and rear brakes. The motorist has one braking control, a pedal. Step on it, and you stop. The motorcycle rider, however, must coordinate front and rear stoppers, balance the mount, steer it safely while his wrists are taking the strain of his body being forced forward by deceleration, and cope with other subtler influences.

Nature has given the motorcycle an inherent stability while it is moving. The motorcycle is known as a single-track vehicle; the front wheel directly follows the rear, leaving but a single track. The automobile is a dual-track vehicle; the right side struggles with the left for control of the vehicle. Not so with the motorcycle; where both wheels and the mass they carry are in line and in balance. The motorcycle is built to stabilize itself, and it does, except in cases where the operator makes it do otherwise. Most often, it is through the operator's fright or lack of understanding that the motorcycle is made to act unnaturally. It is among the rider's responsibilities to use his perception and judgment to avoid this.

Maximum braking is achieved when the brakes are just short of locking the wheels. The front brake, due to forward weight transfer from the front wheel, ends up supplying about 70 percent of the braking effort in a panic stop. It is mandatory, therefore, that the motorcyclist be more than just passingly competent when it comes to front brake control. Once locked, the heavily loaded front wheel becomes very difficult to steer and has a tendency to slew sideways. Farther back, the rear wheel, when locked, tries to drive right on past the motorcycle.

Beginning motorcyclists should practice braking. The skills gained might well save a life, not once but many times throughout your riding career (Fig. 3-3). Practice braking under ideal conditions. Locate an area of clean, dry pavement away from all distractions. Have a parent or friend act as observer and, of course, wear your helmet, boots, and gloves. Begin at stopping from low speeds, about 10 mph. Apply the brakes gradually at first, but with each pass squeeze them tighter and tighter. Learn when skidding occurs. Keep the bike arrow straight as you apply the brakes from gradually increasing speeds; make mental note of all the nuances of your rapidly decelerating machine. In this way you won't be unpleasantly surprised when the real thing happens out there in traffic. Note how the front forks compress, how you tend to slide forward on the saddle toward the tank, and how you must tighten your leg muscles to prevent this—all the subtle quirks that will become prominent in a panic situation.

In practicing this way, you learn about both the motorcycle and yourself. You can also develop confidence. But most important, you will learn the braking finesse necessary to cope with contingencies at freeway speeds. Throughout your practice, however, proceed carefully and gradually. With time, 60 mph-to-0 stopping distances in the neighborhood of 115–120 feet may be achieved with a disc-braked middleweight street bike.

FIGURE 3-3. Motorcycles are generally capable of excellent stopping power. Be aware of what you and your machine can do in a tight situation.

A final word of caution: Beware of overconfidence. Don't make the mistake of thinking you can stop your bike with maximum efficiency any time you want. Things just don't work out that way. An emergency is just that; it can't be predicted. Don't count on having such luxuries as clean, dry pavement and advance warning. Making practice stops at a parking lot or race track is much different than avoiding a thoughtless lane changer. When you're practicing, you know that you will soon have to stop. On the street, you don't. Anticipation makes all the difference in the world in physical reactions.

And don't overlook the traction factor. Street surfaces are not all necessarily clean, dry concrete. You'll encounter all sorts of surfaces, including those that are wet, dirty, gravelly, sandy, and oily. Consider, too, that street surfaces do not have to be soaked by a downpour to affect traction. Changes in humidity as well as other subtle factors can alter braking ability.

In short, don't count on having emergency stops occur under ideal conditions.

rain riding

Many of the hazards posed by rainy weather are obvious, so most motorcyclists don't have to be told to ride carefully. There are some tips, however, that not all riders are aware of.

Realize first of all that your visibility is seriously affected. After all, you don't have the benefit of windshield wipers. Go very gently for this reason alone.

Do not ride in the center of the lane, for the reasons we discussed earlier. But remember that now it's even more slippery. Also, pavement is characteristically most slippery during the first half hour of a rainstorm, when oils and slippery, loose particles have not yet been washed away. Traveling uphill in the mountains? Remember the center of the lane will likely have a thin layer of oil spewn out by laboring engines, which makes things all the worse.

Travel in the tracks of cars ahead of you, not between them. The passage of the auto's tire has forced some water away from its path, making things a bit less slippery. And bear in mind that those narrow rain grooves combed into the pavement's surface in so many parts of the United States are for the benefit of automobiles, not motorcycles. Even in dry weather these grooves can make a motorcycle's steering response feel downright spooky, and this combined with rain can make for a definitely unpleasant riding experience. Thus, we motorcyclists have all the more reason to follow those auto tire tracks closely to realize best traction.

Avoid painted pavement traffic lines. These become very slippery when wet and can have you on your wallet before you know it. When crossing these, be delicate with brakes and throttle and try to keep the bike as vertical as possible.

Railroad tracks also pose a serious hazard, for they might as well be ice, they offer so little traction when wet. And to make matters worse, if you're riding parallel to streetcar tracks, for example, your wheels can easily be caught in the surface groove. By all means, stay away from them. Narrow tires have a most difficult time getting out of the grooves. If this happens, don't try to steer the bike out by turning the handlebar; this often causes the front wheel to slide crazily out of control. Instead, keep the front wheel pointed straight and steer the bike out of the groove with your weight. When you encounter tracks in your path, try to hit them at as close to a 90-degree angle as possible, rain or shine.

road hazards

What may appear to be minor road hazards to automobile drivers pose major threats to motorcyclists. The novice motorcycle rider with four-wheeled experience should bear this in mind. Road debris, ruts, potholes, puddles, and other hazards will often require the rider to suddenly change lanes or direction. There are some techniques experienced bikers use to cope with these problems.

It is very important to watch the vehicle ahead of you for movements suggesting hazards ahead. A car moving suddenly to one side may be dodging a piece of lumber in its path.

Riding in the center third of your lane presents a particular peril for motorcyclists. A hazard in the lane might be straddled by the tires of the car in front of you and yet lie squarely in your way. The auto shields the hazard from your vision until it's too late.

A feisty dog leaping out at your motorcycle from the curb is threatening for two reasons. First, his sudden appearance can be very startling and you may be jolted into a violent, uncontrolled lurch. Keep a cool head, however, and don't try to second guess Bowser. Don't try to kick at him, for that will only upset your balance. The dog has already plotted out his course and he's just chasing you for sport. He just looks like he wants a hunk of your calf. Even a small dog can upset you if you hit it. What you should do is leave the throttle where it is, keep your feet on the pegs and move your weight rearward. (The latter is done just in case you do hit the dog.) Violent braking only upsets the dog's timing

FIGURE 3-4. Alarm! A ball rolling into the street is likely to be pursued by a child. To the motorcyclist, hazards are everywhere.

and dangerously loads weight on the front wheel. In short, try to ignore Bowser, but be prepared to hit him, if worse comes to worse.

And the fact that dogs have a way of chasing cats and other dogs doesn't make things any easier. A dog or cat running across the street might be pursued by another animal. Just keep your head, however, and avoid violent maneuvers while our four-footed friends play their games.

Children are not likely to pursue you like dogs, but you can count on them doing almost everything else. (On the other hand, and thankfully, dogs don't ride tricycles!) Is that a ball rolling across the street? Look for a tot to follow it. Also, kids commonly chase other kids, so if you see one in a residential area, expect to see others nearby.

A final caution: Dogs are predictable, kids aren't. The hazard presented by a child in the street is fraught with many times more danger (Fig. 3-4).

There are many, many more contingencies to be met on the street than we have discussed here. But to deal with them all would fill a book. in itself. In these pages we have tried to describe the situations most commonly vexing to motorcyclists and car drivers alike.

But words of advice and reproach cannot do the job alone. Riding a motorcycle safely is still primarily a matter of practical experience. You must be instinctively aware of what your motorcycle is doing and what it is capable of. You must also be constantly attentive to traffic patterns around you. And you must be able to relate your motorcycle to surrounding traffic with safety foremost in mind. All these things come from riding—the more, the better. . . .

4 away from the road

The ins and outs of not falling off

Away from the road an exhilarating world, a world of clean air and secluded trails, awaits the off-road motorcycle enthusiast. It is a world too, of healthful exercise and, if you get far enough away, peace and solace.

But to realize the most benefit from trail riding, the motorcyclist should observe certain techniques, cautions, and courtesies. Hazards exists for off-roaders as well as for street-riding enthusiasts. Minimize these, and motorcycling's off-road adventure is enhanced accordingly. Of course, the beginning rider will require substantial practice to achieve proficiency. This chapter does not pretend to take the place of practical experience. It does intend to augment it, however, and make the sometimes rocky learning period safer and more enjoyable.

which kind is best for me?

Motorcycles in today's showrooms are emblazoned with all sorts of catchy names. Most prominent in the off-road field are the "scrambler," "enduro" and "motocross," and "trials" models. With the exception of trials motorcycles, which we will discuss later, there are no hard definitions for these motorcycles. Generally, though, each has traits distinguishing it from the others.

Up until about the mid-1960s, the word *scrambler* referred to a motorcycle to be raced on the usually smooth-surfaced, closed-course, off-road race tracks popular at that time. A scrambles track also often had a variety of jumps, left and right turns, uphills and downhills. Because of the comparatively smooth track surfaces, there was much emphasis on machines with high-peak horsepower, and thus rather narrow power ranges. Additionally, tires of smoother tread design were favored over heavily lugged knobby tires, as the former offered better traction on the graded, often hard-packed surfaces. Today, however, even though the scrambles races of yore have been almost totally eclipsed by the twistier, rougher motocross type of competition, the scrambler name still survives to some extent, although as much as an advertising term as anything else. The scrambler of today is often more of a street motorcycle than a dirt machine but, because it is commonly fitted with universal-tread tires, high-mounted exhaust pipes, and perhaps lower (numerically higher) overall gearing, it retains limited off-road capability (Fig. 4-1). In recent years, the scrambler designation has lost much of its marketing strength, and so concern over such off-road suitability is confined mostly to used motorcycles. If your mind is set on this type of motorcycle, you should bear in mind that the machine's probably generous weight and often mediocre ground clearance will limit its use to smooth, preferably hard-packed dirt roads.

FIGURE 4-1. Today the "scrambler" motorcycle is more often a street machine with somewhat limited off-road capabilities.

FIGURE 4-2. The enduro motorcycle is generally much more effective as an off-road machine than the scrambler.

The *enduro* motorcycle is generally much more effective as a dual-purpose machine (Fig. 4-2). And for this reason, enduro bikes are probably the most numerous of all off-road machines. The enduro motorcycle is usually street-legal while also having some features necessary for trail riding. It must be remembered, however, that this motorcycle, too, is a compromise machine. It can cope with both street and trail travel adequately, often better than the aforementioned scrambler, but can rarely accomplish either with truly distinctive performance.

Physical characteristics of the enduro machine typically include the following features. The exhaust pipe is mounted high to maximize ground clearance and avoid damage to the pipe itself. (Jagged rocks, for example, can often rip exhaust pipes open or crimp them shut.) Universal-tread tires are standard, for two reasons: (1) some laws prohibit the sale of motorcycles fitted with knobbed tires for street use, and (2) tire patterns well suited for pavement adhesion tend to lack off-road traction. The universal-tread tire—midway between a dirt-only knobbed pattern and a street-only road design—presents a compromise compatible with, but not ideally suited to, either highway or trail applications (Fig. 4-3).

The enduro motorcycle saddle is usually large enough to allow significant fore and aft rider movement, to allow easy front or rear weight bias for off-road contingencies. Similarly, the seat-handlebar-footpeg relationship is very important. The motorcycle should be easily ridden from the standing as well as the sitting position.

Footpegs should be of the folding (hinged and spring-load to fold upward and rearward) variety. In this way painfully bruised ankles can be avoided. A fall can also be precipitated by a fixed peg digging into the ground when the bike is leaned over, and a folding peg obviates this hazard as well.

Footpeg placement is important, too. Footpegs should allow comfortable riding in both seated and standing positions. If the footpegs are too far forward, the standing rider will be forced to pull on the bars more than he would otherwise. This throws inordinate strain on the shoulder muscles. Generally, footpegs are located about 20 inches below and to

FIGURE 4-3. The universal-tread tire is basically a compromise between street and off-road tread patterns. It is suitable for use on pavement and dirt, but is not ideal for either.

the front of the seat. As a rule of thumb, when you are trying on a dirt bike, attempt to move from a sitting position to a standing position with your hands in your pockets. If the footpeg-to-seat relationship is correct, you should be able to do this easily.

The fit of the handlebar is also crucial. It is important to know that most motorcycle steering is not done by turning the handlebar but by leaning the motorcycle. Thus, the leverage provided by an overly wide handlebar is not only unnecessary, but a hindrance. If the handlebar requires you to move your arms in an uncomfortably long arc, then its length or fore-aft adjustment is wrong.

Correct positioning for the bar is as follows. Stand on the footpegs. From this position you should be able to swing your arms forward and hold the handgrips securely, without discomfort. Now sit down. Your fingers should be able to reach out and wrap over the control levers. Your hands should be horizontal to the ground, and an imaginary line through the bar should be parallel with another line passing through the last three knuckles of your extended fingers.

While sitting as far forward on the seat as you can, you should be able to turn the front wheel throughout its full arc without having to twist or lean your torso away from the upright position. If the bar does prove too long, its ends can be removed with a hacksaw.

Overall weight of the enduro machine can vary from about 240 pounds for a lightweight 250-cc model (such as Ossa or Bultaco) to about 315 pounds for a larger-displacement four-stroke machine (such as Honda XL-350). Bear in mind also that a motorcycle's weight is much more critical in terms of off-road riding ease and performance. A heavy motorcycle on the trail can prove very tiring because the rider plays a much more active role in its balance and overall physical dynamics than he does in leisurely pavement riding, which requires a fraction of dirt riding's physical activity.

Enduro refers to a particular type of off-road competition in which riders are required to maintain a specific time schedule over a given course, sometimes as long as 500 miles. An enduro is more of a challenge to motorcycle and rider endurance than an all-out speed race. Also, because of the precision involved, it is a test of the riders' mathematic skills in geographical computation.

Because of the nature of this kind of competition, the enduro bike is usually untemperamental, reliable, relatively easy to ride, and capable of negotiating almost any kind of terrain.

The *motocross* motorcycle makes no pretense about being street-legal; it is a no-compromise racing machine (Fig. 4-4). A motocross race is run over a closed circuit usually somewhere between 1 and 2 miles in length. The motocross track is characterized by very tight, twisting

FIGURE 4-4. The motocross motorcycle is a racing machine made strictly for off-road use.

turns, uphills and downhills that are sometimes steep and rough, and often undulating surface.

If you have ever seen a motocross event, you should have a good idea of the serious nature of this kind of motorcycle. It is not at all uncommon for off-road enthusiasts to use motocross motorcycles not for racing but for weekend fun on the trail. Indeed, some riders prefer motocrossers for cow-trailing because of the bike's minimum weight, knobby tires, low gearing, and generous horsepower, features typical of such motorcycles right off the showroom floor.

The motocross machine is basically similar to the enduro motorcycle, although pared down to its bare essentials. No lights, of course, are fitted to the motocrosser, no universal-tread tires, nothing that it doesn't really need. Ground clearance is high, usually in excess of 9 inches. The exhaust pipes of newer motocross racers, although fitted with silencers by their manufacturers, do not dampen noise enough for street use. The silencers are fitted to reduce the obnoxious piercing noise emitted by the engines on the race track, and the motorcycle industry, through the Motorcycle Industry Council, has imposed upon itself maximum noise limits on all motorcycles made. Unfortunately, these devices are all too often removed by motorcyclists in the belief that more power will result. Sometimes it increases power, sometimes not. Yet the motorcyclist who does this will surely do damage to this sport because of the excess noise in this lopsided tradeoff for perhaps a bit more power. Fortunately, some race tracks have instituted noise emissions tests for contestants' bikes, and those emitting more than, say, 115 decibels at half-throttle measured at 20 inches from the exhaust are declared ineligible. Interestingly, at an international motocross race, the winning motorcycle put out 104 dB, the quietest of the top ten finishers.

Noise aside, generally, the more expensive a bike is, the less suitable it will prove for fun riding and the more serious its intent. There are some exceptions to this rule; mostly they are the bikes that manufacturers have called motocrossers for advertising reasons, even though such motorcycles would stand little chance in competition.

The *trials* motorcycle is a specialized machine with distinctive mechanical characteristics. As a rule, trials bikes have excellent ground clearance—perhaps 12 inches or more. They also tend to be light in weight; some 250-cc machines scale in at less than 200 pounds (Fig. 4-5). Wheelbase is short for maneuverability, fork inclination is steep—25 to 27 degrees or so—for quick steering, and the engine's state of tune is very mild, with lots of low-speed torque, rather heavy flywheels, and low overall gearing. The trials motorcycle is designed to be ridden from a standing position, so its saddle is usually small, hard, and minimal. In short, the trials bike is not very good for much else but trials competition.

What kind of contest requires such a machine? Well, *trials,* or *observed trials,* to be more accurate, is a type of motorcycle competition

FIGURE 4-5.   The trials motorcycle tends to be very lightweight, with generous ground clearance, quick steering, and low-speed tractability.

FIGURE 4-6.   The motorcycle sport of observed trials stresses throttle control and balance, not speed. The rider is penalized for touching his feet to the ground.

that stresses throttle control and balance, not speed (Fig. 4-6). The trials rider is assessed penalty points for "dabbing" (touching the ground with his feet), for leaving the extremely tight confines of the course and, of course, for falling off his motorcycle. The trials course can be made up of as many as a dozen or so separate areas called "sections." A section might be anywhere from a hundred yards or so up to perhaps a half mile in length. Typically, a trials competitor may encounter, say, a rocky section, sandy sections, uphills, downhills, and obstacles, such as logs, to surmount. The rider will be required to ride each section three times during the entire event. His goal, of course, is to "clean" each section, that is, to negotiate it without incurring any penalty points. And while the spectacular slides and jumps of motocross racing are lacking in trials competitions, the challenge is no less imposing and the rider's physical condition is no less important.

Trials motorcycles are not usually equipped with lights or other street-going accoutrements. Mufflers are used, however, because they significantly help engines maximize low-speed power output.

The trials motorcycle is designed to be ridden from the standing position for several reasons. First, with the rider's weight centered down around the footpegs rather than on the saddle, the motorcycle can be ridden with much more precision. Second, during passage over rough terrain, the rider's flexing legs act as shock absorbers, allowing for less fatigue and better rider control. The motorcycle bounces around beneath the rider, but he remains somewhat isolated from the pounding. Third, the rider's weight can be quickly shifted fore, aft, or to either side as the motorcycle requires. Finally, motocross racers and enduro competitors commonly ride standing up for the same reasons. As a matter of fact, many professional motocross racers spend their training hours riding at race speeds on machines with the saddles removed altogether.

Among other features an off-road motorcycle should possess are fenders that are mounted high up, away from the tires. This is to avoid mud buildup between tires and fenders, for this buildup can cause the wheel to stop turning, sometimes suddenly, with upsetting results.

The U.S. Forest Service requires all off-road motorcycles to have an approved spark arrestor fitted to the exhaust system. Virtually all new machines come equipped with them, but it is a definite thing to watch for when shopping for a used bike. Spark arrestors are easily identified because the law requires that they be stamped "U.S. Forest Service approved" and that they bear their manufacturer's approval number. Motorcycles lacking such a stamping are considered by forest rangers to be illegal for riding in designated areas.

Because of the wide variation in off-road motorcycles, because of their many different engine displacements, overall weights, gearing, and other features, the choice can be difficult for the beginning rider. You must determine what is best for your own needs. Of course, the ideal motorcycle is one on which you feel confident and comfortable and yet whose performance offers you a challenge to improve your riding skill. In other words, you must choose a mount whose performance— acceleration, handling, braking, and so on—exceeds your talent. In this way you can grow into the bike. This is not to suggest, however, that you rush out and purchase a thoroughbred championship motorcycle; just look for a machine of such potential that you won't become bored with it once you achieve riding proficiency.

Many things must be taken into account here, such as your weight, the type of terrain the bike will be used on, the amount of money you can spend, and so on. In making your decision, don't overlook seeking out local expert riders and mechanics whose opinions you value. Motorcycle dealers, too, are anxious to help a new rider make a sound decision because it will assure the return business of a satisfied customer.

where shall we ride?

Just a few years ago, this question would have seemed pointless, for talk about governmental closure of public lands was just that . . . talk. It was not taken seriously by the majority of off-road enthusiasts. Sweeping land closure, however, became a reality in the early 1970s, and the diminishing available riding areas today pose an increasingly complex problem. Until the early to mid-1960s, when motorcycles were not so numerous, a rider could travel almost anywhere off the pavement, bothering no one. However, because of problems of noise control and some environmental concerns, it became apparent that the burgeoning numbers of off-roaders were no longer an innocuous element. As a result, the most readily accessible public lands were closed to off-road vehicles. And soon afterward, other less popular but no less sensitive locales were also closed. So today's motorcyclist has but two choices: either to travel farther away from civilization to pursue dirt riding or to ride at a privately owned motorcycle playground, many of which have opened throughout the country.

The motorcyclist out in the wilderness is not without responsibilities. Most important is that of respecting private property. Unauthorized riding on private land has caused significant criticism of motorcyclists in recent years and, unfortunately, much of it with good reason. Most off-road riders respect fences and no trespassing signs, but there are many who haven't. Private property, even though it may be uninhabited, is still private, and the owner's rights must be respected. Land owners generous enough to grant riding permission want to know who is using their land and how it will be used. Reassure them that you have safety equipment and that all bikes in your group are equipped with mufflers. The land owner should not have to worry about careless riders injuring themselves on his property, nor should he have to worry about excess noise or destructive riding practices. In some areas, government-owned land is restricted. Public land, which belongs to all of us, is under the control of the federal Bureau of Land Management. This overseeing organization has authority to prohibit off-road traffic in many wilderness areas. It is a good idea to determine the status of unposted land before possibly violating a closed area.

The trail rider also has a responsibility to be aware of the circumstances of the nonbiker. A motorcycle can easily frighten a horse. If you meet horseback riders on the trail, pull off the trail and stop your engine until the horses have passed.

before the ride . . .

No one will disagree with the fact that being stranded away from other people can be dangerous. Yet it seems that comparatively few of us take this contingency seriously. Were your motorcycle to break down or run out of fuel, or if you injured yourself even only a mile from help, disaster could result. To prepare for such problems, there are several cautions to observe.

Don't ride alone. In time of emergency, a companion can mean the difference between life and death. Use the buddy system when riding in the wilderness. Unknown terrain offers the excitement of discovery but also can pose hazards to the unsuspecting rider. If you must ride alone, at least file a "flight plan." Let someone know your intended route and destination. Thus, in case you do lose your way, searchers will at least have your approximate location.

Needless to say, your motorcycle should be well prepared and have a full tank of gasoline before you get underway. As precautionary measures, there are several easily stowable items you should take along. In case you become stranded in the wilderness, a book of matches can provide you with fire, be it a signal fire or just heat to keep the cold away. And long after you're too hoarse to shout, remember that a whistle will still be heard over great distances. A tow rope can be of invaluable aid in case of a mechanical breakdown. Having to push a motorcycle o'er hill, dale, and sandwash is exhausting work, if you can do it at all. Further, many a disabled motorcycle has been lost to thieves after being left by its owner in search of help. There is no need to be concerned that a rope would hinder your riding; just wear it around your waist as a belt. About 12 feet of strong nylon twine works nicely. A canteen of water is valuable for obvious reasons, but there are few motorcyclists who carry one even occasionally. For a dollar or two, you can buy an ammunition belt from a war surplus store to which you can attach the canteen. Small cartridge carriers made to attach to ammunition belts can be used to carry other items, such as salt pills, spare chain links, and nuts and bolts.

Now that your precautionary inventory has been collected, all that remains is to give your motorcycle a preliminary check. Gasoline and oil should be topped off. Next, examine the drive chain for proper lubrication and adjustment. Many good, easily applied aerosol chain oils take

FIGURE 4-7. The off-road rider should dress with personal safety in mind. Helmet, gloves, boots, and leather pants are not uncomfortable yet provide excellent protection.

just seconds to use, so there is little reason for chains to get dry. Adjustment of chain tension is outlined in your bike's owner's manual. Include the aforementioned spare chain master link in your tool kit just to be safe. Also, if you have room in your tool kit or on your person to bring a Vise-Grip or equivalent adjustable tool, so much the better, for it can serve a variety of uses, from tightening bolts to clamping components together. Some motorcyclists simply tape Vise-Grips, spark plug wrenches, and such to out-of-the-way places on the motorcycle. Strong, waterproof, fabric-backed duct tape is the overwhelming favorite here.

In terms of personal preparation, the rider should dress for protection but not at the expense of comfort (Fig. 4-7). A helmet should always be worn when riding; ditto, tall, well-padded protective boots. Leather pants are not mandatory; dungarees or other rugged trousers will suffice.

However, leather pants, often featuring additional protective padding at hips, thighs, and knees, are best suited to the job and can minimize injury in case of a spill.

Gloves are not mandatory, but they're a good idea nonetheless. Even if your hands are toughened and calloused, they are still subject to painful abrasion during a mishap. Also, branches and thorns have a way of gouging the backs of your hands when you are traveling through the brush. Because of these factors, gloves can be a useful asset.

If the weather is warm, at least wear a light windbreaker or a motocross jersey. In this way you will be protected from sunburn and insects, as well as having some—albeit slight—shielding from "road rash."

Prices for the various required pieces of riding apparel vary from bargain basement to breathtaking. Don't be intimidated into purchasing clothing just because the sales display tells you that international motocross stars use a particular brand. Make your purchases on the basis of how well the clothing fits your body and pocketbook. Plan on keeping your boots at least one year, maybe two or three, and your leather pants for the same period. Examine them closely for quality and fit, with an especially close eye toward potentially irritating seams and zippers. These are the small things that can prove very bothersome when riding for several hours at a time.

riding technique

If there is any universal trait of a motorcycle in the dirt, it is slipping and sliding. It is this habit of the machine that spooks most new riders. Sure, the effect can be intimidating at first, but once you accept it as a natural part of the machine's behavior and *take advantage of it* on occasion, you will be able to relax and enjoy the sport's finer points, while also increasing your versatility and riding skill.

Trail riding is probably the commonest form of dirt motorcycling. While some don't regard riding on a graded dirt road as true off-roading, it is dirt riding nonetheless and requires a certain technique to master. Graded dirt roads used by other types of vehicles tend to be relatively smooth, perhaps with curves of larger radius than other unpaved paths. As a result, the motorcyclist is tempted to travel faster than he might otherwise. This type of dirt road, sometimes called a *fire road*, requires intense concentration at brisk speeds, for several reasons. The fire road's surface is often not uniform; it may vary from a highly tractive, hard-packed texture on the inside of a turn to a loose, slippery powdery texture at the outside. Surface variations are not confined just to curved portions of the road, either. They may appear anywhere. Additionally, large rocks may protrude from the road. Rocks may be securely fixed in the surface or may be loose on the road. Either way, a serious hazard is presented to the unsuspecting rider, because such rocks can easily deflect the front wheel of the motorcycle with consequent loss of control. Another more obvious peril to the overexuberant dirt rider is meeting a vehicle traveling in the opposite direction. Because of the often marginal tractive conditions, it can be very difficult to stop or take evasive action. And even if you have the traction, you might not yet have the necessary skill for such sudden maneuvering.

So, even though a road may have inviting straightaways and sweeping turns, the safety-conscious rider should ride at reduced speeds and maintain constant alertness for hazards. Avoid sudden moves on your motorcycle. Dirt riding is predicated upon smoothness of movements, and motorcycles are particularly sensitive to sudden changes in direction.

stopping

One of the more difficult maneuvers for the beginning rider, and certainly the most important, is stopping. To practice stopping off the road, take your motorcycle to a flat, reasonably straight area, for here you can gain experience in straight-line stopping. Aboard your bike, approach the straight area at perhaps middle revs in second gear to mid-third gear, about 20 or 30 mph. Keep your body weight rearward on the saddle, using your feet against the footpegs to prevent yourself from sliding forward on the seat. Look straight ahead. Pull the clutch lever in and depress the rear brake pedal. While applying the rear brake, squeeze the front brake lever. Try to apply as much pressure as possible without locking the front wheel. Keep front wheel steering movements absolutely minimal. In practicing this maneuver, just release the brakes if the motorcycle starts to move sideways, and the laws of physics will let the motorcycle straighten up of its own accord.

The three most important points of braking are these: (1) Keep the motorcycle straight. It doesn't take much braking effort to induce a slide when your motorcycle is leaning to the side, and the farther it is leaning, the easier it is to cause a slide. (2) Keep your weight rearward. Under even seemingly delicate braking, weight is suddenly transferred to the front end of the vehicle (Fig. 4-8). Besides removing weight from the rear wheel and making it easier for the wheel to skid, the front tire has to work

FIGURE 4-8.   Beginning riders should learn braking proficiency first. Pick a clear spot of dirt road and practice stopping. Note how this motorcycle's front suspension is deeply compressed under decelera- tion and how the rear tire is relatively unloaded because of forward weight transfer.

much harder to maintain traction. While the rear wheel becomes un- loaded, the front wheel can become overloaded, if you're not careful. The compressed front fork assumes a *diminishing-trail mode*. This means that *trail*, a crucial dimension which describes the distance by which the front tire's contact patch trails the bike's steering axis, is drastically shortened. With trail shortened, the motorcycle steers much quicker, is much more sensitive to steering inputs, and is more easily deflected by road irregularities. Keeping your weight as far rearward as possible minimizes weight transfer and so minimizes the aforemen- tioned perils as well. (3) Do not turn the front wheel. Keep steering movements to an absolute minimum. A skidding front wheel offers no control. The front wheel pointed straight ahead offers greatest traction. Turn it just a few degrees from straight ahead, and the amount of braking force it can accommodate is lessened drastically. Highly experienced motorcyclists are capable of extensive braking maneuvers while leaning and turning, but this talent is rarely achieved without sustaining more than a few bumps and abrasions along the way.

It is common practice among dirt riders to adjust the front brake cable so that when the lever is squeezed to its limit, the wheel is just shy of locking. In this way panic stops can be made without fear of skidding the front wheel. On the other hand, it should be pointed out that a brake so adjusted will lack the total stopping strength of a conventionally adjusted brake. It is suggested that you master use of a conventionally adjusted front brake before experimenting with various cable adjustments.

Another braking technique you may find useful off the road involves using only the rear wheel brake. As you practice on smoother areas, you will notice that a rear wheel skid can be induced easily and that it can be controlled without drastic compensations. If the motorcycle is leaned slightly to either side, however, the rear end shows a marked tendency to slide to the opposite side. Most riders can make the motorcycle do this safely and predictably after a little bit of practice. This technique can be put to use to accomplish reasonably quick stopping. Because the tire is being more or less dragged sideways in relation to the direction of travel, its ground contact patch is altered. You can take advantage of this condition by locking the rear wheel and allowing the rear end to step out sideways and, of course, steering in the direction of travel. In this way the motorcycle is said to be "crossed up." The motorcycle's rear tire realizes increased contact area and so allows faster stopping. This maneuver should be considered only for low-speed riding. At speeds above about 30 mph, it becomes tricky, even for an highly experienced rider.

downhilling

You may ask why we discuss going down hills before we deal with going up them. Well, because the beginning rider finds it so exhilarating to launch full-throttle assaults up a slope, he often finds himself to be much like a cat up a tree. He got up there with ease, but coming down is a much different matter. Besides, often as not, our enthusiast made it up the slope just part way and now must somehow return to the bottom in one piece. So, before you get into such a situation, we'll describe how to get out of it.

There are three basic ways of descending hills: riding, foot dragging, and bulldogging. We'll begin with riding.

The most important thing to remember here is to always keep the wheels turning when you are going downhill. A motorcycle's gyroscopic stability increases as its wheel speed increases. Many professional racers are quick to point out that hill descents should be made at as fast a speed as possible for this reason. You should also bear in mind that a skidding wheel offers no directional control. The wheels must be kept turning, otherwise the motorcycle has no directional control and cannot be steered around obstacles in your way. Skidding wheels also allow the motorcycle to skate unpredictably. Ideally, the wheels should have just enough braking applied so that they are just short of locking for maximum stopping power. Braking finesse necessary to do this can be acquired through moderate practice.

A descent can be achieved with the motorcycle in neutral, but this is not advised because too much emphasis is placed on the rider's braking skill. Also, the rider may have to use his foot to maintain stability, thus forcing him to forsake use of the rear brake. With the motorcycle in gear, this problem is not so acute, because the engine's compression will offer a modicum of control.

The object is to choose a gear ratio low enough to effectively retard the motorcycle's rate of descent but not so low that "overrun skidding" will occur. The latter takes place when the motorcycle exceeds the maximum engine speed allowed by the gear ratio in use. The engine cannot keep up with the vehicle's speed, and wheel skidding occurs. Many people impulsively put the motorcycle in low gear before the descent, where the use of second or even third gear might offer safer riding. Choosing the appropriate gear for descending a particular hill is a matter of judgment. The rider must strike a balance between his motorcycle's capabilities and the steepness of descent. Some beginners will find this difficult, but with experience such judgments take place almost by reflex.

Choosing your path down the hill is extremely important. A motorcycle going downhill is difficult to steer even under good conditions, because in this situation the front wheel is carrying most of the vehicle's weight; braking and the motorcycle's nose-down attitude combine to transfer much weight from rear to front. And complicating matters is the diminished-trail condition of the partially compressed front fork. As a result, changing direction once you're underway can be a very delicate maneuver. Try to avoid rocks, ruts, and other surface irregularities that can deflect the machine's wheels. If some ruts cannot be avoided, try to encounter them at as close to perpendicular as possible. Wheel deflection is minimal if the angle of attack between the wheel and rut is 90 degrees.

Be especially watchful after a rain. Rain can loosen rocks or move them, make potholes, and create ruts. Even if you're very familiar with a particular area, you should exercise caution after a rain because of the way it tends to change terrain.

In choosing your path of descent, always look at the bottom of the hill. Green grass at the base of a slope might indicate a gully; water will collect in the gully and make the surrounding area green.

Remember also that even if there are no rocks in your intended path, there still might be rocks and other hazards at the bottom of the hill. During rainstorms and snowstorms, rocks will roll down a hill and collect at its base, waiting for unsuspecting riders.

Most important, when you are riding down a grade keep your body weight *rearward*. The front wheel must be kept light to afford steering control. This point cannot be emphasized strongly enough, for off-road riding very often requires the rider to keep his weight as far to the rear as possible. There are many situations which require this—riding over rocky streambeds and sand, for example, as well as going over jumps and dropoffs—not just downhilling.

Beware of locking your elbows to hold yourself rearward. When this is done, you lose the ability to make a sudden turn if you see an obstacle in your way. Instead of straightening your arms fully, leave your elbows slightly bent to allow some movement and grip the fuel tank with your knees to hold you back (Fig. 4-9).

FIGURE 4-9.   When riding downhill, you must stand on the footpegs and keep your weight well rearward. The elbows should be slightly bent for smoother control.

Steering while downhilling can be very touchy. You can make directional changes with reasonable speed and safety, however, by leaning the motorcycle in the direction you want to go. Try to keep handlebar steering to a minimum, using lateral weight shifts instead. In this way the overloaded front wheel's traction is not additionally stressed.

The foot-dragging technique of downhilling is largely self-explanatory (Fig. 4-10). While sitting on the motorcycle, put the machine in low gear and turn the engine off. Throughout your descent, manipulate the clutch so that the engine drags with minimal tire slippage. Drag the boot you change gears with. In this way you are operating the rear brake with your other foot and the front brake by hand. If you start to lose your balance and must take your foot off the brake pedal to hold yourself up, just let the clutch out and allow the engine to slow the rear wheel.

If the rear wheel has a tendency to skid and slide to one side or another, release the rear brake and let the rear wheel turn and regain traction.

FIGURE 4-10.   The foot-dragging technique of descending hills allows you to use your legs as outriggers to stabilize the motorcycle.

FIGURE 4-11. If the slope is severe or otherwise dangerous, the bulldogging method can be effective. Lean the motorcycle against your hip and dig your feet into the ground.

Experienced motorcycles resort to bulldogging only in extreme conditions. It is a slow method and requires that you get off your machine and walk it downhill (Fig. 4-11). At the top of the slope, as you stand to one side of your motorcycle, pick your path carefully, looking for soft, loose soil rather than hard dirt. Stop the engine and make sure the ignition is off. Shut off the gasoline supply at the fuel tank petcock. Put the motorcycle in first gear.

Now lay the upper part of your body against the motorcycle's saddle to bear weight on the rear wheel. Use engine compression to slow the rear wheel, using the clutch lever much like a brake. The rear wheel will turn with the clutch in. Apply pressure to the front brake with your right hand. Dig your heels into the dirt so your boots are also used for braking. (Incidentally, this illustrates the difference between the sole of a motocross boot and that of an enduro boot. The motocross sole is smooth, for easy foot sliding on the motocross track. The enduro boot, however, is heavily lugged, allowing the rider's feet good purchase on the ground so that he can push his machine without slipping.) From this stance, the bulldogging rider can lay his motorcycle on the ground if it starts to get away from his control.

hill climbing

Before attempting to climb a hill on your motorcycle, pause to plan your moves. You can "read" the hill by visually examining its features. Rocks, ruts, loose and hard dirt, shrubbery—they will all have an effect on the motorcycle. You must plan your path before you start, because if you try to pick your way as you go, chances are the climb will be sloppy and erratic at best . . . or a painful spill at worst. Rocks and bumps can cause your motorcycle to become airborne, which leads to instability and can sacrifice valuable momentum. The best and the fastest way up a hill is almost always the smoothest, both in terms of terrain and rider technique. Try to maintain a course that does not require delicate on-off throttle work to keep control.

Make use of your momentum. It is not at all difficult to induce energy-wasting wheelspin when climbing a hill, for the gradient of the slope and the dirt surface combine to affect traction sorely. Providing you have chosen the smoothest way to the top, you should try to gain as much momentum as possible before you reach the base of the hill. Momentum can be critical in hillclimbing, and just a few mph at the bottom can spell the difference between success and failure.

Momentum is beneficial in other ways. Often a hill that can be climbed in second or even third gear cannot be climbed in low gear. Why? Many off-road motorcycles have a first gear so low that on a steep hill engine power is wasted through wheelspin. In second gear, engine torque multiplication through the gearbox is less and your speed—and thus momentum—will be greater, two factors helping to minimize wasteful wheelspin and maximize forward drive. The most important use of momentum is to carry you and your motorcycle through areas that offer no traction.

Successfully climbing a hill also requires you to make fore-aft weight shifts, as you try to strike a balance between maximum rear wheel traction and a front wheel pawing for the sky. At times you must have your weight far enough rearward for good rear wheel traction. As the motorcycle surges ahead under power, however, the front wheel will tend to leave the ground. A third factor is throttle technique. Too much throttle, and the wheel spins; not enough, and momentum is lost and the engine may bog and stall.

FIGURE 4-12. When you are climbing hills, stand on the footpegs and keep your weight forward for best control.

So now that you've chosen your path and are acquainted with some of hillclimbing's basics, you're ready to give it a try. Depending upon the amount of space you have to gain momentum, begin your ride by running the motorcycle up to at least second, or perhaps third, gear. Do not sit on the saddle. In climbing hills, always stand on the footpegs; this effectively lowers the motorcycle's center of gravity by concentrating the rider's weight down at the footpegs rather than up at the saddle surface (Fig. 4-12). As you ascend the slope, keep power on; if engine speed starts to drop significantly, don't hesitate to downshift. Many riders fail hillclimbing attempts because they have allowed the engine to bog, or even stall, midway up the hill. A slight mistake, a pause, a too-late downshift, and the motorcycle rapidly loses headway. Trying to get a motorcycle restarted halfway up a hill is very difficult. You might as well turn around and go back to the bottom for another try, in the vast majority of cases. Remember, in hillclimbing it is always best to overrev the engine rather than let it lug. This is because (1) lugging generally does more internal damage to an engine, and (2) an overrevving engine develops more horsepower than its lugging counterpart. Both lugging and overrevving should be avoided because they place abnormal strains on an engine; the good rider can easily avoid both conditions. Our point here is that when forced with a choice between these two evils, overrevving is the less harmful.

As you accelerate up the slope, be sensitive to what the front wheel is doing. Is it starting to loft into the air? It is being pressed firmly into the ground? Or is it just skating across the ground lightly? Of the three conditions, the best is when the tire just lightly skims the ground. Of course, if the front wheel is in the air, you have no steering control; also, the motorcycle can loop over backward from this position. If you feel the front end starting to rise, bring it back down not by rolling off the throttle but by moving your body weight forward. The standing riding position allows you do to this easily with precise balance. If the tire is making full contact on the ground, you'll probably benefit from shifting your weight rearward, lightening load on the front wheel while increasing traction at the rear.

Many riders exhibit a strong tendency to soar exuberantly over the crest of a hill with full throttle. Play it safe . . . don't. Many motorcyclists have learned the hard way that likely as not the hill descends just as quickly on the other side. There are other hazards, too, that aren't readily seen from the base of the hill, such as ditches, cliffs, and fences, all eager to upset the careless motorcyclist.

water crossings

Crossing a stream inspires dread in some motorcyclists. It shouldn't, for water crossings offer both challenge and fun. A little bit of practice and forethought are required, plus a motorcycle of adequate power, because the secret of the entire maneuver is a precisely timed wheelie (Fig. 4-13). Master this and there's no reason at all why you should get wet crossing a stream.

Hypothetically, let's begin with a simple crossing perhaps ten yards wide. Make a smooth approach to the water in a lower gear—first or second. The motorcycle's higher gears usually don't offer enough torque to loft the front wheel when you want to and keep it clear of the water's surface. Stand on the footpegs with your knees straight and your weight well rearward. About 3 to 5 feet from the edge of the stream, bring the front wheel up by suddenly pulling the throttle open. The front end should come up a foot or so from the surface. Using your balance and throttle, make only your motorcycle's rear wheel enter the water. Once you enter the water, you'll probably notice that, due to drag of the water on the rear wheel, the front end will tend to fall back down in the stream. So as you go across the water, you must also open the throttle further.

FIGURE 4-13. When crossing streams at speed, the rider must wheelie across the water to avoid a thorough drenching.

If the crossing is wide—say, 30 yards across—it is most unlikely you'll be able to carry the front wheel the entire distance. Over such a distance water drag will slow the bike so much that the front wheel cannot stay above the water.

You don't need to have a stream to practice water crossings. When you're out trail riding, simply pick a smooth section of ground and mark off a spot to show where the water starts and another spot to show where it stops. Using this section, practice your wheelies, pulling up the front wheel as you approach the first mark and keeping it in the air until you reach the second mark.

Wide streams, water crossings too far to wheelie across, are handled in a different manner. Once you've determined that the stream is shallow enough to ride across, you enter it slowly in first gear. Whether you ride standing or sitting is optional. But whichever position you're in, try to keep a maximum of weight on the rear wheel. Use the throttle delicately. Too much will cause excessive wheelspin, allowing the motorcycle to dig itself a furrow in the streambed. Attempt to maintain an even, smooth flow of power to the rear wheel. Avoid making turns

FIGURE 4-14.   Many small-displacement machines lack the power to wheelie for significant distances. If the water is not too deep, these vehicles can be ridden across streams at low speed.

during your passage, or anything else that can affect the machine's somewhat delicate progress. Small-displacement machines with insufficient power to wheelie should be ridden across at low speed (Fig. 4-14).

There is a good rule of thumb to remember when you're unable to determine positively the depth of a stream or the presence of obstacles just below its surface. When a stream widens, it gets shallower. When it narrows, it gets deeper. So, generally speaking, you should attempt most stream crossings at the widest point. Further, a rippled stream surface may indicate shallow water, while the proverbial still waters are likely to run deep.

Streams and rivers, both deep and shallow, should be treated with respect. They pose potential hazards. If, for example, you have stalled your machine midstream, you will find that your strength alone might be insufficient to push the bike to the other side. Indeed, this can be a serious problem even if the water is only a few inches deep. We spoke earlier in this chapter about the value of riding with someone, the buddy system. A motorcycle stuck in mud, jammed between rocks, or mired in deep, soft sand can be a very serious problem, often with frightening implications. Such a situation is clearly where the buddy system is most valuable.

loose sand

Some motorcyclists are intimidated by sand. They feel that their motorcycle's stability has been reduced to almost nothing and, perhaps, that doom is imminent. Well, even though the motorcycle rarely achieves a stable mode of progress, the rider certainly should not avoid sandy areas. Sand is a relatively safe surface to practice on because it is soft to fall off in, its generally soft texture contributes little to abrasions, and its peculiar tractive characteristics allow plenty of room for learning errors. When learning how to ride in sand, just remember two things: (1) keep your weight rearward, and (2) do not oversteer. But more about these points later.

Starting off in soft sand presents a tough challenge to some motorcyclists, but it is not particularly difficult as long as a few rules are observed. To begin with, make sure the motorcycle is straight up and down and pointed straight ahead. Next, bring the engine up to operating speed and engage the clutch. Try to make a low-gear takeoff with a minimum of wheelspin. Push off with your feet. As soon as the motorcycle starts to move, put your feet on the footpegs. Do not drag your feet any more than absolutely necessary. As the motorcycle gains a couple of yards, you might find it necessary to roll off the throttle slightly to avoid wheelspin. Once reasonable traction is achieved, shift into second gear quickly. The use of second gear should give you enough speed to propel the motorcycle across the top of the loose sand. If the motorcycle begins to bog down, move your weight forward, allowing the rear wheel to spin so the engine can get back into its power range. Once the engine regains its revs, you may move your weight rearward again and continue accelerating and upshift as soon as conditions allow. The torque multiplication of the transmission will often allow too much power to be transmitted to the rear wheel in the lower gears. This results in wheelspin and subsequent instability. For this reason, you want to get into as high a gear as possible without harmfully lugging the engine (Fig. 4-15).

Weight should be kept to the rear because it is crucial that the front wheel does not become overloaded, at which point it takes on a tendency to slew from side to side, dig in the sand, and ultimately toss you off. Weight also should be kept rearward to give the rear wheel maximum traction.

You should take great care steering the motorcycle as you travel across loose sand. The front wheel tends to hunt and move from side to side, a phenomenon that frightens some riders. The secret, however, is to let it hunt. Let the wheel move around and seek its own stability. The anxious rider must learn to relax and let the wheel go through its motions. All you really must do is balance the motorcycle and control

FIGURE 4-15(a). Getting underway on soft sand can be tricky, but it is a relatively safe surface to practice on. Keep your weight rearward, use your feet to push off and to stabilize. Try to minimize wheelspin.

FIGURE 4-15(b). Once underway, keep your weight rearward. Upshift as soon as possible, using the highest gear ratio the engine can comfortably pull. Steer by body leaning and throttle application; front wheel stability can be touchy.

the throttle. The motorcycle is not steered with handlebar movements. Instead, the machine should be steered just by throttle and lots of body English, that is, leaning the motorcycle.

mud

Riding a motorcycle through mud requires a technique very much like sandy terrain. The primary difference is that mud is less forgiving of rider mistakes and things tend to happen more quickly, giving the rider little warning.

Mud can vary a great deal in consistency. The stuff can offer a reasonably tractive, though gummy, surface in one area, yet just a few yards away it might seem to be a bottomless mire. If you are riding in a well-traveled muddy area, pay particular attention to the tracks of those who preceded you. Tracks can reveal much about a particular muddy patch—its depth, water content, and overall consistency, for example. How quickly and to what depth are the tracks of a preceding vehicle filled with water? As a tire spins in the mud, is the goo flung into the air in a murky shower (indicating very wet, slippery mud) or is the mud displaced in larger, firmer hunks (relatively dry mud, probably offering pretty good traction)?

Like sand, mud contributes to a definite loss of steering control. As you motor through it, the motorcycle's handlebars are often easily turned, yet the motorcycle continues going straight. Equally, the machine will often wander on its own even though you're trying desperately to keep the handlebars straight.

To cope with such situations, you should ride the motorcycle much as you would in deep, soft sand. Keep your weight as far rearward as possible while standing on the footpegs. Try to traverse muddy sections in as high a gear as possible to minimize wheelspin, and be delicate with the throttle. Sudden applications of power will break rear wheel traction, probably sending the bike slewing sideways. Keep the front wheel pointed straight. Do not try to steer the motorcycle by turning the handlebars; this will only aggravate the vehicle's instability. Steer the machine through gentle applications of throttle and leaning it in the vector you desire. In other words, suggest to the motorcycle where it should go, but by no means force it.

Another riding tip in sand and mud is to use momentum. The harder the going and the worse the traction, the more valuable momentum is to you. After all, if the drive wheel cannot transmit power, how else are you going to traverse the knotty sections? Momentum offers the additional advantage of gyroscopic balance. Which wheel has more inherent gyroscopic stability, a slow-turning one or a fast-turning one? Entering a poorly tractive area at moderate speed often allows much more stable and safer passage than tippy-toeing through.

conclusion

Within this chapter we have tried to answer the most commonly encountered questions about the many facets of off-roading. Space does not permit detailing all the thoughts and techniques shared by off-road experts. We have tried, however, to condense and distill this vast, complex field into hard facts that (1) inform the curious, (2) inspire those lacking self-confidence, and (3) help the bruised avoid the problems which made them that way.

The one part of off-road that cannot be emphasized enough, however, is that of responsibility. Each year, approved riding areas become fewer and farther between. Of course, there is no more land being manufactured while, on the other hand, converts are being made to the ranks of motorcycling every day. The pressure of numbers is growing, and only demonstrations of responsibility on a 24-hour basis by enthusiasts, both as a group and as individuals, can hope to relieve that pressure.

5 a noise upon the land

Motorcycles, man, and his environment

There has been more than a little confusion about the motorcycle's impact on our environment. This is unfortunate, for a preponderance of material is available that details researches of the subject.

The main areas of concern are those of (1) noise emissions, (2) soil alteration, (3) air pollution, and (4) fuel consumption.

noise emissions

Ever since its inception, the motorcycle has had a reputation of being excessively noisy. This view is so widely held that it is traditional. And, unfortunately, to an uncomfortable degree it has been accurate.

Exactly why many motorcycles have been noisier than their four-wheeled counterparts (up until recent years) is due largely to three factors:

1. *Economics.* Exhaust noise control has not always been relatively simple field it is today. Manufacturers often lacked enthusiasm in fitting efficient mufflers to their machines because of cost effectiveness. Sure, in days of yore, motorcycles could be fitted with mufflers, but the prevailing rationale was that a relatively quiet motorcycle would cost

significantly more than its poorly or completely unmuffled counterpart. And this, of course, would tend to defeat one of the main motivations to buy a motorcycle in the first place. Anyway, some contended, motorcycles are expected to be noisy; it's one of their selling points. Further, some manufacturers have been so insensitive throughout the years as to produce streetgoing motorcycles with absolutely no attempt toward muffling at all.

2. *Technology.* More accurately, the lack of it. The science of sound control has only recently come abreast of the other sciences involved in motorcycle making. The problem has been largely one of size. By necessity, the motorcycle's engine has been relatively small because the overall size of the machine is small. Generally, to achieve acceptable performance from this somewhat limited physical package required that the powerplant be given every possible advantage, minimal muffling for maximum engine breathing being chief among them. Another drawback was that effective mufflers tended to be overly large in relation to the rest of the motorcycle. Remember that an automobile chassis can usually accommodate hefty components with much greater ease than a motorcycle can. For example, 65 pounds of mufflers can be accommodated on an auto chassis with relative ease, but a 25-pound silencer on a motorcycle poses significant problems of mounting and balance.

Today, however, the technological picture is brighter. Mufflers tend to be cheaper, lighter, and more efficient. But more about that later.

3. *Apathy.* The motorcycling public and some manufacturers deserve blame here. They just haven't cared. The fact that a machine several blocks away could noisily intrude on personal comfort and privacy mattered not an atom. The manufacturer was still selling his motorcycles and the enthusiast was still getting his auditory thrills of power.

of two-strokes and four-strokes, but first some background

The two-stroke engine has been around as a mechanical reality for about as long as the four-stroke powerplant, that is, since the latter part of the nineteenth century. The two-stroke, however, never approached the four-stroke's popularity in numbers until the early 1960s. Before this time, the four-stroke engine was undisputedly more popular both as a street and an off-road power source. The reasons for this are several. First, most of the world's motorcycle manufacturers were still operating with tooling dating to World War II and earlier. When this tooling was designed, two-stroke technology was still far behind that of four-stroke engines. Thus, for well over a decade after the war, manufacturers were forced by economic necessity to produce four-stroke machinery until they could afford to retool and refit their plants.

Another reason for four-stroke dominance was that some metal casting, machining, and alloying practices were not developed until the second World War. Among these practices were those that would most benefit the two-stroke engine, which till then was often smoky, gasoline-greedy, and somewhat unreliable. Generally, until the late '50s and early '60s, the two-stroke was poorly suited for anything other than low-speed applications.

The manufacturing climate changed drastically, however, when the large Japanese manufacturing concerns turned their efforts to such things as high-silicon content aluminum casting for pistons and elaborate yet highly efficient crankcase machining operations. As a consequence of these and many other rapidly improving techniques, the two-stroke engine came into its own. It was no longer doomed to a wheezing, rattling, premature death by a necessarily loose fit among its vital reciprocating parts. Lubricating oils were also becoming more and more sophisticated, as were bearings, ignitions and other components.

All of a sudden, then, the two-stroke engine became a viable product, boasting mechanical simplicity, economy of manufacture, and a surprisingly high performance potential. And because of these reasons, the two-stroke engine was a natural for motorcycle use.

For the sport, the two-stroke engine proved a curse as well as a blessing.

The two-stroke engine emits a type of exhaust noise much different from that of the four-stroke. The two-stroke engine breathes through holes, called ports, in its cylinder walls (see Chapter 6). Combustion of the fuel-air charge forces the piston downward. Explosive pressures shove the piston down the cylinder until it uncovers the exhaust port, at which point the still expanding gases are ducted out of the cylinder.

The four-stroke, on the other hand, does things differently. When combustion occurs, the piston is forced downward. As the piston is near the bottom of its stroke, a poppet valve in the cylinder head opens. The piston, continuing through its cycle, now begins its ascent in the cylinder, forcing spent gases past the open valve and out the exhaust port.

And herein rests the difference in sound of the exhaust between the two-stroke engine and the four-stroke. The latter exhausts its gases after their combustive force has been spent more thoroughly than those of the two-stroke. By comparison, the two-stroke exhaust port is opened while an explosion is still running its course in the cylinder. The four-stroke's piston also absorbs much residual energy of the spent gases during its upward stroke. Since the two-stroke has no upward exhaust stroke, this noise-damping benefit is not realized.

There is still another reason for the difference in exhaust noise. The two-stroke engine fires every time the crankshaft rotates. The four-stroke engine fires with every other crankshaft rotation. Thus, at 4000 rpm, for example, the two-stroke will emit the noise of 4000 explosions, while the four-stroke yields the noise of 2000 explosions.

The sum of all these factors is a powerplant with an exhaust note that is, to the general public, extremely piercing in its unmuffled state. It is a sound of timber and frequencies that can carry over long distances with irritating efficiency. Also, because of technical characteristics typical of the two-stroke engine, a different type of muffler technology is required to maintain acceptable power output. This technology is a relatively recent development on the internal combustion engineering scene, but still, as of 1977, there were some manufacturers who, for one reason or another, have not incorporated it into their products.

But historically, the shortcomings of existing sound control were never more apparent than in those years of the 1960s, when two-stroke motorcycles became numerous and the economics and technology of noise control were lacking, as was motivation of the motorcycling public and some manufacturers toward curing a rapidly worsening problem.

As a result, many states have enacted stringent noise control laws—in many cases excessively stringent. And some motorcycle manufacturers are now scratching their heads wondering how to make a motorcycle that will emit less noise than that of a busy office (about 80 dB) and still retain the proportions and price of a practical vehicle.

A realistic middle ground exists. The entire motor vehicle industry now supports efforts to control noise. Industry leaders feel, however, that noise control should be consistent with the principles of acoustics, based on demonstrated need, and within the capabilities of attainable technology at reasonable cost.

sound parameters

To control noise, we must first define its characteristics and then translate them into terms and scientifically measurable traits, to eliminate the subjective shortcomings of human judgment. These traits must then be fed into scientific instruments capable of making objective evaluations.

Sound as we know it is composed of pressure variations in the atmosphere. The human ear is extremely sensitive to these variations. It is so sensitive, in fact, that it can detect pressure levels that are about 10 million times stronger that the lowest pressures it can perceive. In other words, its spectrum of perception from the lowest threshold of hearing to the point of maximum noise and physical damage encompasses a 10 millionfold pressure range.

To measure sound pressure on a linear scale would be unwieldy, requiring an astronomical range of numbers with a scale from 1 to 10 million. So, by concentrating the spectrum of audible sound pressures into a scale based on mathematical ratios and logarithms, a scale spanning 0 to 160 dB has been formulated.

A *decibel* (dB) is a technical term representing a relative quantity of sound pressure. Just as we use the term *miles per hour* to describe the relationship of time and distance, the decibel expresses the relationship of sound pressure to a reference point of zero dB. The low threshold of sound perception is 0 dB; the opposite end of the scale, 130 to 160 dB, is the threshold of pain.

The human ear is more sensitive to sounds of certain frequencies than it is to others, so the ear will perceive a sound level as louder at one frequency than at another, even though both sounds are identical in pressure levels. To compensate for this, sound measuring instruments approximate human hearing fidelity by a *frequency weighting filter system*. The system that simulates human perception is called the "A" decibel scale, and is expressed as dB(A).

To provide perspective, the rustle of leaves on this scale measures about 10 dB(A); a soft whisper, 35 dB(A); average street noise, 80 dB(A); a jackhammer, 120 dB(A); and a jet aircraft taking off may cause pain at 140 dB(A). Current motorcycles can vary from about 80 dB(A) to about 105dB(A), the former representing showroom-stock street machinery and the latter representing unmuffled racers, both measured at the legally prescribed distance of 50 feet. (Interestingly, the practice of measuring noise emission from a distance of 20 inches is finding favor in certain sectors of the industry in recent years. Measuring sound in this way eliminates many of the external variables that could affect scientific evaluation. The American Motorcycle Association uses this method in post-race noise checks for sound control enforcement.)

noise—what is its effect?

That exhaust noise is a damaging ecological factor is the frequent argument of off-road vehicle opponents, who contend that it disturbs animals in their natural settings and reduces their ability to survive there. As this is written, however, impartial scientific studies relating to wild animals and vehicular noise are lacking. It is safe to conclude, though, that vehicular noise likely does have an effect on wildlife, but still it is not known just how important this effect is. Significantly, it has been the experience of some vehicle recreational parks that wildlife has much greater resilience than was previously expected. A heavily trafficked motorcycle park in Southern California, for example, temporarily closed a portion of several hundred acres of trails. Within a matter of weeks, the closed area was teeming with wildlife of the same species in numbers approaching that of pre-motorcycle years, almost half a decade earlier. On the other hand, there is no doubt that noise plays a very important role in some situations and is negligible in others.

All motorcyclists should be aware, though, that people, as opposed to other forms of wildlife, are quite sensitive to vehicular noise. The Motor Vehicle Manufacturers Association commissioned an independent research firm (Bolt, Beranek and Newman) to survey attitudes at 60 separate sites in Boston, Detroit, and Los Angeles. Motorcyclists should be well aware of the results of their report, entitled *Motor Vehicle Noise Identification and Analysis of Situations Contributing to Annoyance.* (Motor Vehicle Manufacturers Association, Detroit, 1969.)

1. Motor vehicle noise is not a health problem, but one of annoyance.
2. The vehicle noise levels that rise above background noise levels should be reduced, for it is the occasional, particularly loud, noise that produces the most complaints.
3. Persons expressing annoyance at a specific noise usually felt that it was a situation the driver could control, such as tire squeal, hot-rodding and so on.
4. Annoying noise sources are usually relatively close to the person hearing them.
5. Most people who expressed annoyance indicated that they were at home when it occurred and it was generally in the evening.

It is important to note that a modest level of noise is acceptable by society, but it is also doubly significant that those polled in the study expressed particular annoyance with practices unfortunately not uncommon to some motorcyclists, that is, squealing of tires and brakes and exhaust roar from faulty or intentionally altered exhaust systems. These are the results of neglectful and inconsiderate riders. The study goes on to say that a large number of public complaints were directed at heavy-duty trucks, motorcycles, and high performance sports cars.

In most states, under present law, you simply can't buy a new, noisy motorcycle. A dealer selling machines of substandard noise control can be liable for stringent action by authorities, and the same applies to the distributor who supplied the dealer with the noisy motorcycle. It is not at all unusual, however, for motorcyclists to purchase special exhaust systems from accessory manufacturers that allow better performance, fuel mileage, lightness, and ground clearance. It is a commonly held opinion in the motorcycle industry that the majority of motorcycle noise annoyance complaints can be traced to the abuse of motorcycles so equipped. With the exception of motorcycles sold expressly for competition, just about all motorcycles sold today are legal for highway use. Thus, they are relatively quiet, for they ostensibly meet legal muffling requirements as dual-purpose (street and trail) motorcycles.

A study made by Harrison, under the auspices of the U.S. Department of Agriculture Forest Service, lends yet another slant to this issue. According to this study,

"Some people associate dust, odor and rowdy conduct with motorcyclists. Much of the dissatisfaction expressed with motorcycle noise may not be directly attributable to the noise itself, but to other unpleasant characteristics of motorcycles and motorcycle operation. Since noise is the most easily identifiable unpleasant characteristic of motorcycles, motorcycle noise is likely to continue to be a prominent source of complaint from the public as long as motorcycle noise is heard." (Robin Harrison, *Motorcycle Noise*. Noise Reduction of Forest Service Equipment. ED&T 2428, February, 1974, p. 8.)

soil alteration

This is an area which does not affect the street and highway motorcyclists, whose riding is solely confined to the 5 percent of America's surface area that is paved. However, it is the concern of every off-roader, no matter how many wheels he has under him.

From an environmental standpoint, there are many areas of this country suitable for competitive and casual trail riding. Many established pathways allow excellent riding. This includes fire roads, fire breaks, unused railroad rights-of-way, mine spoils, and even trails made specifically for trail riding, not to mention those purely natural climes approved for motorcycle use.

Strictly speaking, everything we do as a group and as individuals has an effect on our environment. In other words, everything affects something else. The person having a good understanding of his impact on the environment is better equipped to keep that impact to a minimum. On the other hand, we also must be honest with ourselves in realizing that some kind of impact is inevitable. This goes for hikers, campers, horsemen, and other nonmotorized sorts, too. The attitude that the wilds would be intact to this day, were it not for the rapacious off-road vehicle, is no more realistic than the contention that all efforts at land control smack of creeping totalitarianism and should be opposed with patriotic fervor.

Our country boasts a huge variety of climes and soil types, so the effect of a motorcycle wheel on soil alteration is far from constant. Some types of soil are highly sensitive to any type of intrusion; others are ecologically resilient. All have weaknesses and strengths. There are three primary ways by which soil can be altered through off-road vehicle traffic. Some soils are more susceptible to one, maybe two, types of alteration and yet can be relatively immune to the third. Others are fragile in other respects, with innumerable permutations of susceptibilities and strengths.

1. *Soil Compaction*. How this phenomenon occurs is self-explanatory. The weight of the vehicle—or foot, for that matter—squeezes the soil particles together tighter than their natural state. This has several harmful effects.

First, water cannot penetrate compacted soil as it should. In this way subsurface organisms do not receive the moisture they require, and it is these organisms that play such an important role formation and maintenance of a given soil. This effect is confined to the immediate area of compaction, however, and in a low-traffic area its implications are not usually cause for great concern.

Lack of water penetration does have other effects, however. Puddling often results where compaction has occurred, sometimes drowning very small animal life and plant life normally found there.

Compaction has yet another effect. Water, if it hasn't puddled over compacted soil, has the tendency to run off, possibly leading to erosion.

Generally, the direct effects of soil compaction are limited to the immediate area of tire contact, so if traffic density and soil composition are compatible, the long-range effects may well be minimal. But the indirect effects of compaction must also be taken into account. For example, were compaction to occur across the face of a hill or in an area otherwise sensitive to water flow, compaction could have serious implications, ducting an erosive trail of water across land, perhaps leading to permanent and ever-widening scars on that land. Also, problems can arise when, instead of water slowly seeping into the soil surface, a nearby compacted trail can drain vital water away.

2. *Displacement*. Displacement occurs when soil ingredients are removed from their natural surroundings, as when a wheel spins a furrow into the ground, or when a camper clears ground cover for his tent. Displacement might also happen when twigs, dead leaves, and such are pulverized at the soil surface. With the weight and size so reduced, these components are said to be more susceptible to being blown away by the wind or carried away by water. There is some debate

about motorcycles and their environmental effects in this area, for, unless the area is heavily trafficked, accurate measurements are difficult.

Displacement can, however, affect a surface much like compaction in forming ruts and thus encouraging erosive water flow. In this respect, the motorcyclist must be aware of damage potential, for a spinning tire can remove (or kill) soil-retaining plants and litter, forming an ugly groove in a sensitive surface.

Litter is the term for the large pieces of organic matter on the soil's surface which tend to protect the more delicate components beneath from the direct impact of raindrops. If litter is displaced, these smaller, more delicate soil ingredients can be more vulnerable to erosive influences. Litter also performs an insulative function, offering the soil a degree of thermal protection against temperature fluctuations. Consequently, the displacement of litter further insures the loss of soil organisms already made likely by compaction.

3. *Mixing*. Depending upon its type, within the top 3 inches of soil there may be several clearly defined layers. These layers represent different levels of organic decomposition, bacterial life, and soil texture. Mixing takes place when the soil's layered profile is altered, thereby changing its ability to support plant life. The indirect effect of this is to increase a soil's potential for erosion.

Mixing most commonly occurs in wet and loose soils and is commonly the result of excessive wheelspin, as are most of the environmental maladies attributable to motorcycles.

In leaving the topic of soil alteration, there are several points the motorcyclists should bear in mind about soil vulnerability. If we are all cognizant of these while riding, soil alteration can be avoided. Here are some conditions to look out for:

Soil type: Sands, like many other relatively well-drained soils, tend to be resistant to water erosion. This is because there is little surface flow.

Soils with a high proportion of large particles, such as gravel, are less readily eroded than soils composed of fine particles. Soils containing cohesive materials, such as clays, are less subject to erosion than dry soils completely composed of fine particles, or soils made of comparatively heterogenous mixture of textures.

Water content: High water content encourages mixing and attendant erosion.

Seasonal factors: Winter periods often have frozen soils. Spring and fall seasons may have high soil water content.

Slope: The potential for water erosion of soil increases with the degree of steepness of a slope.

air pollution

There is no evidence to suggest that motorcycles contribute significantly to air pollution as we know it. Moreover, a 1975 statement by the President's Council on Wage and Price Stability held that "motorcycle emissions are not now and would not become a problem sufficient to require nationwide regulation in the public interest."

According to figures supplied by the Environmental Protection Agency, in 1970 motorcycles contributed only 0.15 percent of total unburned hydrocarbon emissions and only 0.17 percent of total carbon monoxide emissions.

Furthermore, the EPA estimates that by 1980 these percentage figures are expected to grow only to 0.7 and 0.3 percent, respectively.

EPA data also indicates that of the areas facing air pollution problems in the next decade, only nine will have substantial motorcycle populations, all of them in the western United States (Salt Lake City, Denver, Sacramento, San Francisco–Oakland, the San Joaquin Valley, Los Angeles, San Diego, the southeast California desert region, and Phoenix-Tucson).

The President's Council on Wage and Price Stability also cautioned the EPA against implementing emission control standards that would sharply drive up the costs of regulated motorcycles. According to the EPA's own 1975 estimates, the agency's proposed standards would have cost consumers between $304 and $665 million during the five-year period between 1978 and 1982.

fuel consumption

In the area of fuel consumption, the motorcycle compares very well with other forms of transportation. During the sometimes frantic days of the fuel shortages of past years, sales of street motorcycles burgeoned. Clearly, many individuals who had previously thought of motorcycles as purely recreational devices were confronted with the practical and economical appeal of the machines.

Of the large-displacement motorcycles sold today, probably the poorest mileage is gleaned from the Kawasaki H2, a 750-cc, three-cylinder, two-stroke machine. This motorcycle delivers between 18 and 26 miles per gallon under most circumstances. It is, however, a machine of great power, capable of sprinting through the standing start quarter mile in about 12.5 seconds.

There are motorcycles of so many different displacements, states of tune, and overall size that representative generalizations cannot be made about mileage. There are several motorcycles sold today, however, with engine sizes ranging from 750 to 1000 cc, that commonly deliver 45 miles per gallon and upward. Smaller, lighter motorcycles deliver commensurately better mileage, with middleweight mounts (350- to 500-cc displacement, 325 to 400 pounds overall) capable of yielding 50 to 65 miles per gallon at freeway speeds.

One final observation: bear in mind that every motorcycle is at least 50 percent occupied when on the road. In comparison, the American sedan typically seen on freeways and city streets has a seating capability of five persons, yet seldom carries more than two.

In conclusion, the motorcycle enthusiast should be fully cognizant of the effects his mount has on his environment, both good and bad. The potential for causing damage is significant in many cases when riding in the wilderness, with certain areas to be avoided entirely—a prohibition the Bureau of Land Management has been charged with enforcing. Other parts of the off-road world have much more resilence than some environmental protection groups realize. Either way, it is the motorcyclist's responsibility off the pavement to use the public lands, lands that belong to all of us, with responsibility and maturity. In the past, regrettably, not all of us have done so. Time still remains.

On the other hand, however, the road-riding motorcyclist, because of the inherent frugality of his mount, according to available evidence exerts an indisputably beneficial effect in comparison to his four-wheeled contemporaries.

6 your engine: why it does what it does

*The bits and pieces, circuits, and systems
(plus a little witchcraft) that make your
motorcycle go*

how your engine works, but first some theory

An engine is a device for producing power . . . everybody knows that. And, in our field of interest, it is what makes a motorcycle go. But for the sake of clarity, before we get really deeply involved in the various systems that compose an engine and cause it to do what it does, there are some basic terms that should be explained.

Force: Force is an effort exerted against an object that will tend to move that object from a state of rest or to accelerate or otherwise alter the movement of that object. For our purposes, when calculating engine torque or horsepower, force is measured in pounds.

Work: When we exert force to move or alter movement of an object, work is done. We measure the amount of work done by multiplying the force applied by the distance the object is moved. In other words,

$$\text{Work} = \text{Distance} \times \text{Force}$$

Moreover, if a 75-pound object is moved 10 feet, the amount of work done would be 75 pounds multiplied by 10 feet or, in simpler terms, 750 foot-pounds.

Power: Power is commonly defined as the rate at which work is done. In other words, while work is the product of force and distance, power is force times distance divided by time, or

$$\text{Power} = \frac{\text{Force} \times \text{Distance}}{\text{Time}}$$

Horsepower: This commodity was defined by James Watt, Scottish inventor of the steam engine in the late eighteenth century. Horsepower is a unit measurement of power. One horsepower is equal to doing 33,000 foot-pounds of work in 1 minute (550 foot-pounds per second). Today, this is the universally accepted definition. The formula for determining horsepower is:

$$\text{Horsepower} = \frac{\text{Pounds} \times \text{Feet}}{33,000 \times \text{Minutes}}$$
$$(\text{or } 550 \times \text{Seconds})$$

Torque: Just as horsepower is a measurement of engine performance, so is torque. This is simply the twisting effort realized at the output shaft of an engine when under load. It is possible to calculate the horsepower of an engine by measuring its torque (in foot-pounds) and the engine's output speed (revolutions per minute, or rpm).

Engine torque and rpm are measured on a machine called a dynamometer. The dynamometer characteristically has a controllable method of applying load to the engine. The engine's output under load is measured at various engine speeds. Horsepower is then calculated from these figures. The term "brake horsepower" is commonly used because a certain type of machine, the brake dynamometer, was used for power measurement.

Internal combustion cannot occur without air. Engine efficiency is predicated upon the amount of air (and fuel, of course) ingested on a given intake stroke. Because of this fact, air density plays a crucial part in an engine's efficiency.

Temperature and barometric pressure affect air density. The colder air is, the denser it is; the higher the barometric pressure, the denser it is. Consequently, changes in weather and elevation will cause engine power output to vary. There are three rules of thumb to remember here:

1. For each 1-inch drop in barometric pressure, engine power will decrease by about 3 percent.
2. For each 10-degree rise in Fahrenheit temperature, engine power will decrease by about 1 percent.
3. For each 1000-foot increase above 1000 feet in elevation, engine power will decrease by about 3 percent.

With such variables, it is apparent that a set of correction factors must be used to obtain representative power evaluations under varying conditions. The Society of Automotive Engineers has specified a thorough, complex correction formula as a result . . . too complex to describe here. Suffice it to say, however, that engine power readings are corrected to atmospheric conditions of 29.92 inches of mercury (in. Hg) and 60 degrees Fahrenheit.

the basics of the matter

For a spark-ignited engine to provide power, a sequence of five events is required. This sequence is called the *cycle* and is repeated in each cylinder of an engine as long as work is being done:

1. Atmospheric pressure forces the mixture of fuel and air into the cylinder when the pressure within the cylinder is reduced by the piston traveling downward in the cylinder (or by applying pressure to the mixture through crankcase compression, as in two-stroke engines).
2. The piston, now moving upward in the cylinder, compresses the fuel-air mixture.
3. A timed electric spark ignites the compressed fuel-air mixture.
4. The fuel-air mixture burns, rapidly expanding. This forces the piston downward in the cylinder, converting combustive energy into mechanical power.
5. The spent, gaseous by-products of combustion are exhausted from the cylinder so that a new cycle can take place.

the four-stroke engine

In the four-stroke engine, the aforementioned five events occur in four strokes of the piston—that is, two complete revolutions of the crankshaft. These strokes are referred to as (1) intake, (2) compression, (3) combustion, and (4) exhaust.

A Parisian engineer, Beau de Rochas, first formulated and publicly presented what we accept today as four-stroke theory. In 1862, he described the four essential conditions for harnessing internal combustive energy:

1. Maximum cylinder volume and minimum cooling surface
2. Maximum rapidity of expansion
3. Maximum ratio of expansion
4. Maximum initial pressure of the ignited charge

It was also de Rochas's contention that these essential conditions could be achieved through what we now know as the four-stroke cycle.

But while de Rochas laid crucial theoretical groundwork, it was his contemporary, Nikolaus August Otto, who developed the first workable system of mechanical valving for the four-stroke powerplant. Otto was also responsible for countless other engineering contributions to the field of internal combustion. Such was the scope of his work that to this day, piston engines relying upon electric spark ignition are known academically as Otto cycle engines.

Let's follow this cycle from start to finish, assuming that the piston is at TDC (top dead center), ready to begin its intake stroke (Fig. 6-1). As the piston comes up and past TDC, the mechanically actuated intake valve opens. This allows a fresh fuel-air mixture to enter the cylinder, because the downward travel of the piston reduces air pressure in the cylinder to below atmospheric pressure. Air is forced through the carburetor, where it is mixed with fuel, through the intake port and past the open valve. The intake valve stays open until the piston approaches the bottom of its stroke (the lowest point of which is called BDC, or bottom dead center). The piston now begins its upward stroke. The intake valve closes, sealing the combustion chamber and cylinder. The piston continues its ascent. Just before the piston attains TDC, the spark plug emits an electric spark to ignite the compressed fuel-air mixture. As the piston rolls past TDC, combustion (which is far from instantaneous and universal throughout the combustion chamber) is developing expansive strength, forcing and accelerating the piston downward in its power stroke. As the piston again reaches BDC, the mechanically actuated exhaust valve opens. Hot, spent gases, whose pressure is higher than atmospheric pressure, start to flow out the exhaust port. The piston

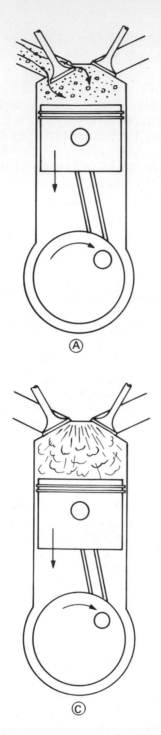
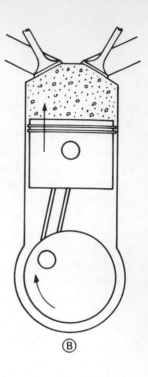
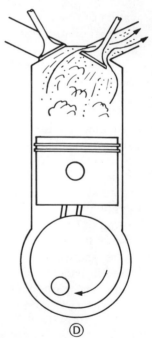

FIGURE 6-1. The four-stroke cycle. (A) Intake stroke. (B) Compression stroke. (C) Combustion stroke. (D) Exhaust stroke.

continues past BDC into its upward exhaust stroke, wherein it forces the residual gases from the cylinder. Then, just before TDC, the exhaust valve closes, and we're right back where we started, ready to begin another complete cycle.

The intake and exhaust valves are the arteries of the four-stroke engine, and the camshaft is its heart. By controlling the breathing characteristics of the engine, the camshaft determines the engine's demeanor—whether it's to be a high-performance fire-breather or an industrial plodder.

The camshaft is basically a metal shaft with eccentric bumps on it, called *lobes*. The camshaft is driven by the crankshaft and spins at half the crankshaft's speed. (Why? Well, if it were driven at the same speed as the crankshaft, the valves and piston would collide and no breathing could be realized. Remember, the four-stroke engine requires two full crankshaft revolutions to complete its cycle.) It is the function of the camshaft to actuate the valves at appropriate points in the four-stroke cycle. Because the vast majority of motorcycles made today are of overhead camshaft configuration, let's use such a single overhead camshaft design as an example. In this design, a lone camshaft is located above the combustion chamber. It is driven by the crankshaft, commonly through chain or gears. The camshaft has an *intake lobe*, which operates the intake valve and an *exhaust lobe,* which does the same for its respective valve. Small levers, called *rocker arms*, act like seesaws. There is one for each valve. The rocker arms ride on the cam lobes at one end and bear on a valve end at the other; they pivot in the middle. As the camshaft spins, its lobes come around, and contact the ends of their rocker arms. The arms teeter-totter and so force their respective valves open. Positive mechanical effort from the cam lobes is used to open the valves, but springs bearing on each valve exert a continual closing force. When the cam lobe rotates away from the rocker, the compressed spring is allowed to push the valve back to its seated position.

In four-stroke engine practice, however, there are complications; all is not so simple.

Valves have mass. So does the fuel-air charge in the intake manifold, so does exhaust gas, so does everything else in an engine. Things with mass cannot be started and stopped instantaneously. Instead, they must be gradually accelerated and decelerated. To achieve efficient operation, we must begin to open valves before TDC and BDC. Take the intake valve, for example. Its opening should actually begin somewhere around 30 degrees before TDC. In this way, the valve has achieved significant opening by the time the piston reaches TDC. It is important to note that giving the valve such a head start over piston travel has little negative effect on intake charge flow. Contrary to what you might think, the fuel-air charge is not expelled backward out the intake tract. Why?

Because the intake charge requires acceleration time, too. It cannot make instantaneous responses. Instead, the charge is just beginning to move down the intake port when the piston has traveled about 30 degrees *past* TDC. Furthermore this intake charge in general terms will not achieve its maximum speed until the piston is about 75 degrees before BDC.

The intake charge has real momentum now. It wants to keep flowing. As a matter of fact, this tendency is so pronounced that we can keep the intake valve open well past BDC and achieve even more cylinder filling despite the piston's now-upward travel. Additionally, the valve's opening movement has to be halted and closing started. It takes time to do these things. Consequently, the intake valve can be closed at around 60 degrees after BDC. (Indeed, some high-speed racing camshafts delay intake closing until 80 degrees or more after BDC.) Note that while the natural tendency for us is to assume intake charging takes place in 180 degrees crankshaft rotation, the laws of internal combustive physics require the intake valve to be open for about 270 degrees duration.

The same holds true for exhaust gas behavior. Our hypothetical engine can get along just fine with its exhaust valve opening about 60 degrees before BDC of the power stroke. Moreover, the exhaust valve is generally kept open for some distance *past* TDC of the exhaust stroke, sometimes as much as 50–60 degrees in racing machines.

. . . which brings us to overlap. Those of you who have followed the foregoing closely will have determined that there is a span in the engine's cycle during which both valves are open simultaneously. This is called *overlap*. So, for example, if our engine opens its intake valve 30 before TDC while the exhaust isn't closed until 30 after TDC, its total overlap is 60 degrees. Generally, valve overlap is used to capitalize on intake and exhaust inertia. The inrushing intake charge helps push exhaust gases out the exhaust port. Another slant on the matter occurs when the inertia of the outgoing exhaust gases actually creates a void behind them, adding further incentive for the intake charge to rush inward.

The four-stroke engine can be viewed as an air pump . . . a hot, noisy one, but a pump nonetheless. It pulls air in, mixes it with fuel, burns it, and pushes it out. Some readers will find its machinations hard to visualize at first, but with application, understanding will come. Bear in mind that of the engine's 720-degree cycle (two complete crankshaft revolutions), only about 120 degrees are used directly for power production.

We have used a single overhead camshaft for our hypothetical engine here (Fig. 6-2). There are several other basic designs, however.

The *L-head engine* is also known as the *flathead* or *side-valve engine* (Fig. 6-3). In terms of performance, this is the least efficient engine; it is still popular in industrial and marine applications, how-

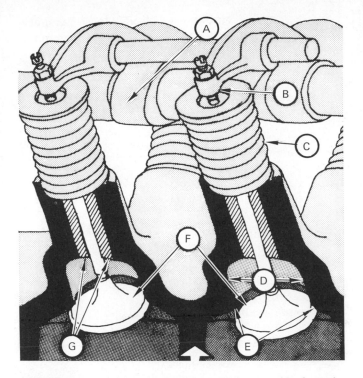

FIGURE 6-2. A single overhead camshaft assembly from the XL-250 Honda. Rotation of the camshaft (A) transfers motion to rocker arms (B). The valves (F) are held closed by pressure of coil springs (C) until forced open by the rocker arms. The valves fit into sleeves in the cylinder head called guides (G). When the valve is opened, gases can flow through the port (D). The port is sealed when the valve rests on its seat (E).

ever, for reasons of economy and simplicity. In this type of powerplant, the valves are located in the cylinder block itself. The faces of the valves are on the same plane as the top deck of the cylinder. In other words, the valves are located alongside the cylinder bore. Intake and exhaust ports run through the engine block. The camshaft is under the valves and often bears directly on them. The cylinder head is basically just a cap for the cylinder with a spark plug in it, thus the nickname "flathead." The reason the L-head is inefficient compared to overhead valve (sometimes called "valve-in-head") designs is because of breathing ability. While the overhead configuration allows the cylinder to breathe through its ceiling, the L-head must breathe through the back door.

The conventional overhead valve design utilizes valves located in the cylinder head while the camshaft is in the engine block (Fig. 6-4).

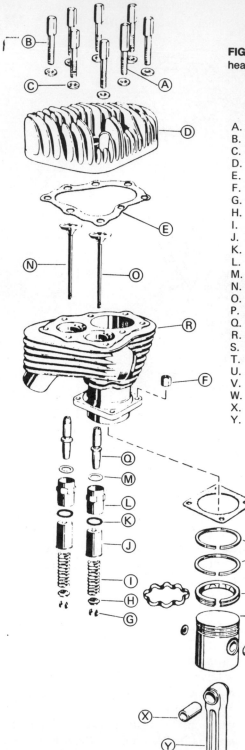

FIGURE 6-3. Piston, cylinder, valve, and head assembly of an L-head engine.

A. Cylinder head bolt (1 3/4 in.)
B. Cylinder head bolt (19/32 in.) (7)
C. Head washers (8)
D. Cylinder head
E. Cylinder head gasket
F. Cylinder base stud nut (4)
G. Valve key (2)
H. Valve spring collar (2)
I. Valve spring (2)
J. Upper valve spring cover
K. Valve cover seal (2)
L. Lower valve spring cover
M. Valve guide oil seal (2)
N. Exhaust valve
O. Intake valve
P. Cylinder base gasket
Q. Valve guide
R. Cylinder
S. Compression ring (2)
T. Oil control ring and expander
U. Piston pin lock ring (2)
V. Piston pin
W. Piston
X. Piston pin bushing
Y. Connecting rod

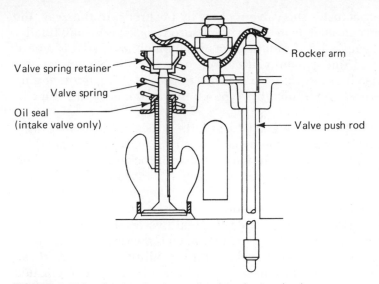

Rocker arm

Valve spring retainer

Valve spring

Oil seal
(intake valve only)

Valve push rod

FIGURE 6-4(a). Overhead valve pushrod, rocker, and valve assembly.

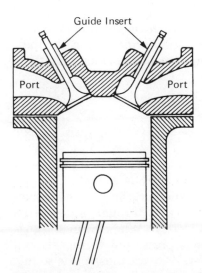

Guide Insert

Port   Port

FIGURE 6-4(b). Intake and exhaust valves of an overhead valve assembly.

The camshaft actuates the valve rockers by pushrods. In this way, the engine uses a camshaft, cam follower, pushrod, rocker arm, and finally, the valve. The majority of American-made automobiles used this type of configuration. And generally, this approach is suitable for low-to-moderate-speed motorcycling use. This is because maximum engine revolutions (revs) are limited by—you guessed it—inertia, this time in the valve train.

The use of dual overhead camshafts is becoming increasingly commonplace in today's motorcycle industry. This system is good for engine performance because it does away with rocker arms, plus their related bits and pieces and attendant inertia. An absolute minimum of valve-actuating equipment can be used. For example, in some motorcycles the cam lobes press directly upon coin-like spacers called shims, which are located on the valve ends. Dual overhead camshafts offer excellent power potential, but generally at an increase in cost, for their manufacture and assembly must be tightly controlled. Dual overhead camshaft systems also often have the drawback of more complicated valve clearance adjustment, which drives up the cost of routine maintenance.

An interesting slant here is that of *desmodromic* valve actuation, in which valve actuation is 100 percent positive. A cam opens the valve; yet another cam closes it. Valve float—the high-speed phenomenon of valves not returning to their seats despite spring pressure, due to valve train inertia—is not possible. Desmodromic systems are rarely encountered, though. The Mercedes-Benz 300 SLR racing auto of the early and mid-1950s had desmodromic valves. Of recent years, the Italian firm of Ducati has offered certain of their models with desmodromically operated valves. Why don't we see this system more often? Once again, it is due to expense and complication.

the two-stroke engine

Compared to the complication of the preceding engine types, the two-stroke is incredibly simple . . . and incredibly subtle as well.

Rather than breathing through valves and ports and related actuating machinery, the two-stroke engine breathes through holes in its cylinder wall. The piston is used as a sliding valve. When the piston goes down in the cylinder, it uncovers various ports, and so ingests and exhausts. On its way back up the cylinder, it covers those ports so that combustion can take place. The two-stroke's cycle requires but 360 degrees of crankshaft revolution for completion, compared to 720 degrees for the four-stroke.

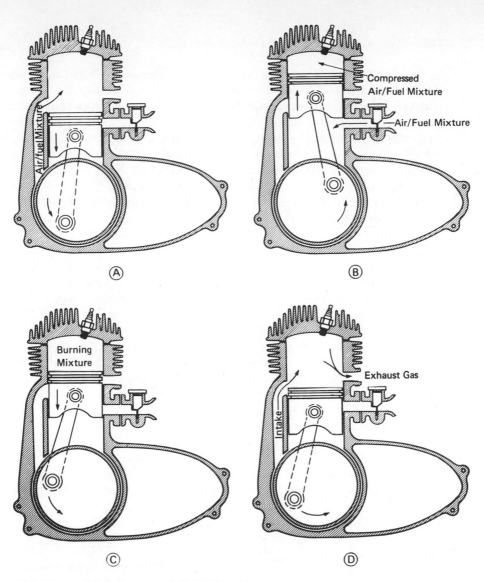

FIGURE 6-5. The two-stroke cycle. (A) Intake: crankcase to cylinder transfer. (B) Compression: crankcase intake. (C) Power: crankcase compression. (D) Exhaust, then intake.

To understand how the two-stroke operates, let's start with the piston at TDC (Fig. 6-5). The spark has just ignited the charge in the combustion chamber and the piston is forced downward, delivering energy to the crankshaft. As the piston travels down the cylinder, it uncovers the exhaust port. The still-expanding but largely spent exhaust gases escape through the open port. (To help visualize the two-stroke sequence, remember that the port highest in the cylinder is the exhaust duct. Next farther down are the transfer ports, and lowest in the cylinder is the intake port.) Still traveling downward, the piston now uncovers the transfer ports. While the exhaust port is ducted out to the atmosphere, the transfer ports run from the crankcase up into the cylinder. The pressure in the crankcase is rising as the piston descends. When the descending piston also uncovers the transfer port, the pressurized fuel-air charge, hitherto trapped in the crankcase, is vented up into the cylinder. Also, since the exhaust port is open at this point, the incoming mixture helps force out spent gases from the cylinder. Still downward the piston travels, until it reaches BDC, at which point the transfer ports are fully opened. Now the piston starts to rise, carried through this part of its cycle by inertia from the relatively heavy flywheel. Remember, the cylinder has been fully exhausted and freshly charged. Remember, too, that the intake port hasn't started to work yet. The rising piston now covers the transfer ports and then the exhaust port. Also, the fuel-air charge is now being compressed in the cylinder at this time. As the piston continues to rise, its lower portion now uncovers the intake port, which is vented to the crankcase (Fig. 6-6). As the piston ascends, negative pressure grows in the crankcase, when the intake port opens, it inhales a fresh fuel-air charge. Moving upward in the cylinder, the piston now approaches TDC, and the ignitive spark occurs. The resulting expanding gases force the piston down, and the whole cycle starts all over again.

Of course, the placement of the ports in the cylinder is of utmost importance in the two-stroke engine, for they, like the four-stroke's camshaft, determine the engine's demeanor and efficiency.

Because at any one point in the two-stroke cycle at least two functions are taking place, these engines have not always been easy to

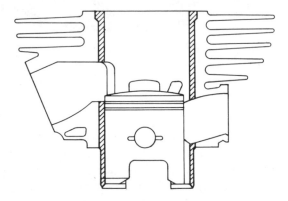

FIGURE 6-6.   Two-stroke piston in cylinder with exhaust and transfer ports open and the intake port closed.

get along with. In some past instances, they could be frustratingly temperamental. To explain further: The critical two-stroke breathing functions of exhaust, transfer, and scavenging tend to take place when piston speed is slowest. The designer hopes to make an engine that ideally will attain greater movement of gases when piston speed is low. With today's technology, this is readily achieved, but it hasn't always been so. Only since about the mid-1960s has the two-stroke engine's potential been realized.

Crankcase compression ratio is of great importance in two-strokes. Generally, you want to have as little compressible crankcase volume as possible when the piston is at BDC. The reason for this follows: Remember when, as the piston rises, it uncovers the intake port? Okay, from this point on, all that internal engine space, from the underside of the piston to the crankcase, is filling with fresh charge. On the piston's downstroke, this charge will be forced up through the transfer ports. With a minimal crankcase volume, the force, and so the velocity given the transfer charge, is maximized. Crankcase compression ratio is a critical determinant in the movement of gas and charges during exhausting, transferring, and scavenging.

Because they breathe through cylinder wall ports two-strokes have symmetrical timing. That is, if the exhaust port opens at 90 degrees after TDC, it must also close at 90 degrees before TDC; after all, the piston in this case is just a sliding valve going up and down in a cylinder.

This symmetry can make for problems, and a phenomenon called "blow-back" is one of them. You see, as the intake port passes fuel-air charge into the engine as the piston ascends, a portion of this intake charge is ejected back out the intake port as the piston descends. This, of course, wastes fuel and power.

The solution to this problem is to incorporate a valve into the intake tract. This is done by two methods: the rotary valve and the reed valve. The *rotary valve* is a disc driven off the end of the crankshaft. This disc has a portion cut away and runs flat against the crankcase's flank. There is a hole in the crankcase flank, the *intake port*. The rotary valve spinning on the end of the crankshaft opens the port as its cutaway portion rotates past and closes the port when the solid portion spins by (Fig. 6-7). Because of reasons of manufacturing expense and less-than-ideal flow characteristics, the rotary valve is not as common as it was several years ago. But the rotary valve offers one great advantage—asymmetrical port timing. Lately, though, with the stellar performance of some current rotary-valved motorcycles (notably the Canadian-made Can-Am machines), there has been a resurgence of interest in this method throughout the industry.

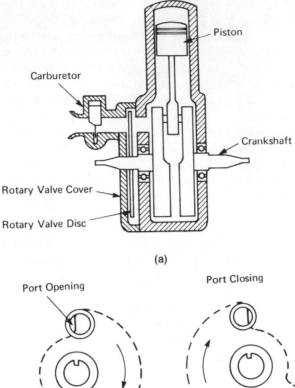

(a)

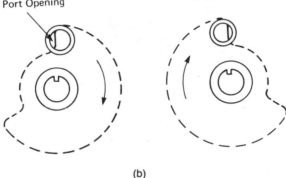

(b)

FIGURE 6-7(a) and (b).   How a rotary valve works.

The second approach to controlling intake blow-back is the reed valve. This device is predicated upon a wedge-shaped metal framework. Two sides of this triangle taper together to form a leading edge, similar to the roof of a house. Thin reeds, sometimes called *petals,* cover the framework of these two sides. The reeds are fastened to the wedged cage only at their bases. The reed valve works like this: When pressure exists at the inside of the wedge, the petals are forced away from their framework. But when pressure exists on the outside of the wedge, the petals are just forced tighter against their framework. The base of this wedge is open, of course, much like the attic of a house. Locate this valve in the intake stream with the open base directed at the carburetor outlet and the valve's leading edge facing the piston-controlled intake port. As the piston ascends in the cylinder, see how the negative pressure in the crankcase allows the petals to lift from the reed cage and fuel-air charge to flow inward. Some degrees later, as the piston descends, positive pressure exists in the crankcase, forcing the petals against their seats and so sealing the duct (Fig. 6-8).

The same problems attendant to symmetrical intake port timing apply to the exhaust port as well. Because of this, the two-stroke tends to let the intake charge flow right through the cylinder and out the exhaust port at certain engine speeds. Besides being wasteful of fuel and power, this also does little for clean exhaust emissions, so two-stroke exhaust gases tend to register high in unburned hydrocarbon content. And here's the clinker: Due to high temperatures, carbon buildup, and very difficult lubrication in this area, a mechanical valving system for the exhaust tract is currently impracticable. For this reason, we have the *expansion chamber exhaust pipe.* Not just an ordinary pipe, the expansion chamber can be an incredibly complex item—not because of moving parts, because it doesn't have any, but because of its various dimensions, which can be critical to an engine's performance and efficiency.

The expansion chamber appears to the layman's eyes as an exhaust pipe conspicuously swollen in its middle and tapering down to a rela-

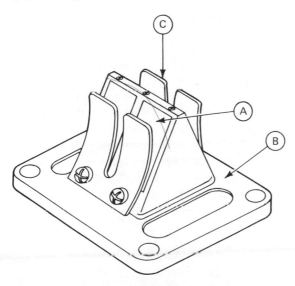

FIGURE 6-8.   The reed valve. (A) Valve petal. (B) Valve cage. (C) Valve stopper, limiting outward movement of petals.

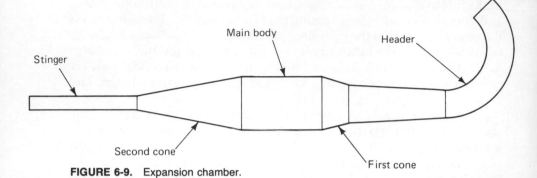

Stinger

Main body

Header

Second cone

First cone

FIGURE 6-9. Expansion chamber.

tively small diameter stinger at its end (Fig. 6-9). The internal dynamics of the expansion chamber and why it works are very complex. Some of the factors a designer must consider are harmonics, speed of sound versus temperature relationships, and wave accelerations. There are few hard-and-fast scientific rules in expansion chamber design and, to be sure, there is no "formula." There are different formulas for different situations. But at this point in technology, an individual claiming irrefutable possession of scientific design parameters—and there are some, regrettably, in positions of authority or instruction—for overall motorcycle performance should not be taken seriously. It is paradoxical in this field of nuts, bolts, and hard facts that gaps still exist in expansion chamber technology. Indeed, research has made good progress in the past several years but, as Jerry Burak, a respected Southern California expansion chamber manufacturer, candidly admits, "Expansion chamber design is still as much an art as a science."

All this aside, however, there is no doubt about the basic function of the expansion chamber. Basically, what the unit does is set up a shock wave at the cylinder's exhaust port. The shock wave acts as a barrier at the port to prevent the passage of unused fuel-air mixture, to close the port effectively with an invisible wall of pressure after exhaust gases have gone but before new charge is wasted. Through varying chamber design, the shock wave can be weak or strong, intense or gradual, or degrees between these extremes. It can also be made to occur at particular areas of an engine's rev range.

how the carburetor works

If you can grasp how Aunt Lucille's perfume atomizer works, you can understand why a *carburetor* does what it does. The function of a carburetor is to atomize the fuel and mix it with air in the varying proportions demanded by the engine. The carburetor feeds the intake manifold, which pipes the explosive blend to the various intake ports in some engines; in other engines, the carburetor feeds the port directly. Industrial or marine-type carburetors, which are used on engines that are operated at relatively constant load and speed, can be of much simpler design, for the spectrum of fuel-air mix they have to deliver is limited. On engines such as those that power our motorcycles, however, the carburetors must be more intricate to meet the varying demands of the engine.

As an internal combustion engine performs different functions, it requires different fuel-air ratios. For example, starting in cold weather commonly requires fuel-air mixtures as rich as 1 pound of fuel to 7 pounds of air. Accelerating may require a slightly leaner 9:1 ratio. No-load idling, as at a stoplight, will call for an 11:1 mixture. Part load, open-throttle operation—cruising, for example—will get along with a 15:1 blend, while full-load, open-throttle operation will be closer to 13:1.

The perfume atomizer principle is simple. There is a reservoir of a fluid. This reservoir is vented to the atmosphere—nothing fancy, just a little hole in the lid to let air in. A tube extends from below the surface of the fluid in the reservoir up to the outside. There is a plunger or air-squeeze ball at the top end of this tube. Using such a device, air is forced past and across the top of the tube . . . and what happens? The fluid rises in the tube, is caught in the rapid air stream, and becomes an atomized spray. The carburetor works very much like this, except that pressurized air is not normally used to induce fluid flow. Rather, it is the negative pressure caused by the engine's descending piston(s) that allows air to be drawn through the carburetor at atmospheric pressure. Also, instead of having just one orifice that feeds fuel into a moving airstream, the carburetor has several to take care of the aforementioned different mixture strength demands. These air and fuel metering systems are commonly called *circuits*. Motorcycle carburetors generally have a starting circuit, a pilot circuit, needle jet metering circuits, and main jet circuits, among others (Fig. 6-10).

The carburetor also has something else Auntie's atomizer doesn't have: a *venturi*. The carburetor, like the atomizer, depends upon accelerated air. The venturi is that smoothly necked-down area of the carburetor's throat. Air flowing into the carburetor undergoes an increase in velocity and a decrease in pressure as it passes through the venturi (Fig. 6-11). If we had a tube that was immersed in fuel at one end and opened into the venturi at the other, we'd have the basics of a carburetor. Because of low pressure in the venturi, otherwise known as

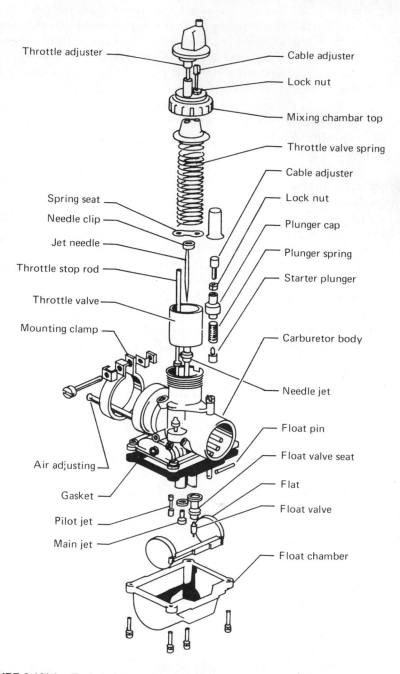

Throttle adjuster
Cable adjuster
Lock nut
Mixing chambar top
Throttle valve spring
Spring seat
Needle clip
Jet needle
Throttle stop rod
Throttle valve
Mounting clamp
Cable adjuster
Lock nut
Plunger cap
Plunger spring
Starter plunger
Carburetor body
Needle jet
Float pin
Float valve seat
Flat
Float valve
Air adjusting
Gasket
Pilot jet
Main jet
Float chamber

FIGURE 6-10(a). Exploded view of a carburetor.

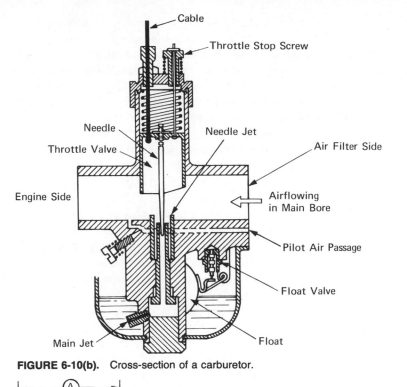

FIGURE 6-10(b). Cross-section of a carburetor.

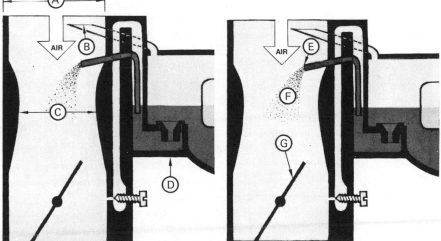

FIGURE 6-11. (Left) Air flows in through carburetor throat (A). Vent (B) leads atmospheric pressure into float bowl. Air is accelerated in venturi (C). Float bowl (D) is fuel reservoir. (Right) Low pressure siphons fuel from tube (E), and it becomes atomized into a spray (F). Butterfly-type throttle (G) controls air flow.

high vacuum, fuel is drawn out through the fuel nozzle by atmospheric pressure on the fuel in the reservoir. As fuel is emitted from the fuel nozzle, it is atomized by the high velocity air flow and mixes with the air.

The next step is to incorporate some type of control for fuel and air quantities in this rudimentary carburetor. A throttling mechanism is located in the venturi to restrict air flow through the carburetor and, consequently, fuel flow as well. There are two basic types of throttle, the butterfly and the throttle slide. The *butterfly throttle* resembles a disc placed in the venturi. Through a linkage we can turn the disc so it faces the incoming air at varying angles. The profile the disc presents in the venturi regulates flow. If you turn it so that only its side edge is in the air stream, the throttle is considered wide open. Turn it 90 degrees so that the disc obstructs the venturi, much like a cover on a manhole, and the throttle is closed completely. The butterfly throttle, while almost universally used in automobiles, is not widely used in the motorcycle field today, largely because of its mediocre air flow characteristics. Until the 1960s, however, it was quite popular, particularly with manufacturers of large-displacement touring machines.

The *throttle slide,* the commonest type today, is a cylindrical item of a diameter slightly larger than the carburetor throat (Fig. 6-12). This piston moves up and down in a bore which is perpendicular to the carburetor throat. At its lowest point, which is while the engine idles, the slide covers almost the entire throat. At full throttle, its wide open position, it is completely withdrawn from the airstream and offers minimal restriction. The slide is normally spring-loaded, so it snaps to a fully closed position as the throttle is released. Most often, the slide is controlled simply by a cable connected to your motorcycle's twistgrip, although some multicylinder machines also use more complex push-pull cable arrangements, along with some rod-and-bellcrank systems. But however the means may be, the end is still the same, to move the throttle slide in and out of the airstream.

At idle, however, the carburetor throat is so effectively throttled that it would starve for air. And even if it weren't gasping for breath, it would die for lack of fuel, because of low air velocity past the main fuel nozzle. To cope with this problem, carburetor engineers developed the *pilot circuit* (Fig. 6-13). What the pilot circuit does is bypass the throttled area of the carburetor by drawing air from the open mouth of the carburetor through a passage drilled in the carburetor body. This passage is routed through the body downstream to the rear edge of the throttle. A very low pressure condition exists here when the throttle is closed, so that air-fuel metering can be achieved efficiently. Like the perfume atomizer, the air passage is usually routed to pick up fuel droplets and then discharge them into the main airstream behind the throttle. Gener-

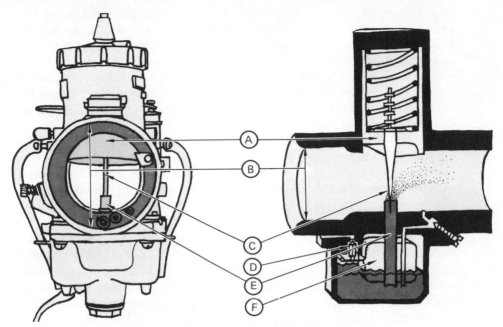

FIGURE 6-12.   (A) Throttle slide. (B) Carburetor throat. (C) Metering needle. (D) Float needle valve. (E) Siphon tube. (F) Float.

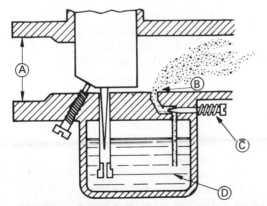

FIGURE 6-13.   The pilot metering circuit. (A) Carburetor throat. (B) Pilot circuit fuel outlet. (C) Idle mixture air screw. (D) Fuel supply.

ally, carburetors allow adjustment of both air and fuel content of the pilot circuit. Fuel passage is controlled by a small screw with a smaller, precisely drilled hole through its middle. This is called the *pilot jet* and is available in different sizes for different conditions.

Air content of the pilot mixture is usually controlled by a small needle valve in the pilot air passage. Turning a screw moves the needle valve in or out of the air stream, constricting or opening the passage as desired.

As the throttle is opened slightly more, air passes through the venturi. This causes a rise in velocity past the tube leading up from the fuel reservoir. Unfortunately, this results in too much fuel being drawn into the airstream at this stage. The overrich engine runs poorly or not at all. A remedy is needed; something to meter fuel effectively at partial throttle openings.

And so came the *metering needle*. This is a precisely tapered rod or needle that projects from the bottom of the throttle slide. The lower end of the needle fits into the main metering tube, which, you'll remember, leads up from the fuel bowl. The needle's dimensions are such that when the throttle is closed, the needle is at its lowest point and the tube is completely plugged. At full throttle, however, when the slide is pulled up out of the airstream, the metering needle is also pulled up out of the tube's fuel stream. And so the metering needle's taper, when correctly coordinated with throttle slide opening, allows efficient fuel-air proportioning between the extremes of idle (at which point the engine is running on the pilot circuit) and at full throttle, where the engine is fed fuel solely by our next focus of interest: the main jet.

When the engine is at three-quarters to full throttle, the metering needle becomes ineffective. After all, it is pulled just about completely out of its metering orifice. So, some form of additional fuel control is required, this time for very wide throttle openings.

The diameter of the siphoning tube, if it's too big, allows the engine to gag on excessive fuel. If it's too small, the engine doesn't get enough. To control maximum fuel flow through this tube, a precisely drilled jet was fitted to it. This is called the *main jet*, for it controls the carburetor's maximum fuel supply capability. The main jet is commonly located at the bottom of the siphoning tube, technically called the *riser tube*, submerged in gasoline. The carburetor's maximum fuel flow characteristics are thus controlled. Main jets are available in a variety of sizes, as are most other carburetor metering components.

The fuel reservoir is more accurately called the *float bowl*. Its function is to be an intermediate chamber for fuel between the fuel tank and the carburetor. The level of fuel in this reservoir has great influence on how your engine runs. Remember, the main jet and fuel riser tube

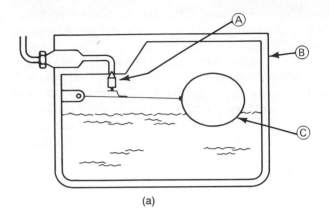

(a)

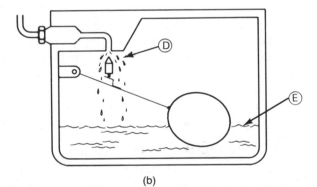

(b)

FIGURE 6-14(a) and (b). Carburetor float fuel control. (A) Needle valve. (B) Float chamber. (C) Float. As engine consumes fuel, the level in the chamber drops (E), allowing (D) stream of fuel to enter chamber.

extend down into the gasoline held here. If the fuel level in the bowl is too high, the engine will run rich because fuel will flow more quickly up the riser tube. When the fuel level is low, the engine will run lean because the precious fluid lies deeper down the well.

Fuel level in the float bowl is controlled by a device much like a toilet tank float valve (Fig. 6-14). Here, a buoyant float rides on the surface of the fluid. The float is connected to a valve; in the motorcycle carburetor's case, it is a needle valve. As fluid level rises, so does the float. And as the float rises, the valve is closed more and more, until it is shut completely. The engine's appetite for gasoline remains, however, and then the fuel level drops, thus allowing the float to open the valve. This method of maintaining a precise level of fuel in the float bowl is quite accurate. The difference between full-open and full-closed in most motorcycle carburetors is usually a matter of a surface variation of just a few thousandths of an inch.

The *choke* is largely self-explanatory; it chokes the engine of air. Usually a butterfly or some such valve in the air stream, the choke is used to cause the engine to ingest a very rich fuel-air mixture for starting ease, particularly in very cold weather, when the gasoline fluid is reluctant to atomize into the incoming air. Of course, the choke is not normally needed when the engine is relatively warm, because the fuel droplets stay more readily in suspension in the air flow.

A more current variation on this theme is the *mixture enricher*. This device—or circuit—is actually very much like the pilot circuit we discussed earlier. Like the pilot circuit, air is tapped into the carburetor from a small hole by the carburetor mouth. This air passage runs down the carburetor to an opening in the carburetor throat just downstream of the slide. This air passage is also vented to the float bowl; it draws up fuel from here through another small, precisely drilled orifice, the *starting jet*. The only thing that keeps this circuit from coming into operation every time the slide comes down is an on-off valve located right in the middle of its air passage. When the passage is plugged, the circuit is inoperative. To achieve extra-rich mixtures needed for starting, the starter jet system restricts air flow in no way. What happens when you move that little plunger is that the starting circuit is unplugged, allowing the engine its special fuel-air blend.

Traditionally, lubrication of the two-stroke engine has been simplicity itself. Oil is mixed with the fuel. Thus suspended in the fuel, lubricant goes everywhere the gasoline-air blend goes. On the intake stroke, when the fresh charge is brought into the crankcase, lubricating oil is also present. Crankshaft and connecting rod bearings are oiled by the swirling mist, as are the cylinder wall and piston. Additionally, the hot surface of the piston crown that receives the brunt of combustion is cooled somewhat by the new, cool charge bathing the underside of the piston.

However, not all two-stroke engines are lubricated through gasoline-oil premixing. Oil injection is a commonplace approach today, although it was pioneered on a mass production basis only as late as the 1960s. Oil injection is actually a very simple process. Most often, the motorcycle's oil tank gravity-feeds the oil pump. The oil pump is usually driven directly by the crankshaft, or by an ancillary shaft elsewhere in the powerplant. The oil pump delivers oil directly to the intake port. The pump operates on varying demand through two methods: (1) because the pump is mechanically connected to the crankshaft, the faster the crankshaft turns, the faster the pump works; (2) and the volume of each pump stroke varies with throttle opening. At idle, for example, the pump may be likely to deliver oil at a relatively lean 200:1 ratio. At the other extreme, full throttle, however, the pump will be delivering lubricant at a much richer 16:1 fuel-oil ratio. In this way the engine gets the most oil when its need is greatest, while at idle it requires and receives very little oil, for minimal exhaust smoking and spark plug fouling.

Some oil injection systems also squirt undiluted oil directly to the crankshaft bearings and other components. This is beneficial because the oil reaching these critical load-bearing surfaces is at its normal viscosity. Its film strength is not broken down by the addition of gasoline.

If there is an inherent weak spot in the two-stroke powerplant over a long period of time, it is lubrication. Compared to the four-stroke engine, where the crankcase is a repository of undiluted oil and where components have relatively good access to oil, the two-stroke engine's lubrication appears somewhat haphazard. The four-stroke engine does not rely upon a medium, namely the intake charge, to convey lubricant to moving parts.

No group of motorcyclists is more conscious of this fact than motorcycle racers. The two-stroke's mechanical simplicity and superb power-to-weight potential make it the unquestioned choice of the majority of motorcycle racers. However, these powerplants can be quite sensitive to variations in humidity, air temperature, and gasoline quality, for all of these factors and more affect fuel-mixture and lubricity. Road racers can attest to complete engine seizures brought about by just slightly lean carburetor jetting or improper float level adjustment. A high-speed two-stroke engine running at full throttle for just a split second without the proper fuel-oil-air blend can be reduced to rubble (explode, or at least suffer serious damage) in the blink of an eye.

how the ignition works

In 1820, Hans Christian Oersted discovered something truly momentous, although at the time he was probably unaware just how momentous. Oersted observed that when a wire was moved through a magnetic field, electrical current is generated. To this day, nobody knows why this happens, but Oersted gets the credit for first documenting it. And this effect is the keystone for harnessing and controlling electrical power.

The motorcycle ignition is based upon this effect, although we now pass finely wound coils of wire through magnetic fields at fairly rapid speeds to realize greater electrical energy.

Ignitions today commonly use one of two types of magnetic power sources: the permanent magnet and the electromagnet. The *permanent magnet* is just that; a permanently magnetized piece of metal. Its strength cannot be turned on and off or altered. However, by winding wire around and along a metal core and then connecting each end of the wire to a battery terminal, we have an *electromagnet*; one we can turn on and off, whose field strength, which is sometimes called *flux*, we can vary.

The contemporary motorcycle generator mounts electromagnets in a circular housing. This stationary part of the generator is called the *stator*. The individual electromagnets in the stator that produce the magnetic fields are known as *field coils*.

Within this circle of electromagnets rotates an *armature*. This part of the generator is also composed mainly of *wire windings*, although they are arranged differently than the field coils, and are connected to commutator bars. The armature is spun within the stator while the electromagnets are energized; electrical energy is generated. This power is picked up and carried away from the armature by contacts that rub against the spinning *commutator* surface.

Okay, so now we have current; what shall we do with it? Well, the most important thing to do is to light the spark plugs, so that the engine will run. However, the combustion chamber of the internal combustion engine is not what you'd call a friendly place. Its air pressures are high and so are its operating temperatures, neither of which is conducive to good sparking. In sum, what we have to do is magnify the voltage of that electrical current. Trying to make a low-voltage spark jump a gap under those conditions is fruitless. While the generator has produced a lot of current (*amperes*) and relatively low voltage, the ignition needs few amperes at very high current. We want to take maybe 12 volts or so and multiply them to about 15,000–20,000 volts, perhaps more. And this is exactly what the high tension coil does. Moreover, we can do this thousands of times per minute if we use a triggering device of some sort, and the breaker points are our mechanical trigger.

The ignition coil is based upon the phenomenon of induction. Here, a current generated in one circuit is used to induce a current in another circuit. To understand how this works, let's look inside a high tension coil. The unit is composed of two separate windings of wire. In the typical coil, these windings are wound over each other and have the same electrical ground. The primary winding consists of several hundred turns of comparatively large-gauge wire. The secondary winding is made up of many thousands of turns of finer wire. When you apply current to the primary coil, a strong magnetic flux is created, an energy that will be picked up by the other coil. The large number of finer windings in the secondary coil allow for easier saturation by the primary flux. Also, the primary and secondary coils are wound over a common iron core, whose purpose is to intensify the magnetic field.

Remember, the high tension coil has no moving parts, so primary flux does not pass through the secondary windings as the result of anything mechanical within the coil. What happens next is hard to explain to the layman because of its complexity (so we won't) and is hard for him to visualize. Nevertheless, *inductance*, that is, the transference of flux from primary to secondary windings, does not occur as the result of flux building up to a high peak intensity and then surging across windings. Rather, this transference of energy occurs when the primary field *collapses*. When this happens, voltage is magnified through the secondary windings and then travels to the spark plug.

To explain: The magnetic flux in the primary windings is controlled by the opening and closing of the breaker points. When the points are closed, current flows directly to the primary windings of the coil. As the engine rotates through its cycle, the breaker points will be bumped open by the points cam. When the points open, all that magnetic energy stored in the primary windings suddenly collapses *and in so doing passes into the windings of the secondary coil,* which results in a big jolt of current (Fig. 6-15). Because of the greater number of wire windings in

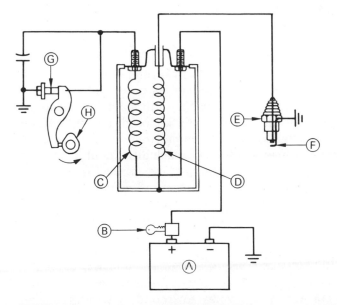

FIGURE 6-15. Ignition circuit. (A) Battery. (B) Ignition switch. (C) Primary coil winding. (D) Secondary coil winding. (E) Spark plug. (F) Spark plug firing tip. (G) Breaker points. (H) Breaker cam. When cam pushes breaker points open, no current flows to primary coil windings. When cam allows points to close, current flows.

the secondary coil, voltage is magnified many times over. An insulated wire carries this energy from the secondary coil directly to the spark plug.

For the sake of clarity, we have taken a few shortcuts. This was done because explaining ignitions, points, coils, and related gimcrackery to those not acquainted with electrical principles is often highly confusing. Trying to understand an author's rendition of where sparks come from is, as we've said, hard to visualize. Moreover, what with all those technical terms and concepts, it's like trying to take a sip of water from a fire hose.

An ignition system of the type described here commonly has a *battery* incorporated in its circuitry. In this way electrical current is generated by a *generator* (which puts out DC, or direct current) or an *alternator* (which produces AC, or alternating current). This current is regulated by a device called, logically enough, a *regulator*. It is this unit's job to lend a modicum of regularity to the battery's life. If, say, a generator produced enough current to keep the battery charged and lights burning when the engine is idling, what would happen when the engine is operating at freeway speeds? Something would have to give, and in all likelihood the battery would be destroyed. So a regulator is placed in the system to prevent such maladies as overcharging.

Current for ignition, then, is drawn from the battery, which is actually a reservoir of energy also feeding such ancillaries as lights, horn, and so on. And thus we have briefly described what is generally known as the *battery-coil ignition system*.

The *magneto* is a less complex ignition system that does not rely upon battery power. The magneto generates its power by spinning a magnet past a fixed energizer coil; each time the magnet comes past, current is generated. With the breaker points closed, current coming from the energizer to the high tension coil is short-circuited to a ground. But just as the permanent magnet and coil reach alignment, maximum voltage and flux occur. When this alignment takes place, the points are opened. In other words, when maximum energy is generated, the points open. This allows current flow from the energizer coil to the high tension coil. So here we see a great surge of current, perhaps 4 amperes and 300 volts, in strength, coursing through the primary windings of the high tension coil (Fig. 6-16). Unlike the battery-coil and related ignition systems, however, the magneto's secondary spark voltage is generated by the rapid *increase* in primary flux. (If you'll remember, the battery-coil system passed current from primary to secondary windings when the primary field *collapsed*.) Magnetos, although generally efficient, are not as common today as they were several years ago. Alternators, generators, solid-state electronics, and some motorcycle lighting laws of

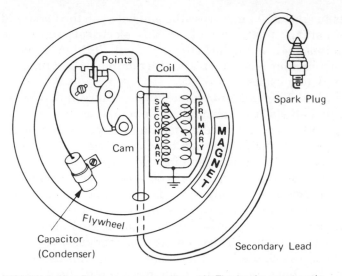

FIGURE 6-16. Basic magneto ignition. (A) Flywheel magnets spin with crankshaft. Current is generated in primary windings (C). Secondary coil windings (B) receive electrical energy upon control of breaker points (D), allowing spark to occur at spark plug (E). This type of magneto does not use a separate high tension coil as do some others.

this country have made the magneto largely impractical for little else than racing purposes, so their street use is limited.

We haven't discussed the role of the *condenser* up to this point, even though its function is essential to the life of the breaker points. But perhaps now you have sufficiently assimilated a feeling for electrical dynamics so that we may describe what it does and why.

The breaker point assembly is a mechanically operated switch controlling flow of electrical current to the primary windings of the high tension coil. In normal use, the points are opened and closed thousands of times per minute. Mechanically they are simple, but their job is difficult. In Chapter 8 we describe that, by necessity, the point contact surfaces are made of very hard wear-, corrosion-, and heat-resistant tungsten alloy. Nevertheless, breaker points still fall prey to burning, pitting, and plain old wear and tear.

Plain old wear and tear we can't do much about, outside of normal inspection and maintenance. Burning and pitting, however, is another matter.

When the points are closed, current flows through them. Electrical energy, however, does not stop flowing the very instant the points are bumped open. It wants to continue flowing across the widening point gap. This results in an electric arc across the gap between the two point surfaces. While perhaps pretty to look at, this electrical arc proved harmful to the points, for it would burn the metal with its high temperatures much like a miniature arc welder, and in a relatively short time the points were completely useless.

And this is where the *condenser* comes in. A century or two ago, it was discovered that an electrical charge can be temporarily stored between two metal plates. The area of the plates and their distance apart determine the amount of charge that can be stored (Fig. 6-17).

Thus, it is the job of the condenser momentarily to absorb, then stop the flow of current across the points. This is because when current flow is interrupted in a circuit containing a condenser, the condenser will retain a potential voltage and so spare the points the torture of unnecessary arcing. The condenser, as shown in the figures, is connected in parallel with the contact points. The capacity of a condenser to absorb current (*capacitance*) is limited by the small area of the plates. To increase current-absorbing ability, the condenser used in today's ignition systems is constructed as shown in Figure 6-18.

Since the early 1970s, a different, more powerful type of ignition has been adapted to some motorcycles: the *capacitive discharge ignition*. In comparison to a battery-coil arrangement or a magneto, the CDI, as it is called, is quite different, although in basic function it's not overly difficult to understand. There are several different CDI configurations found on today's motorcycles. Krober, Bosch, Femsa, and Motoplat are commonly fitted to European machines, while the major Japanese motorcycle manufacturers also produce their own units. For example, let's take a peek at the Honda CDI system used on their motocross racing machines.

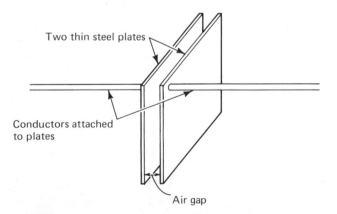

FIGURE 6-17. Construction of a simple condenser.

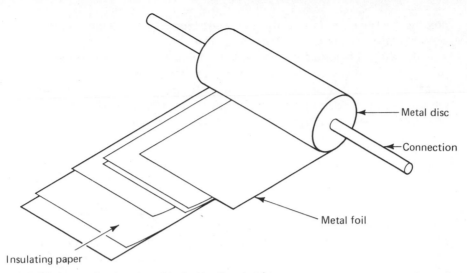

Metal disc

Connection

Metal foil

Insulating paper

FIGURE 6-18.   Construction of typical ignition condenser.

Electrical power begins with an assembly of more or less conventional coils and electromagnets. Specifically, current comes from an alternator, which is an alternating current-producing generator. This unit consists of two coils: an *exciter coil* and a *trigger coil*. AC electricity from the exciter coil is *rectified* (changed into DC) and then carried to the *capacitor*. (In function, a capacitor is just like a condenser; just the names are different.) A short while back, we pointed out that the condenser-capacitor stores an electrical charge temporarily. However, the capacitor-condenser used here is of much greater capacitance than used in a conventional system, so here the similarity ends. The Honda ignition capacitor holds its charge until the CDI's trigger circuit allows it to be released. This release, or capacitive discharge, happens very quickly, perhaps in a millionth of a second. This results in a lightning rush of electrical energy through the high tension coil, and here voltage is multiplied many hundreds of times to fire the spark plug with perhaps 50,000 volts, depending upon the condition of the plug.

Basically, the triggering system works like this. Earlier we mentioned the trigger coil. Like any other generating coil, the trigger coil gets its energy from rotating magnets. Power generated here is carried to what is casually called the "black box." Actually it is a complete solid-state assembly of some rather complicated electronic circuitry, along with the aforementioned capacitor. When trigger coil energy attains a certain point, the trigger circuit sends an electronic message to the "black box" to release the capacitor's charge. The capacitor will discharge only when elements of the "black box" tell it to, and the "black box" gives the command only when energized by the trigger coil. This type of ignition has no need of mechanical breaker points.

Finally, it is significant to note that spark occurs in this system at peak primary coil flux, as in magneto systems, and not at flux collapse, as in battery-coil systems. Ignitions that fire upon flux increase are generally known as *energy transfer ignitions*. Thus, the Honda CDI can be described as an energy transfer ignition with electronic points.

in conclusion

The elements we have described in this chapter, though perhaps confusing to some readers, are basic and general. In the motorcycle marketplace you will surely encounter mechanical and electrical variations, but the basic theme remains the same: To get power, you need fuel, a place to burn it, and a fire to light it with. No matter how exotic a piston engine may seem to be, it still is bound by the same physical, electrical, and thermodynamic laws that make your lawn mower go and power your neighbor's buzz saw.

7

tools...
you gotta
have tools

The right tools for putting things on
or taking them off

It has been a largely accepted tenet that ownership of a motorcycle also necessitates having a generous complement of suitable tools. And, to be honest, this belief has not been entirely without foundation. In past decades, the motorcycle had earned itself a reputation of being less than totally reliable, perhaps mechanically whimsical, even in its best moments.

Of recent years, to be sure, important strides have been made in design, manufacturing, assembly, and quality control, with consequent benefits realized in dependability and longevity. Despite such progress, however, motorcycles generally still fall short of the level of long-term reliability displayed by much of the automobile industry. That most motorcycles lack the mechanical complexity of all but a few automobiles is beyond dispute, even though such contemporary considerations as exhaust emission controls and federally mandated equipment have changed matters some of late. Unfortunately, though, the motorcycle's relative simplicity has not spared it from a seemingly inordinate appetite for both preventive and curative maintenance. And despite the growing numbers of commercially available motorcycles that will travel 100,000 miles with just routine maintenance, the large majority of remaining models will demand serious mechanical attention well before that distance.

The reasons for the mechanical sensitivity of these motorcycles are found in (1) the nature of the machine, and (2) the nature of the owner. By this it is meant that the type of motorcycle should be compatible with its projected type of riding. In other words, under normal usage, is it happy doing what it is doing? To illustrate: The high-winding 250-cc Kawasaki triple develops very little practical power below 6000 rpm. The engine just loves to rev and is a suitable mount for a rider who doesn't mind frequent gear changing and recognizes when the powerplant is operating comfortably or laboring excessively. On the other hand, the machine is not what you'd call a beast of burden. For mountain touring laden with camping gear, this motorcycle would prove unsatisfactory for most of us. Additionally, being forced to labor thusly adversely affects the motorcycle's lifespan; it is being forced to do things it's not supposed to do, which amounts to abuse.

And the nature of the owner is important here, for his is the responsibility not only to ride the machine in accordance with its design, but to maintain it properly as well. Oil must be changed, all the necessary adjustments must be made, and the other routines of regular maintenance must be carried out. In this respect, the machine becomes much like its human owner, who requires his own kind of maintenance, such as food, cleanliness, exercise, and prompt aid when he's ill.

There is no unwritten rule requiring the motorcycle owner to have a brace of exotic tools at his fingertips. And there are enough dealerships scattered throughout the land that the owner need only drop his bike off for service and pick it up when it's ready—just like a car. In doing this, however, the owner will soon find out that his motorcycle's servicing bill at the cash register may also be just like a car's—a rude shock. After all, the bike is just a fraction of the auto's size but may cost the same to service.

Actually, size has little to do with the bill. Sure, the machine may have a few less spark plugs to replace than a car and its oil sump may require less lubricant. But the cost of human labor remains for the most part constant, and usually this comprises the lion's share of servicing costs.

In light of this fact, the first-time motorcycle owner can realize significant savings by familiarizing himself with his mount and the appropriate tools to treat it with. There is, for example, little sense in paying a dealership anywhere from $3.50 to $7.50 merely to adjust a clutch, usually a very simple chore seldom taking more than 5 minutes.

The same goes for spark plug changing and gapping, oil changing, spark timing, brake adjusting, and all the other minor chores that are simple to perform but sometimes cost inordinately to have a shop do.

There is, however, one caution that should be observed: If your motorcycle is new, it will be covered by a warranty, and manufacturers warn us that the motorcycle's warranty is void if service is performed by persons not authorized by the manufacturer during the warranty period. If you have purchased a used motorcycle, the warranty may no longer be in effect. Racing motorcycles, also, are rarely covered by warranty.

Stripped threads, broken studs, rounded bolt heads, skinned knuckles, and blue air are all symptomatic of inadequate preparation by the would-be mechanic. So the first step you should take is to arm yourself with a comprehensive workshop manual. A factory manual is generally easily procured from dealerships selling your type of motorcycle or from one of the after-market manual publishers, such as Chilton, Clymer, and Carbooks, among others. Sheer mechanical enthusiasm is no substitute for the sound guidance a manual can offer.

Do not confuse the owner's manual with the workshop item. Owner's manuals are adequate if you're adjusting the drive chain or inspecting breaker points. If your mechanical ambitions and curiosity are more intense, however, you'll probably find them of marginal aid. They're not much help to a man installing a camshaft or rebuilding a clutch assembly.

The complete novice may find the workshop manual confusing because it tends to assume that the reader possesses an understanding of basic mechanics and technical terminology. Generally, though, their nature is not so technical that some confusing areas cannot be understood through careful reading and studying of accompanying illustrations.

Most important, if your motorcycle needs mechanical attention but you are unsure of how much and where, the manual will usually tell you which parts can be left alone as you're sorting your way through an engine's vitals. The tyro mechanic's tendency is to make things more complicated for himself than need be, which compounds the complexity of the original problem and, in turn, its frustration.

The illustrations included in the workshop manual are valuable in helping you avoid assembly mistakes. For example, spacers, shims, and other parts to be assembled on a shaft will have to follow a specific order. Carelessness here can lead to further equipment malfunction or, worse, damage.

impact driver

Most Japanese-made motorcycles—which is to say, most motorcycles in the world—utilize many Phillips-head screws in their assembly. Unfortunately, these screws are often made of rather poor steel; they are comparatively soft and have a low tolerance for overtightening. Upon factory assembly, the screws are usually installed with air-driven power tools to maximum torque. Compounding the problem is the fact that the steel screws and aluminum parts are often bonded together by corrosion. This is the result of electrochemistry between dissimilar metals. Thus, being tight and somewhat soft, these screws can be difficult to remove without gnawing the Phillips head shapeless with the screwdriver bit. And once this cross-shaped recess in the screw head is too deformed to retain the bit, the screw is all but impossible to take out if you don't have an impact driver.

The impact driver is thus a most valuable device, and no mechanic —tyro or professional—should be without one when working on motorcycles (Fig. 7-1).

This tool appears to be a rather stubby screwdriver with a large diameter handle 4 to 5 inches long and a short, often interchangeable bit. The bit is conventionally inserted in the screw head, while the butt of the driver is struck with a hammer as you twist it in the direction you want to turn the screw. Internally, there is a cam in the handle of the driver that converts the impact of the hammer on the butt into a screw-twisting surge. Additionally, the force of the hammer blow simultaneously seats the screwdriver bit into the screw head. In this way the screw is dealt a one-two punch that loosens it yet manages to keep metal distortion to a minimum.

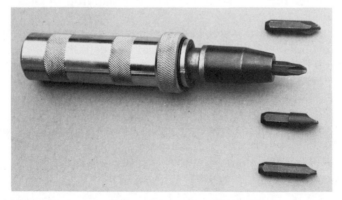

FIGURE 7-1.   Impact screwdriver with assorted bits.

The impact driver is not considered an exotic tool and is found for sale in hardware stores, auto parts outlets, and motorcycle shops, plus many other places, not to mention the ubiquitous Sears chain. The tool is not inordinately expensive at most stores. Sears, for example sells an impact driver kit, which includes the handle, four bits (two straight, two Phillips), and socket drive for about $15. Incidentally, the socket drive is handy, for it allows you to use the driver in conjunction with sockets as well. The extra bits that come with the driver are not just spares but bits of different sizes. Screws, be they Phillips head or straight slotted, come in different sizes. Using the wrong type of bit in a screw can ruin screw heads, sometimes leaving you a ruined tool as well.

Motorcycles most often use Phillips-head screws of sizes #1, #2, and #3. You'll probably find the #3 most useful, for they are most often found on engine cases and covers. The #1 screws are commonly encountered for lighter, more compact fastening duty about the motorcycle. Straight-blade screwdrivers are available with bits from 1/8 in. to 3/8 in. across for normal motorcycle application, although much larger ones are used in other fields. But for our purposes, the most useful sizes are 3/16, 1/4, and 5/16 in. A quick browse through the hardware store's tool department will show you the many different shank lengths available for a given blade size. The very short screwdrivers will sooner or later prove invaluable for certain uses, but the 6- and 8-in. shanks will probably see the most use on your motorcycle.

Of course, the impact driver's clout depends upon the stout blow of a hammer . . . but not just any hammer. You need one particular kind. The impact of steel on steel is to be avoided for safety's sake (hazardous flying metal chips sometime result) along with maximizing life of the driver. What you need is a hammer made of a material softer than metal. Probably the most useful type is the double-duty type of hammer with a hard rubber knob on one side of the head and a resilient, tough plastic knob on the other. Both of these materials are softer than the softest aluminum alloys found on your motorcycle, so you can also use the hammer to carefully thump apart recalcitrant parts without irreparably deforming or even denting metal components. The hard plastic knob is just right for striking the impact driver. Generally, there is little use for a steel hammer in motorcycle applications.

Some motorcycles come fitted with Allen-head screws rather than Phillips-head or bladed screws. Allen head screws have an hexagonal recessed socket which accommodates a similarly shaped wrench (Fig. 7-2). Because of the difficulty often encountered with gouging the more conventional screw heads, many motorcyclists replace them with Allen heads, for if you use the correct Allen wrench on a screw, distortion and chewing of the metal is almost impossible. Also, the Allen head is

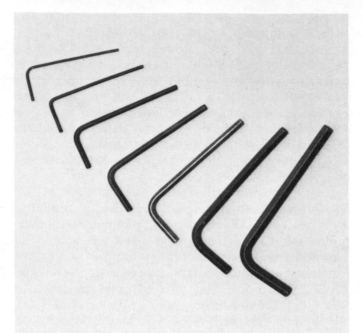

FIGURE 7-2. Allen wrenches.

favored by many because it is generally made of a much better grade of metal. Many motorcycle accessory manufacturers offer Allen-screw replacement kits to eliminate possible future difficulties. A set of Allen wrenches spanning 3 to 8 millimeters (mm) should handle most contingencies.

socket wrenches

There are several points to bear in mind when choosing a set of sockets (Fig. 7-3). These items, together with your combination wrenches, which we'll discuss later, are one of the most important portions of your tool kit.

Sockets have the characteristic of being exceedingly kind to the nuts and bolts they're used on. Sockets boast a comparatively greater contact area to bear upon the bolt or nut than do open-end wrenches. Thus they offer less opportunity to round off flats and corners. In keeping with this point when you purchase sockets, be sure to specify 6-point tools instead of the 12-point kind. The 6-point (the inside diameter has the contours of a 6-pointed star) wrench allows slightly more bearing area than the 12-pointer.

Another facet to consider when buying sockets is choice of thin-wall or thick-wall tools. The thick-wall items are usually less expensive and structurally stronger than the thin-wall sockets. Sometimes, though, you'll find yourself working in very limited confines where the thick-wall unit just won't fit. The primary concern here is cost; the thin-wall sockets' lesser strength is not all that significant under normal usage. Consulting experienced mechanics on this matter should yield sound advice.

The final consideration when buying sockets is that of standardizing their drive size. Sockets for motorcycle applications can be of three sizes: 1/4-in. drive, 3/8-in. drive and 1/2-in. drive. This specifies the size of drive stub that fits into the socket. The 1/4 in. drives generally lack the strength for our intended use, although they will prove adequate for some jobs. Half-inch drives, on the other hand, certainly lack no strength. However, most of the wrench handles to fit these sockets will prove too big and cumbersome for working on motorcycles. They can also be uncomfortably expensive. As a consequence, the 3/8-in. drive is the best compromise among size, strength, and expense. If you standardize your socket collection from the outset, you will encounter less confusion and inconvenience later on.

FIGURE 7-3. Twelve-point metric sockets.

Along with your sockets, you'll need something to turn them with. There are three suggested implements to acquire for your tool collection: flex handle, speed handle, and ratchet handle. The *ratchet* allows quick, easy, one-way operation. It has a ratchet and pawl assembly in its hub. This allows the handle to drive in one direction and freewheel in the opposite direction. The ratchet handle allows for fairly rapid loosening and tightening of nuts and bolts.

The *flex* handle, often called a *breaker bar,* is not ratcheted. It is a steel bar with a hinged drive stub. Because it lacks the internal gadgetry of the ratchet, the flex handle is generally stronger. Flex handles are available in several lengths, and the 12-in. configuration is regarded as good to start with.

The *speed* handle is actually a crank with a provision for a socket at the end (Fig. 7-4). A speed handle of, say, 15 in. in length will allow access to hard-to-reach places.

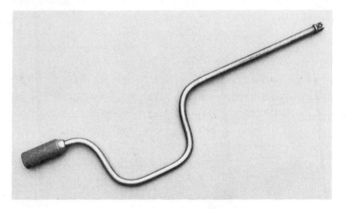

FIGURE 7-4.   Speed handle socket wrench.

FIGURE 7-5.   Ratchet handle with 3- and 6-inch extensions.

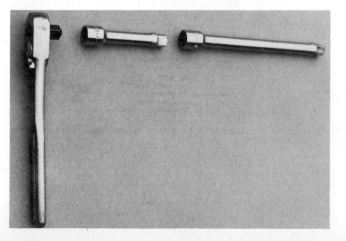

A final note about handles: Get a 3-in. and a 6-in. extension to fit the ratchet and flex handle (Fig. 7-5). These can be used individually, or end-to-end for a 9-in. extension.

which sizes to get . . .

The vast majority of motorcycles made today are assembled according to metric sizing, nuts and bolts included. And with time the motorcycle industry will be totally metrical. Currently, though, metric tools are not available everywhere, so you might have to do a little shopping to find what you want. The American inch sizes have some application in today's motorcycle world, but their popularity is fading for three reasons: (1) Simplicity—metrics are based upon multiples of 10. Size calculation is easier than with 32nds, 16ths, and 8ths. (2) Economy —although metric tools are sometimes more expensive to buy now, within a few short years their prices will be in keeping with the norm. (3) Universality—with a comprehensive set of metric tools, you'll be able to work on any contemporary motorcycle as the metric system becomes accepted.

Metric tools also offer a degree of precision not available with Whitworth-based or inch tools. (Whitworth standard tools were seen mostly on British motorcycles of past years. At this point, however, they are relatively seldom encountered and, for our purposes, are largely obsolete.) Inch tools are available in 1/16-in. increments, which corresponds to 0.0625 in. Metric tools are 1 millimeter apart or 0.0394 in. In other words, if you have a complete set of metrics, you won't be more than about 40 thousandths of an inch from a perfect fit. Using the inch standard, you're more than 60 thousandths away from a perfect fit.

A small collection of sockets ranging from 9 to 22 mm, plus ratchet handle and 13/16-in. spark plug socket, can be bought for about $25. This assembly should take care of most immediate mechanical needs and provides a good starting point. With more mechanical experience, you'll be better able to determine your need for other items.

Quality tools will outlive your motorcycle, so don't begrudge spending an extra couple of dollars for a tool you need but don't have. There will be plenty of future opportunity to use it.

pliers

As a rule, pliers are inexpensive tools, which is good, because your tool collection should include several. Ordinary household pliers will prove useful for a wide variety of applications, and while not always ideal for a specific job, good pliers will often prove handy and adequate in a pinch. An improvement on this theme are *slip-joint* pliers, particularly the kind with narrow jaws. Slip-joint pliers are capable of handling a wide spectrum of sizes to be secured within the jaws, and the narrower jaws will allow better access to objects in tight confines. Channel Lock is one of the most popular makes (Fig. 7-6).

Needle-nose pliers are a must-have item in your tool kit. Their narrow, long jaws are made for probing into tight places and grasping small objects. Needle-nose pliers are not to be used for getting a strong grip on something big, however, and besides proving ill-suited for such chores, the pliers can easily be distorted and ruined by this abuse.

Another highly useful adjunct is a *locking-grip* or *Vise-Grip* plier (Fig. 7-7). These tools function much like conventional pliers, with one big difference. Where regular pliers demand a constant hand pressure to

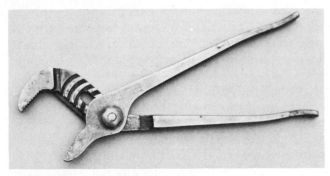

FIGURE 7-6. Channel Lock slip-joint pliers.

FIGURE 7-7. Locking-grip pliers.

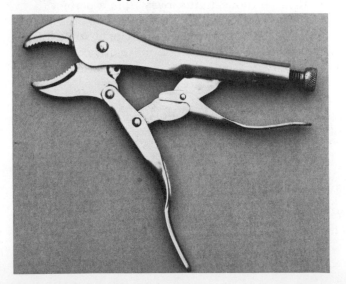

keep a part secure, the lockable variety can be firmly secured to an object and locked there. In this way they are much like a third hand, allowing the part to be held firmly while leaving your two hands free. These are not made to be used as wrenches, although their versatility will provide strong temptation. No tool box is complete without them.

Other types of pliers are available to the aspiring mechanic, but their uses tend to be more specialized. Miniature ignition pliers are an example, and so are snap-ring pliers and pliers with unusually shaped handles, hinges, and jaws. For certain more isolated chores, such tools will be valuable. But to many, their infrequent use will not justify their expense.

wrenches

Your investment in this area, as we pointed out earlier, is very important because, like sockets, you will probably be purchasing several wrenches at a time. There are many types of hand wrenches: box, open-end, combination, offset box, plus swiveling wrenches, ratchets, and many others. You can spend a great deal of money here and still have a tool kit that lacks versatility and takes up a lot of space.

Fortunately, because motorcycles are not generally hampered by the under-hood complexity and plumbing of automobiles, most of the more elaborate wrenches are not necessary. The motorcyclist can usually get along with standard types of tools.

There are three basic kinds of wrenches we will discuss: open-end, box-end, and combination (Fig. 7-8). The open-end wrench has a fixed

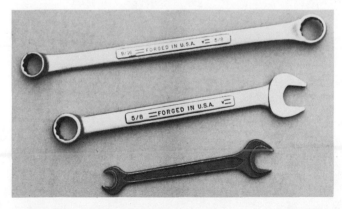

FIGURE 7-8. Top, box-end wrench; middle, combination wrench; bottom, open-end wrench.

open jaw that allows the wrench to be slipped into place from the side. The *box-end* wrench terminates in a ring that slips over the nut or bolt. The *combination* wrench is an open-end at one side and a box-end at the other. The latter style is considered by many to be the best choice in a limited, nonprofessional tool chest. This is because of the versatility the combination wrench offers, for there are nuts and bolts on motorcycles that can be reached only with one or the other end of this type of tool. In composing a tool kit from scratch, it is suggested that you begin with this type of hand wrench. Once this is done, and once you have used your tools in different situations, you can go on to purchase a set of open-end wrenches, then a set of box-ends. By this time, you will have more of an idea of your specific needs in terms of types, sizes, and perhaps brands.

Another extremely handy tool to have available in a tough situation is the type with jaws shaped to lock on nuts too badly battered to accept a conventional wrench. Gnarling nuts and bolts irreparably is the bane of mechanics, and sometimes even the seasoned hands of a professional blunder and damage them. Usually, though, rounding off bolts is due to using the wrong type or size of wrench on a bolt, tendencies of the inexperienced or ill-equipped mechanic. A tool to remove distorted nuts and bolts can shed optimism on a seemingly hopeless situation.

While on the subject of rounding off nuts and bolts, many professional mechanics are quick to caution us about use of the adjustable-end wrench, also known as the crescent wrench (Fig. 7-9). Careless use of this tool can easily round flats and corners, because its grip is seldom as secure as that of a box-end or socket.

FIGURE 7-9.   Crescent or adjustable-end wrench.

There are occasions, however, when the adjustable-end wrench must be used—for example, when you're trying to remove a 14-mm nut from a 14-mm bolt and have just one 14-mm combination wrench available. In such a case, you should use the adjustable-end wrench to hold the bolt and the combination to turn the nut. This minimizes the danger of damaging the flats of the nut.

torque wrench

Serious engine dismantling and assembly should not be attempted without a *torque* wrench (Fig. 7-10). All major nuts, bolts, and studs in a powerplant have a specified tightness rating. This tightness is a function of the type of nut, bolt, or stud, its size (length and diameter), material (aluminum, graded steel, and so on) and thread, plus other considerations, such as the type of material it is threaded into or what is threaded onto it. Disregarding torque specifications can lead to stripped threads and sheared bolts, not to mention bashed knuckles. Generally, a feel for the tightening capacity of nuts, screws, and bolts comes with experience, and many veteran mechanics display a surprisingly accurate sense for this. Even so, no professional mechanic would shun using a torque wrench for the more important parts of engine assembly, no matter how good his touch. In this respect, cylinder head bolts, cylinder base bolts, and manifolds should all be tightened to manufacturer's specifications using a torque wrench. If not, not only can threads be stripped or studs broken, but farther-reaching effects can result. An improperly tightened cylinder can warp, leading the way to head gasket failure. Additionally, this situation can cause serious harm to a water-cooled powerplant, as hot combustive gases force their way into the water jacket, forcing

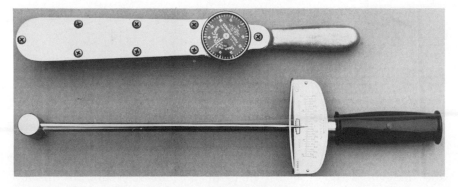

FIGURE 7-10. Torque wrenches. Top, dial readout; bottom, beam type.

precious coolant out. This can cause engine seizure, perhaps even complete engine destruction. As another example, in past years the owners of many motorcycles fitted with British-made Amal carburetors complained of excessive throttle slide wear, even slide breakage. Following this, an in-depth investigation revealed that the carburetors and slides were not at fault. Instead, the fault was in overtightening of the carburetors on their manifolds by unaware owners and mechanics. This resulted in distorted carburetor bodies. The carburetor slide, forced to work in a distorted bore, developed accelerated wear patterns and eventually broke.

A torque wrench, even a bargain basement model of marginal accuracy, is better than none. Shop manuals and some of the better owner's manuals list torque values for engine components. Tables listing bolt sizes and threads and recommended torque figures are found in local libraries in many mechanic's and machinist's reference books. Also, the catalogues of many nut and bolt manufacturers have these specifications; hardware shops and auto supply stores commonly carry these catalogues. Torque figures are usually listed in foot-pounds or inch-pounds. However, as the metric system spreads, we will be seeing the specifications in kg-m (kilogram-meters) and kg-cm (kilogram-centimeters).

Some very elaborate torque wrenches are commercially available, and prices can exceed $100. Devices suitable for our needs, however, cost nowhere near this price, and a torque wrench of the beam type costing $12 to $16 will be satisfactory. When buying your torque wrench, make sure it is adaptable to your sockets. If you have a 1/2-in. drive torque wrench but 3/8-in. drive sockets, you'll need an adapter, which requires an investment of another couple of dollars. The beam-type wrench indicates torque via a needle that swings across a scale near the wrench's handle. This is generally the least expensive method of readout. Other methods include a bell that rings when a preset torque is achieved and one that yields a click you can hear and feel when preset tightness is reached. There are also some that have dial readouts that visually indicate tightness. Torque wrenches of these types tend to be more expensive and are largely preferred by professional mechanics.

miscellaneous tools

Even though needle-nose pliers are often adequate for removing circlips and snap-rings, they are less than ideal. *Snap-rings* and *circlips* are commonly used for various fastening chores on motorcycles and the work will usually go faster—with less fasteners fumbled or dropped into

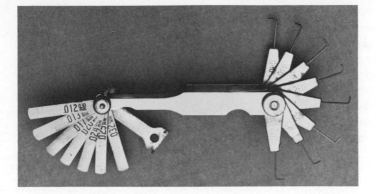

FIGURE 7-11. Feeler gauge.

inaccessible places—if you have the correct tool. A pair of snap-ring pliers will cost you $7 to $8. These come with interchangeable tips and are suitable for both inside and outside snap rings.

A must item for any tool kit is a good *feeler gauge* (Fig. 7-11). This instrument is used for setting spark plug gaps, breaker point gaps, valve clearances, and many other functions. A versatile gauge that measures between, say, 0.0015 in. and 0.025 in. will be necessary, along with a gauge spanning the spectrum from 0.025 in. to about 0.050 in. The reason we indicate that two gauges may be needed is that not many such single gauges are available that measure distances between 0.004, or smaller, to 0.050 or so. Too many individual blades, and the tool becomes cumbersome, but if you find one to your liking, good.

A *dial indicator* is a device commonly used to achieve accurate spark timing on motorcycle. It is actually a gauge with a projection that fits in the spark plug hole. The tool's projection contacts the piston crown in the combustion chamber and measures the piston's vertical movement against Top Dead Center. Many motorcycles, particularly those with two-stroke engines, specify the spark to occur at a given point in piston travel before TDC. This specification is commonly given in millimeters B (before) TDC. The dial indicator helps achieve accurate measurement here.

Another timing device that goes hand in hand with the dial indicator is a *points meter*. This electrical tool has a dial and wire leads that connect with the motorcycle's ignition system. While the dial indicator tells you where the piston is in relation to TDC, the points meter tells the instant of points opening, and thus spark generation. The points meter is also valuable because it can give indications of the points' state of health. When the needle swings sharply across the scale as the points are separated, a clean opening exists. If the sweep or motion of the needle is hesitant or ragged, however, the points are dirty or burned, or the condenser could be faulty.

Don't rely on service station air pressure gauges for proper tire inflation. The gauges on the air hose handles see so much use and abuse around the clock that they are often inaccurate. A good pocket-type gauge, the kind that service station attendants have clipped to their shirt pockets like pencils, costs about $3 or so and is accurate for the job. More expensive, more accurate dial types are also available.

Not all motorcyclists will want to get as deeply involved in the servicing of their machines as the tools discussed in this chapter will allow. Indeed, many of us lack the time to go to such efforts; are reluctant to spend the money for, say, a dial indicator and points meter; or lack self-confidence for these chores—all understandable attitudes. Consequently, the foregoing items are recommended only if you're certain you'll use them. Otherwise, it's better in the long run to have a competent professional do the work.

8 basic motorcycle care

What to do with it after you've got it

We are not all "skilled mechanics." Indeed, not all "skilled mechanics" are truly skilled mechanics. It is a regrettable situation. Some dealerships and accessory shops—and every state in the United States has a few—are poorly prepared to service the machines they sell. Not every aspiring motorcycle mechanic is fortunate enough to go to a service school. Further, not every dealer is willing to pay a competitive wage to woo a talented mechanic away from other fields, aircraft or automotive repair, for example.

And then there is the matter of your personal finances. Even though your owner's manual might suggest that you rush your motorcycle to the shop every time it needs something more than an oil change, and even though your dealer's service facilities are competently manned, your middle-class checkbook can take a beating. It's expensive running for professional assistance whenever the slightest mechanical complication crops up. Wouldn't it be better to tackle the routine mechanical chores yourself? After all, in doing so you will (1) save money, and (2) get to know your motorcycle well. Besides, working on a motorcycle is not like working on an automobile. Few cars can boast the simplicity of a motorcycle. Accessibility is excellent. Generally, carburetor, ignition, and other adjustments are either out in the breeze or very close to it.

157

Slide rule proficiency, race tuning experience, and a bank of blinking, beeping, buzzing electronic analyzers are not necessary for a tyro mechanic to achieve a satisfactory state of tune for his engine. Of course, some of today's multicylinder powerplants are of awesome complexity. The six-cylinder Benelli Sei 750, for example, and the Honda GL-1000 should be considered out of the tinkerer's league. But if the mechanically inexperienced owner approaches the tune-up of his motorcycle methodically and coolly, there is little reason for him not to be successful. A motorcycle is just a machine and a machine is, basically, just pieces with a plan. Understand the steps of that plan and you've got it knocked . . . in theory, at least. On the other hand, manual proficiency comes with experience, as with anything else. At this stage, however, your wrench-twirling speed is not important, only the accuracy of your work. Don't rush things.

Another point: we're talking about the tune-up here, not major mechanical work. If an engine is seriously ill, there's nothing to be gained from a nonprofessional tune-up. You can't make a motorcyle run correctly if its worn pistons and rings allow too much oil in the combustion chamber, if its vital carburetor metering passages are clogged with goo, or if its worn bearings are clattering in an expensive death rattle. A highly skilled mechanic just might make such an engine run a little better, but this is only temporary relief and outside of the scope of this chapter.

the service manual

Unless you've had prior experience with your type of motorcycle, you'd be asking for trouble if you don't also have a service manual . . . not an owner's manual, but a service manual (Fig. 8-1). The owner's manual is generally basic, telling you such things as recommended tire pressures, how to start the bike, and where to put the gasoline (Fig. 8-2). A notable exception to this is the owner's manual that comes with Husqvarna motorcycles. This booklet is very comprehensive, with excellent illustrations and charts; it is better than some service manuals, in fact. The service manual, however, is what professional mechanics use for mechanical repair. Motorcycle manufacturers produce service manuals for each basic model they make. These manuals are then sold to dealers much like special tools and spare parts.

Along with the official factory-produced service manuals, there are also independent manual publishers. Clymer, Chilton, and Glenn are among the most prominent in this field. Manuals from independent publishers are sometimes even better than the factory literature. Factory

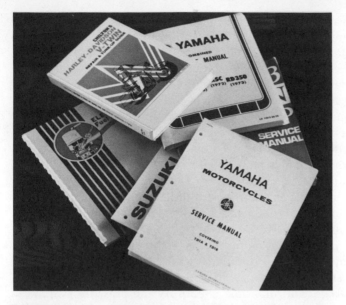

FIGURE 8-1. Service manuals can be of invaluable aid in servicing and repairing your motorcycle.

FIGURE 8-2. Owners' manuals tend to be general in content, although there are some exceptions.

manuals for imported motorcycles occasionally suffer from poor translation. For example, due to inherent differences between the English and Japanese languages, word-for-word translations from Japanese to English tend to be unclear, even downright confusing. Shop manuals produced in the United States often have extensively reworked, polished texts. On the other hand, many manuals on the market today have been copied directly from the factory publication.

The real headache occurs when you have, perhaps, a limited-production motorcycle, a model that is no longer made, or a bike produced by a manufacturer indifferent to shop manuals. Ducati owners can attest to this last state of affairs; these manuals can be a real hassle to locate. But fortunately, the Ducati owner's manual is more comprehensive than the norm, so at least you're not entirely on your own.

Sometimes manuals are produced in small, infrequent quantities. These must often be ordered from a dealer or distributor, and then you might have to wait for it to arrive. To be fair, publishing manuals is a low-priority service of some manufacturers; they are, after all, in the business of manufacturing motorcycles. The independent publishers, however, see the manual as their bread and butter. As a result, these publications are usually widely merchandised and easy to obtain.

There is considerable variation in shop manual content among manufacturers. Some go for lots of photos, some for lots of text. Some offer straight nuts-and-bolts removal and replacement information while others are steeped in theory and conversational tidbits.

The Harley-Davidson manuals exemplify the no-frills pragmatic approach. They are directed toward the working mechanic, not unlike U.S. Army instruction manuals—hard facts, straight to the point.

The CB-450 Honda manual represents the opposite approach. Here you'll find explanations of such things as piston ring flutter and valve spring surge. Such discussions are most informative and help us to understand why our bikes go (or don't go). But the workaday mechanic will probably find such theory of little practical use. Fortunately, though, this manual also provides much practical knowledge as well.

Suzuki's approach to shop manuals is both good and bad: good for the dealer and bad for the lay mechanic. You see, information on specific models tends to be scattered through several manuals. To get all factory information on your Suzuki might require you to buy several different manuals. For example, material for the Suzuki GT-750 is spread through separate manuals, one for the engine, transmission, and related running gear, one for the brakes, one for the electrics, another for the chassis, and so on. If your original plan was to gather a complete Suzuki technical library, as a Suzuki dealer would, fine. But this can be a bothersome expense otherwise. Luckily, some models are treated in one manual, the T-500, for example. Moreover, Suzuki manuals do go into great technical detail and leave few questions unanswered. In the past, Suzuki manuals suffered from rather haphazard translation. Recent years, however, have shown a marked improvement in this area.

Honda manuals can be confusing because of poor translation. This is too bad, because beneath it all is a lot of technical information—lots of photos and illustrations, too. There are tables and charts, which will surely come in handy from time to time. Textually, the manuals do not assume great mechanical expertise on the part of the reader. Because of Honda's stature as the largest motorcycle manufacturer in the world, many manuals for Honda are put out by independent publishers, so there is room for shopping around.

Regrettably, some Yamaha shop manuals in the past lacked depth. Specifically, their pages were sometimes filled with tables and promotional puffery. Also, the manuals of some models did not include lists of special tools needed. Imagine yourself hesitatingly disassembling a component. You're up to your elbows in loose parts when you discover that the whole project is stymied for lack of a special tool nobody told you about. Manuals for newer Yamahas are thankfully better—the XS750 manual is a superbly crafted example to the rest of the industry. But if your bike is an older model with no updated manual, you might be out of luck.

Kawasaki's earlier service manuals were less than ideal. They were poorly organized and required intensive combing through to find what you wanted. Much of this confusion was because each manual covered several different models and specifications were sometimes lumped together. However, if the manual for the Kawasaki 903-cc Z-1 is any indicator, this trend is changing for the better. Material is well organized and, besides providing all the technical information you'll need, it gives you good advice about working on the motorcycle.

Manuals for British motorcycles tend to be good. Matter-of-factual, they are written for mechanics and will realize no awards for cocktail humor. Their procedures have step-by-step clarity, although some Americans may be confused by English word usages. For example, only some of us know that a "gudgeon pin" over there is a "wrist pin" here, or that what they call "paraffin" is "kerosene" to us. For working on an English motorcycle, though, there are not better manuals then those put out by the manufacturers themselves. Other less prominent makes with exceedingly good shop manuals are Moto Guzzi, Ossa, Bultaco, and Hodaka. The latter's manual is particularly striking, for its coated paper (easy for wiping off greasy fingerprints) and hard covers ensure a long life.

Whatever publication you use for technical consultation, you're still much safer and wiser than attempting adjustments or repair without any help whatsoever. Motorcycles have their quirks. To be unaware of them when performing mechanical chores is to take a big chance. Mechanical mistakes tend to be expensive, or, at best, an inconvenience. Manuals tell us what to expect when tearing into a motorcycle, and they provide us with at least a basic idea of what connects to what, and why. Additionally, a good manual will be of great help when you order replacement parts.

Manuals often have troubleshooting tips, too. Some of the symptoms and cures may sound general and vague ("Malady: Motorcycle won't run. What to do: Check gas tank."), but they can save you from frustration nonetheless.

The most important thing to remember, though, is commonsensical. Read the manual before you start taking things apart. Know what you're going to do. Give your work some semblance of logical order. You're asking for big (read: expensive) trouble if you mindlessly remove one part after another in the hope of finding something interesting.

Also, proper reassembly requires a manual. Torque specifications for nuts and bolts are shown in all but the chintziest of manuals; correct procedures are shown as well. It's no fun at all to reassemble major components carefully, then discover overlooked parts at our feet and thus have to take the whole thing apart again. I repeat, it's no fun.

the routine inspection . . . what to look for

A motorcycle is a relatively complicated machine, based on the cooperation of many different parts and systems. Gears must get along with other gears, shafts have to cooperate with bearings, chains must tug when they're supposed to and so should control cables. Oil must squirt and gasoline must flow. And tires must maintain a cushion of air between you and the ground.

Making sure these mechanical chores are done presents no real challenges to the inexperienced mechanic, just a few extra minutes each time you plan for a ride. A brief inspection of your entire motorcycle may reveal a potentially dangerous condition. Also, it will familiarize you with wear patterns normal to your motorcycle. Being well acquainted with your bike's idiosyncrasies may save you a lot of grief in avoiding dangerous mechanical failures on the road.

Street motorcyclists, of course, should scrutinize their machines' lights. As we mentioned in Chapter 3, some states require that motorcycles burn headlights in daylight as well. So headlights should certainly be inspected to avoid traffic citations, if not accidents, in the dark. Taillight and stoplight are of particular importance to the motorcyclist. That auto driver behind you needs every bit visual stimulation you can muster to bring him out of his insulated reverie. Street riders could benefit from carrying along a few extra bulbs, especially on long trips.

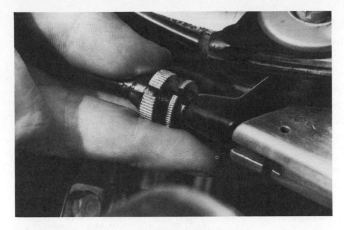

FIGURE 8-3. As a rule, motorcycle control cables can be adjusted by hand.

Cables and control rods should also be inspected. With time and use, cables stretch, brakes and clutches wear, and lube runs dry. Adjust these controls to specifications outlined in your manual (Fig. 8-3). Owners of new motorcycles will probably notice that more control cable or rod adjustment is required in the first few hundred miles than in the next couple of thousand miles. This is largely due to wearing in and stretching. With use, cable sheaths will compress; the cables within will stretch to their normal limits and then more or less stabilize dimensionally. It's normally nothing to worry about but bears watching nonetheless. Brake shoes wear in against their drums and clutch plates also sometimes experience slightly accelerated initial wear. Maintain these correctly and you should realize many miles of faithful service.

Control cables should be lubed. Some cables have oil fittings on them to make this chore easy, others don't. Cables on many new motorcycles are completely dry. If your type of cable has no lube fittings, there are still ways to administer the necessary oil. One method requires that you remove the cable from the motorcycle. Suspend it vertically. Using aluminum foil, make a funnel to fit over the top opening of the sheath. Snug the neck of the funnel around the sheath with rubber bands, tape, a tie-wrap—something to prevent oil from dribbling all over. Now pour oil—just a little bit at a time—into the funnel. Slowly it will penetrate the length of the cable's interior. If this sounds like a hassle, you can buy a cable oiler for a few dollars. This item looks like a large hypodermic needle which fits over the end of the sheath. Pushing the plunger forces lube down the tube. You'll know when there is adequate oil in the sheath when oil drips out the bottom opening.

If, in your inspection, you discover a cable that is frayed, replace it as soon as possible. There is potential for danger here. Imagine yourself at a stoplight, your engine idling and your clutch lever pulled in. And then the worn cable snaps, sending you out into the traffic stream. It's not a pleasant thought, but this very thing has happened. On the other hand, a frayed throttle cable can snag its metal strands on the inside of its sheath, causing erratic, perhaps disastrous, throttle behavior. And nobody needs to be told of the consequences of a broken brake cable, which, of course, will surely happen when you need it most yet least suspect it.

When making your visual inspection of cables, pay particularly close attention to areas where they rub against other parts of the motorcycle and where they make tight bends. Most internal cable wear comes from the latter areas, while external rubbing can wear through the insulative sheath.

the drive chain

The motorcycle drive chain lives in a hostile environment. Its responsibilities are great and its failure can sometimes be catastrophic, yet motorcyclists often neglect it anyway.

No matter what the advertising says on the box of that nifty new chain you just bought, drive chains should be lubricated at least every 300 miles (Fig. 8-4). And that's for street bikes. Dirt bike chains should be lubricated much more often. Give it generous dollops of lube every time it even appears dry and at the beginning of each ride.

Some motorcycles are fitted with devices that automatically and constantly drip engine oil on the chain. These, however, while being of some value, are no substitute for your personal attention to the chain. Your motorcycle's chain should still be regularly inspected and hand lubricated.

Many kinds of chain lubes are available today, and to argue their respective merits would be like arguing religion or politics. Dry chain lubes are quite effective in reducing friction in those small spaces between the chain's rollers and bushings. Additionally, dry lubes are favored by some motorcyclists because after application the chain appears dry, and a dry chain does not attract and hold dirt on the chain. The dry lubes are generally based upon a molybdenum disulphide powder dispersed in a volatile solvent. Upon application, the solvent dries, leaving the molybdenum disulphide lubricant. Such lubricants have been criticized, however, for failing to provide an element of hydraulic

FIGURE 8-4. Correct adjustment and frequent lubrication are essential for minimal chain wear. Be sure to use a good lubricant.

cushioning between the chain's rollers and bushings. The issue remains unsettled, however, with no universal agreement among experienced motorcyclists on the issue.

There are many *wet* chain lubes that utilize a volatile propellant and a nondrying lubricant. Often these are basically oil or grease thinned with a solvent. Thus thinned out, the lubricant can penetrate into the very small recesses of the chain. Again, its job done, the solvent dries, leaving just the basic lubricant. Today's motorcycle after-market offers many types of chain lubricants, some to be applied by squirt can and some in aerosol form. Prices tend to range from $1.50 to $3.00 per can.

Yet a third family of chain lubricants is finding favor among motorcyclists. This type utilizes both molybdenum disulphide and various types of petroleum distillates and synthetic sperm oil. In this way the chain realizes excellent hydraulic cushioning between components, good film strength, and penetration and friction reduction at high temperatures. It is available from several manufacturers in 4- to 5-ounce aerosol cans for less than $2.

When you are lubricating the chain, make sure oil goes to all the correct places. The tendency is merely to oil the rollers, for they are easiest to get at. This alone is of marginal value. Instead, make sure the lubricant penetrates into the spaces among the chain's side plates, pins, rollers and bushings. These are the surfaces that are in constant contact with one another. If you find tight, binding links on a section of your chain, it may be necessary to remove the chain and soak it in a good-quality industrial solvent for a while to break down rust and corrosion. Of course, this will also remove any vestiges of lubricant on the chain, so a complete reoiling will later be needed.

Chain stretch is the commonest type of chain wear. In truth, how-ever, while the overall length of a chain does increase with use, it is not due to actual stretching of its metal parts. Wear of roller bushings and pins create slack which allows the chain to elongate. Chain manufactur-ers commonly allow a maximum of 3 percent chain elongation before suggesting replacement. In other words, when a chain that measured, say, 60 inches overall new measures close to 62 inches after use, it should be replaced.

Even though your loose, saggy chain still transmits power, with no more adjustment room left, resist the temptation to squeeze as many more miles out of it as you can. Chain components, particularly the rollers, are made of very hard metal, much harder than that of most sprockets. So the result of your false frugality can be some seriously worn sprockets . . . and more money to spend.

Adjust chain tension by putting your motorcycle up on its center-stand so that the rear wheel can spin freely. Most dirt or trail motorcycles have no centerstand, so it will be necessary to place a milk crate or similar prop under the center of the machine. Loosen the rear axle nut; sometimes you will encounter a cotter pin securing this nut. This done, the rear axle can slide to and fro in its adjustment tracks at the end of the swing arm. Moving the wheel back and forth tightens or loosens the chain as you desire. The correct chain tension is outlined in your owner's manual. If that specific information is not available, there is a general rule of thumb which, while not ideal, will surely put you in the ball park. Leave from 3/4- to 5/8-inch vertical movement measured at the center of the lower part of the chain. Unlike the previous example, some motorcycles require that their chains be adjusted with weight on the wheel, so swing arm position is an important consideration here. A chain that may seem ideally adjusted with the wheel unladen may become overly tight when weight is applied. After you have adjusted your chain, recheck its tension with weight on the saddle. Most motor-cycles have adjusting nuts at each end of the axle (Fig. 8-5). Turning these nuts one way will pull the axle rearward, tightening the chain. Turning the nuts in the opposite direction will allow the axle to move forward, loosening the chain. Wheel alignment is also controlled by these nuts. Unequal tightening of them can result in the rear wheel being cocked out of line in relation to the front wheel. When you are adjusting chain tension, make it a point to turn each of these nuts just a little bit at a

FIGURE 8-5.   Chain tension adjusting nuts are often located at swing
arm ends.

time. For example, assuming the wheel's alignment is okay to begin
with, turn each nut just 90 degrees at a time when you adjust the chain. It
is important to make sure that all slack is taken up between the adjusting
nuts and their seats in the swing arm. Standing squarely behind the
motorcycle, give the rear of the tire a sound kick with your boot to force
the nuts against their seats. Recheck chain tension. If everything appears
correct, you may now tighten the axle nut.

There are many different makes of drive chain, but almost all of
them share the same size reference system. It makes things much easier if
you can telephone from shop to shop when you're hunting for a new
chain, rather than carrying around an unidentified piece of chain and
trying to match it with what's available. For example, a No. 530 chain
will be of the same major dimensions no matter who makes it. You can
use the following table to determine what type of chain you have and,
perhaps, if it can be replaced by a stronger model of compatible dimensions. For example, if your motorcycle comes from the manufacturer
with a No. 520 chain, the table tells us that the No. 525 offers 1/16 in.
more roller width and, depending on the sprockets, maybe 25 percent
greater load bearing area per roller.

Chain Dimensions

CHAIN NO.	PITCH (IN.)	ROLLER DIAMETER (IN.)	ROLLER WIDTH (IN.)
420	1/2	0.306	1/4
425	1/2	0.312	5/16
428	1/2	0.335	5/16
520	5/8	0.400	1/4
525	5/8	0.400	5/16
530	5/8	0.400	3/8

motorcycle tires

Because those two hoops of rubber are the only things between you and the road, their state of health bears directly on yours. An automobile suffering a flat tire on city streets usually poses more inconvenience than hazard. Moreover, even blowouts at freeway speeds, while sometimes frightening, seldom lead to disaster. The motorcycle, though, is not so fortunate. Sudden tire failure at any speed other than slow is not only frightening but dangerous. The flattened tire wobbles and flutters on its rim and the motorcycle yaws grotesquely beneath you. The flat tire, be it front or rear, wants to steer the motorcycle, first one way then the other. And, generally, all the motorcyclist can do is to avoid making sudden moves and ride the nightmare out.

Off-road motorcyclists are not as susceptible to these perils as are street riders. The pavement-going motorcyclist is often traveling at higher speeds on a much heavier vehicle. Additionally, because of surrounding traffic he may have no alternative but to try desperately to keep his wobbling mount within his traffic lane. And, finally, the street rider faces much worse consequences if he does hit the pavement. The dirt rider is generally traveling much slower, and his machine may weigh perhaps one third that of a large-displacement tourer. He has a great advantage in controlling his bike's gyrations.

Because of their different applications, dirt and street tires are commonly made of different rubber compounds. Natural rubber possesses a high resistance to internal heat buildup, and heat is a major contributor to tire wear. On the negative side, however, a tire made solely of natural rubber would tend to lack the road-gripping power needed for safe street use.

Synthetic rubbers have different traits; they tend to be relatively soft and flexible, thus gripping the road well. But this virtue is balanced by the pure synthetic rubber tire's susceptibility to internal heat build-up, and so the synthetic tire may wear at a very high rate. This destructive heat is the result of tire flex—as it rolls, it flexes; cords, fibers, and molecules stretch and contract, thus generating heat. A little heat is okay, but not a lot. Excessive heat not only accelerates tire tread wear but also tends to weaken the cord body of the tire.

Most modern tires are made of synthetic and natural rubber compounds. Compounds for various uses differ accordingly. Gnarly off-road tires, for example, tend to have a greater amount of natural rubber in their construction, to take the ripping, spinning, pounding punishment usually encountered in the wilderness. The flexible, softer compounds tend to come apart easier under such conditions. Street use demands a different compound because such destructive elements as tire spin and sharp rocks are not normally encountered on the pavement. Also, it is important that the tire surface be soft enough to grip the pavement securely, so relative softness lends to adhesion.

The vast majority of cases of abnormal tire wear can be traced to improper inflation. If the center of the tread shows greater wear than the sides, the problem is likely to be overinflation. This is because the tire is distended, which does not allow for a normal footprint but only contact at the center portion. An underinflated tire will show greater wear at the sides of the tread than at the center. Both underinflation and overinflation will hurt your motorcycle's handling, particularly if it's a street machine. Always keep your tires inflated to the manufacturer's recommendations.

Whether you are a street or dirt rider, it is always a good practice to check tire pressures before going on a ride (Fig. 8-6). Experienced motorcycle riders will tell you that motorcycle tires will sometimes go

FIGURE 8-6. Checking tire air pressure.

flat with disuse. Sometimes even a regularly ridden machine will become unexplainedly flat-footed overnight—fill it up with air and everything's fine . . . no detectable leaks . . . all very befuddling. If this happens, check air pressures as often as possible and make sure the air valve is in good condition.

Interestingly, tire tubes made of pure natural rubber tend to leak because of inherent porosity, while their synthetic rubber counterparts don't. And because this porosity is characteristic of the entire tube, no amount of after-market tube sealant will cure this problem.

When you check tire pressures, the tire should be cold. The tires of a motorcycle that has been ridden generate internal heat that will result in a higher pressure reading. Touring and long distance riders should never bleed off pressure from hot tires. Pressure buildup within the tire is normal during running. Reducing tire pressure at this point will result in additional tire flex, additional heat buildup, and a potentially dangerous condition.

Badly worn tires are highly susceptible to punctures. If a street tire has less than 1/16th-inch tread depth, it's time for a new one.

fuel system adjustments

To begin with, this is a basic discussion about bringing motorcycle fuel systems into adjustment. In these pages, however, we cannot detail the complexities of tuning the carburetion systems of most multicylinder machines. Among other things, you will need special tools, notably a carburetor synchronizing manometer, and some formal technical training wouldn't hurt, either. The Honda GL-1000, with its quartet of constant-velocity carburetors, should not be fiddled with by inexperienced hands. The Suzuki RE-5 Rotary is also much too complicated for beginning motorcyclists and thus out of the scope of this chapter. On the other hand, the procedures outlined here apply to most singles and twins, plus many of the three-cylinder machines on the road today.

Fuel system maintenance involves checking the entire system, making sure it is doing all that is necessary to yield correct fuel-air mixtures to the engine. Start by checking fuel flow. Remove the fuel line from the carburetor and open the fuel tap. Do this with the fuel tank cap on. Fuel should flow freely in a full stream. If not, remove the gas cap. If fuel now flows smoothly, it would indicate that the gas cap breather vent is clogged. If fuel flow is still obstructed, examine the fuel tap for an obstruction. There could also be dirt or a kink in the fuel line or a plugged fuel filter.

Many motorcycles do not come standard with fuel filters, but it is always a good idea to install them. Special filters for motorcycles are sold in most motorcycle shops and can be installed in a matter of minutes. Elements in filters are often simple screens but are sometimes more complicated devices. Some filters are not reusable, but most are. The usual way to clean screen-type filters is to flush fuel or a solvent backward through it, thus cleansing out the dirt particles. If a filter is clogged with varnishlike deposits, gasoline will not clean it out and, if it's a reusable unit, a special carburetor cleaning solvent (usually some sort of chlorinated hydrocarbon solution) will be required. In some instances, when the old filter might not be able to withstand cleaning, due to age and hard use . . . toss it out, get a new one.

Remove the air cleaner and examine it closely. A damaged or dirty air cleaner can choke an engine, inhibiting its performance and possibly causing fouled spark plugs, increased fuel consumption, and excessively smoky exhaust.

There are several types of air cleaners; not all are cleaned the same way. The usual way to service foam-type filter elements is to wash them in gasoline or similar solvent, squeeze them dry, and then lightly oil them with motor oil. The paper-type elements (usually accordion-pleated for increased surface area) can be cleaned to some extent; compressed air is blown against this filter's inner surface to dislodge dirt from the outer surface. Generally, though, this type of cleaning is less than complete, and the element should be replaced from time to time, depending on your type of riding. Dirt bikes will require more frequent replacement than street bikes, and so on. Within recent years, the metal mesh air filter has been forsaken for more efficient types. Nonetheless, there are more than a few on today's motorcycles. Clean this type by agitating and rinsing it in a solvent, letting it dry, and then lightly oiling it. The accordion-folded cloth element air filter is one of the most popular with performance enthusiasts, for it allows excellent filtration with minimal air flow restriction. This type has the advantage of offering finer filtration, because more dirt accumulates on its exterior with minimal compromise in air flow. Before installation on the intake tract, the element is sprayed with a special oil which retains dirt particles. In use, as these particles become layered on the surface, filtration is enhanced. When surface dirt becomes too thick, it is suggested that you merely lightly tap or brush off the excess dirt. Only very dirty elements of this type need to be washed in solvent.

caring for the carburetor(s)

The following describes the method for idle, throttle stop, and pilot jet adjustment suitable to most Mikuni, Bing, Jikov, and other conventional throttle slide and sediment bowl carburetors. Constant-velocity and diaphragm carburetors are not always within the home mechanic's mechanical capabilities.

Your first step is to loosen the throttle cable adjustments. Adjust all tension from the throttle cable(s), and ease off on the throttle stop screws to allow the throttle slides to drop totally closed. Follow your manual here to determine the correct screws and adjusters.

Next, find the point at which the throttle stop screw just begins to contact its respective throttle slide. You do this by gradually screwing in the stop screw and gently tugging at the appropriate throttle cable at the same time (Fig. 8-7). Pull the slide up from the bottom of the throttle bore about 1/8 inch and let it drop back. As you perform both these actions, you'll be able to feel and hear just when the throttle slide makes contact with its adjustable stop; the click of the dropping slide will change slightly, and you'll also be able to feel a light shock transmitted back through the stop screw. This can take the novice mechanic several minutes to achieve, but there's no hurry and to botch the job could be expensive, if not a nuisance. Perform this chore on each of your bike's carburetors.

Once this is done, carefully turn each throttle stop screw inward 1 to 1-1/2 turns, for a ball park figure. Otherwise, consult your manual for the recommended figure. What we're trying to do here is have each throttle slide the same distance off its seat. In this way we're bringing everything back to zero—a known point—and recalibrating carburetor adjustments from there.

FIGURE 8-7.   Adjusting throttle stop screw on Dell 'Orto carburetor.

FIGURE 8-8. Adjusting idle mixture screw on Dell 'Orto carburetor.

The same thing is now done with the idle mixture screws, also called air screws or pilot screws. Turn each of these screws inward until it bottoms against its seat. Be gentle here, for overtightening can distort the seat of the needle-pointed screw. A distorted seat can make further adjustment here impossible. Next, back out these screws the amount specified in your manual. If no figure is available, once again use 1 to 1-1/2 turns outward as a general figure (Fig. 8-8).

Now it is time to start the engine. The carburetors' present state of adjustment will now allow the engine to run well enough for them to be accurately tuned. Let the engine warm up well before making further adjustments; a cold engine demands a fuel mixture much different than a warm engine does. At this point you'll probably notice that the idle speed is too fast. In this case, back off each throttle stop screw a set amount at a time; 1/8 of a turn will do. Work gradually—after all, you're feeling your way around a sometimes complex machine. Step by step, work the throttle stop screws of each carburetor until the desired idle speed is achieved.

That was the easy half. The more difficult part now is to balance the idle speed adjustments against the idle mixture screws. This involves turning these screws in and out slowly while listening to the engine and watching the tachometer, if your bike has one. Generally, idle mixture screws control the passage of air through a particular carburetor passage. Thus, turning the screw outward (counterclockwise) leans the idle mixture, and turning it inward richens it. So begin by turning each carburetor idle mixture screw in at about 1/8-turn increments. Listen carefully. Does this result in a change of engine speed? Let's assume that engine revs pick up in doing this. Now, using the throttle stop screws, bring idle speed back down to where factory specs say it should be. Turn in the mixture screws more. Do revs gain or lose? Try, through leaning and richening the idle mixtures, to locate the setting that yields the highest engine speed. When turning these screws, be patient. Engine speed does not always respond rapidly to these adjustments. Adjust, wait . . . adjust, wait. Because of their more frequent power pulses, multicylinder engines seem harder to adjust; minor imbalances or misadjustments of one cylinder are dampened out by its mates. In time, you will have all idle mixtures working to yield highest idle speed. So now you must again readjust the idle speed down through small steps on the throttle stop screws. Then . . . you guessed it . . . readjust the mixture screws for highest idle speed. In time—depending upon your intuition, patience, and the number of carburetors you have to work with—you will have determined the optimum idle mixture setting and throttle stop adjustment. Now readjust cable tension to factory specs.

We haven't discussed the many other carburetor adjustments that could be made, for this reason: For our basic, simplified, practical purposes, they don't apply. Changing main jet sizes, metering needles, throttle cutaways, and all the other variables are more elements of modification and very fine tuning. But will the average rider be overly concerned if his go-to-school or weekend playbike is missing a fraction of a horsepower at 7000 rpm in a tradeoff for economy or midrange smoothness? We think not. Hyperfine tuning is a subject worthy of volumes. But that can come later. In this book we are concerned with learning the practical aspects of our motorcycles and maintaining them in good fettle.

ignition point care

With the exception of certain motorcycles fitted with pointless electronic ignitions, the vast majority of today's motorcycles still rely upon breaker points to trigger ignition spark.

Breaker points are a mechanical device to interrupt electrical flow to the high tension coil. Through a rather complicated series of events described elsewhere in this book, a spark occurs at the spark plug when the breaker points are opened. (There are certain types of magnetos that provide a spark to the plug when the points close, but their numbers are relatively few nowadays.)

The breaker points should be approached with deliberation. Their gap adjustment is crucial in determining whether your engine is a stormer or a wheezer. Also, incorrectly adjusted or worn points can cause serious engine damage. Spark timing can be affected, with a chance of resultant overheating, and excess heat can turn an engine to scrap in short order.

The breaker points also tend to be physically fragile. Most often, each arm of the contact breakers are made of metal stampings that can be bent or distorted by careless or impatient hands. If either of the breaker arms is tweaked, the contact points will be misaligned, preventing efficient current triggering while seriously hurting point life.

In examining your breaker points, there are several conditions to be especially watchful for.

The ideal set of breaker points should be smooth and clean. This is not always so, however, for in normal operation the points are opened and closed several thousand times per minute. And even though the contact surfaces are made of a tungsten compound—very high melting point, extremely hard, and corrosion resistant—they cannot last forever, even under ideal conditions.

The points commonly operate in a sealed environment to prevent harmful dirt from creeping in. It is not unusual, however, particularly as the motorcycle grows older, for various seals and engine gaskets to leak and allow contamination of the points, usually by oil. Also, it is not uncommon for simple condensation of moisture in the air to have an effect. Whatever the cause, miniscule amounts of dirt and moisture can find their way onto the breaker points, and some cannot be avoided. A certain amount of point surface erosion cannot be avoided, either, for the points carry a large electrical load.

Therefore, visual inspection of your breaker points should reveal no oil or contaminants. Often a very fine layer of condensed engine vapors is found on various components, but this is to be expected, especially in used motorcycles. Commercial aerosol solvents made especially for the cleaning of these components are available for a couple of dollars per can, enough to last several months under normal usage (Fig. 8-9).

Very often, after many miles of operation, the contacts assume a relationship of crater-mountain rather than one of flat surfaces. In other words, material from one breaker surface is removed and deposited on the other breaker surface. This is due largely to incorrect condenser capacitance. (The condenser, remember, is wired in parallel with the points. Its purpose is to prevent destructive electrical current from flowing across the points as they open.) When one of the point surfaces, for example, develops a tiny, mountain-shaped deposit, and the other

FIGURE 8-9.   Spraying breaker points with aerosol solvent.

point surface develops a corresponding crater, this indicates that something is wrong. Arcing is taking place and point material is being broken up and redeposited. Very likely the condenser is not doing its job efficiently. By malfunction, faulty design or assembly, the condenser is over- or under-capacitance. Under ideal conditions, this pitting and cratering would not occur. But because of operating conditions, maintenance and condenser quality, "ideal" conditions are not always achieved, much less maintained for any length of time.

The majority of today's motorcycle ignition systems are negative ground. Among other things, this means that the fixed breaker contact is negative. The moving one actuated by the breaker cam is then positive. If the fixed surface develops a crater and the moving surface develops a mountain, it suggests that the condenser's capacitance is too great. On the other hand, if a mountain develops on the fixed (grounded) contact and the crater on the other, then the condenser's capacitance should be increased.

Craters, mountains, and contamination notwithstanding, contact points in good condition can be expected to take on a slightly eroded surface texture after a while, but this erosion should be an even grayish film.

Breaker point adjustment requires a feeler gauge. But before you begin to adjust point gap, examine the breaker surfaces for the conditions just described. Of course, if the points are pitted, burned, or unevenly worn, you should replace them with a new set. Frazzled breaker points are difficult to adjust in the first place and are not likely to stay in adjustment in the second place. To clean the points, it is suggested you use a points file, Flexstone, or similarly abrasive tool. Don't file the points vigorously, but dress them gently with even strokes. Clean them either with aerosol spray solvent or with a piece of stiff, unwaxed paper soaked in ignition solvent.

Breaker points in almost all motorcycles are adjusted by loosening the lockscrew that allows the point assembly base to move. Using a feeler gauge of appropriate thickness (follow factory specifications to the letter here), insert the gauge between the points as they are opened to their widest position (if you remove the spark plug and turn the engine over by hand, you can achieve reasonable accuracy). With the lockscrew loosened, move the point plate to the position where just a light frictional drag is felt on the feeler gauge as you move it through the point gap. This done, you may now tighten down the lockscrew and consider your points adjusted. Bear in mind, though, that these instructions are far from universal, because different motorcycles can demand different procedures. However, they do apply as basic tenets of point care. On the other hand, the chore of ignition timing cannot be described here because (1) many motorcycles require specialized equipment, (2) procedures can vary widely from model to model, and (3) it will probably prove difficult, frustrating, and, in the end, possibly expensive to repair for the beginning mechanic.

spark plugs

The spark plug lives in a violent world. No wonder it fails on occasion . . . and no wonder it is sometimes blamed for weaknesses in other parts of the engine. If a motorcycle starts to burp and spit, miss and sputter, why, by golly, replace them blankety-blank plugs, boys, so we can get this thing back on the road. This is an unfortunately common attitude, for the trail and street rider rarely encounters a defectively made spark plug. The engine may miss and no spark may occur at the plug, but seldom is it the spark plug's fault. Most often, the spark plug no longer sparks because the points are fouled, carburetor adjustments are off, there are vacuum leaks in the intake tract, the plug is of the wrong heat range, or any other fault or combination thereof. Instead of using the spark plug as a scapegoat for mechanical ills, the thinking mechanic uses it, through visual examination, as a window into an engine's state of health.

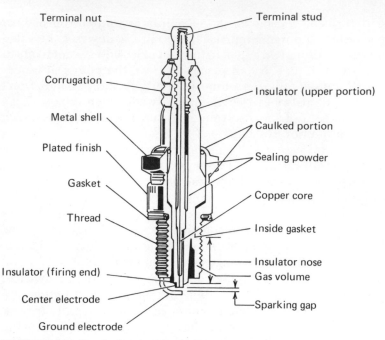

FIGURE 8-10. Spark plug construction.

The spark plug indeed has its work cut out for it (Fig. 8-10). When the fuel-air mixture explodes in the combustion chamber, the temperature rises within milliseconds to approximately 4500 degrees Fahrenheit. Also, pressure rises to about 750 psi. Moreover, during the exhaust stroke, cylinder pressure and temperature drop radically with the discharge of exhaust gases, as well as with the incoming fresh fuel-air mixture of the intake stroke. The spark plug, then, must be able to withstand rapid and extreme variations of temperature and pressure. Further, it must be able to cope with high voltage (as much as 50,000 volts in some cases), mechanical vibration, and the corrosive chemical effects of exhaust gases.

Spark plug experts tell us that all that spark plugs need to do is keep consistently sparking with proper timing.

To achieve this, the firing end of the plug must be maintained within a certain temperature range, so that it does not become so overheated that it is ultimately destroyed or so cool (relatively speaking) that it collects carbon deposits. Also, the plug must be provided with sufficient voltage to permit it to spark. There are hot and cold types of spark plugs. Those that tend to burn within their heat ranges and from which comparatively little heat escapes are called "hot" plugs. Those that tend to get relatively cold and from which heat escapes readily are called "cold" plugs (Fig. 8-11). The heat range of a spark plug will vary with the type and operating condition of the engine. Heat range is commonly defined as the temperature gradient within which the spark plug is neither overheated nor cooled to the point of plug failure (Fig. 8-12).

The main difference between cold and hot types is in the length of the insulators of the firing end. The hot types tend to have a longer insulator, which retains combustion heat. This type, besides requiring more time to dissipate heat, also runs hotter because of its larger area of insulator surface. In comparison, cold spark plugs tend to have shorter, smaller insulators to facilitate heat dissipation through the plug body to the cylinder head.

Generally, hot spark plugs are more suitable for low speed riding than cold plugs. This is because the hot plug's higher ambient operating temperatures do not allow the carbon particle buildup common to low speed and light load riding. At high speeds and high engine loads, however, the hot plug cannot cope with all the heat it is subjected to and failure becomes imminent. On the other hand, the cold plug, while more susceptible to low-speed, light-load carbon fouling, can cope with higher operating temperatures because it does not accumulate and retain as much heat. In this way the cold plug is generally better suited to high-speed riding, heavy loads, and other severe conditions.

Several factors are important in determining the heat range of spark plugs an engine will require.

The ratio of air-fuel mix: Extremes of mixture richness and leanness will likewise cause extremes in operating temperatures. For example, changes in carburetion metering will often require a different heat range plug in an otherwise unchanged engine.

Compression ratio: If the compression ratio of an engine is increased, the temperature and pressure of unburned fuel become hotter immediately before ignition. The temperature of the spark plug also goes up as a result.

Fuel: Some fuels are not as efficient as others in absorbing combustion chamber heat; thus the temperatures of the spark plug and combustion chamber walls will rise.

Engine rpm and vehicle load: As the number of engine revolutions is increased, the temperature of the spark plug rises almost proportionately. Engine load significantly affects spark plug temperature. Under an increased load, the fuel-air charge is also increased, usually leading to a rise in plug temperature.

Spark plug torque: Few people realize that spark plug temperature is also affected by the tightness of the plug in the cylinder head. A spark plug installed insufficiently tight or without gaskets will have its heat radiation qualities reduced; temperatures will rise.

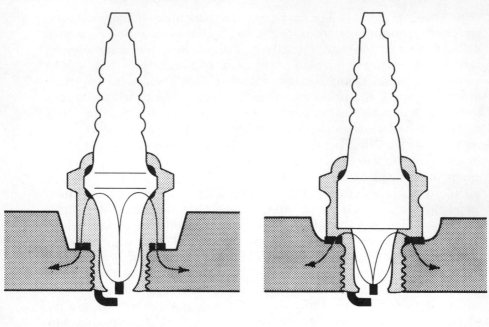

Hot   Cold

FIGURE 8-11. Spark plug heat range is determined by a plug's ability to retain or dissipate combustion. A hot plug retains heat; a cold one dissipates heat comparatively quickly.

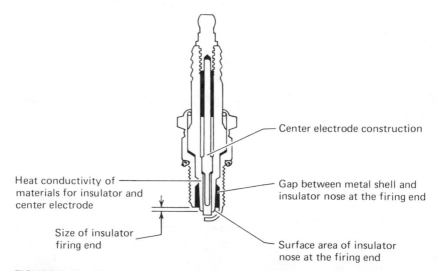

Center electrode construction

Heat conductivity of materials for insulator and center electrode

Gap between metal shell and insulator nose at the firing end

Size of insulator firing end

Surface area of insulator nose at the firing end

FIGURE 8-12. Factors determining spark plug heat range.

It is crucial to use a spark plug with a heat range compatible with the characteristics of your engine. Unless the engine has been modified, or the motorcycle is operated in a different altitude than originally set up for (for example, Denver, Colorado versus San Diego, California), or some other significant reason, use the plugs specified by the manufacturer. After all, they designed and developed the machine. They're not total dummies. In other words, unless you have good reason, don't second guess the people who should know best.

The spark plug that will last forever has yet to be made. For the time being, we will have to content ourselves with items that deteriorate even under ideal operating conditions. The plug's useful life is dependent mostly on the operating condition of the engine. Incorrect selection of plugs or fouling and burning attributable to causes other than the plug itself have an effect on the life of the spark plug.

A dissipated spark plug compromises performance, wastes gasoline, and requires a higher than normal voltage to fire it. Because of this last factor, other parts of the ignition system are forced to work harder to compensate. Spark plugs should be inspected and replaced according to the specifications of your bike's manufacturer. Trying to eke out a few more thousand miles from blunted, corroded spark plugs will only cost you more in long-term maintenance.

The final factor in effective motorcycle maintenance is not mechanical. It is rather the owner's attitude. Just as riding a motorcycle requires so much more participation of its rider than driving an auto does its driver, the motorcycle, for better or worse, also requires its owner to play a more active role in its upkeep. Motorcycle owners should be encouraged to think of that two-wheeled machine as not just a means of getting from A to B. Better, you might look upon it as an extension of your personality. Under these circumstances, routine motorcycle maintenance can become just as natural as looking after your own personal health.

9 fundamentals of troubleshooting

How to stop it from doing what it shouldn't be doing in the first place

Your motorcycle is a machine. And basically, a machine is just *pieces with a plan*. It cannot think. It cannot do what its pieces will not allow. And, despite what you may think in more frustrating moments, it cannot plot against you. Whatever happens in your motorcycle, be it good or bad, has a logical reason. The science, sometimes *art*, of troubleshooting hinges on the tenet that nothing mechanical happens without reason.

So, even though your motorcycle may be technically a bit foreign to you, with the proper set of hand tools and attitudes there is no reason at all for you to feel intimidated by the machine.

If your motorcycle begins to run poorly or stops running altogether, you must fight the urge to panic, even though you may be miles from home or assistance. By following the suggested procedures and keeping your wits about you, chances are that the root cause will be identified, isolated, and remedied within a reasonable period of time. Now, there are almost as many different approaches to problem solving as there are models of motorcycles. Our approach here, and the most widely used method, is that of probabilities and priorities. Follow these in a logically ordered regimen, and the lay motorcyclist's chances of exorcising mechanical gremlins are bright, indeed.

Variations in design and manufacture of the hundreds of different makes extant today do not allow us to include all probabilities and possibilities of malfunction. Condensed herein, however, are procedures formulated to apply to most two- and four-stroke engines commonly found in today's motorcycles.

To begin with, we must define the areas of the motorcycle to be investigated; otherwise, our chances of losing valuable time and further complicating the mechanical problem(s) soar dramatically. After all, what good is it to treat an inflamed appendix with a knee brace? The brace provides absolutely no benefit while the appendix will surely get worse.

We will, therefore, confine our investigation to three areas: (1) fuel supply, (2) ignition, and (3) timing. When all is A-OK in these departments, you're on your way. Additionally, the chances that your motorcycle's malfunction is not in one of these three areas are slim. All that is really required from the troubleshooter is a few basic hand tools, a reasonable grasp of why the internal combustion engine works, and patience. . . .

engine will not start

Here, let's start with the most obvious possible cause (Fig. 9-1). Look in the fuel tank. Is there gasoline? You'd be astounded by the number of people who overlook this. Of course, running out of gasoline can mimic

FIGURE 9-1. Engine doesn't run. Step 1: make sure you have gasoline.

spark plug fouling sometimes, but still, make sure there is sufficient fuel in the tank. Okay, let's suppose the fuel tank has lots of gasoline in it. Our next step is to make sure the fuel tap is turned on and that fuel is flowing to the carburetor. Don't overlook the fact that there might be a low level of fuel in the tank. If your bike does not have transparent neoprene fuel lines where you can visually check fuel flow, remove the hose leading to the carburetor. Move the fuel tap to both On and Reserve positions. If liquid level is low in the tank, it may flow only in the Reserve position. If you have plenty of gasoline but none flows to the carburetor, check the fuel tap filter, if there is one, and the vent in the fuel tank cap. It is not unusual for aftermarket fiberglass tanks to have loose fibers clogging the tap (Fig. 9-2). Normally, when you buy such a tank you are instructed to rinse the thing out thoroughly before installation, but this, like all instructions, often goes unheeded. If the fuel cap vent is plugged, gasoline won't flow. Usually it is a small hole on the underside of the cap, but sometimes it is located on the perimeter or crown. Wherever it may be, make sure that air moves through it freely.

Okay, now that we have ensured that fuel is getting to the carburetor, let's investigate the ignition system. Your motorcycle's fuse

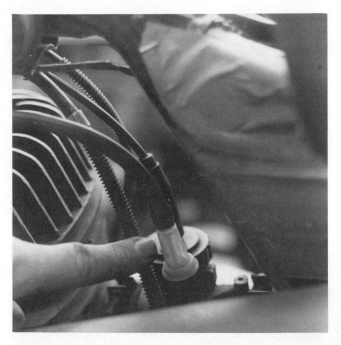

FIGURE 9-2. If your engine has a fuel filter, make sure it's not clogged.

FIGURE 9-3. Checking for spark. Spin the engine with the spark plug grounded. If all is well, spark will appear at plug end.

holder is generally located in an easily accessible area, be it under the saddle, behind one of the side covers, and so on. Has the fuse blown? This can bring a complete shutdown of motorcycle operation. If a fuse has failed, a short circuit may be evident, at worst, or the fuse may just have failed from old age. (Fuses do have a life curve that varies directly with current flow through it. Consequently, even though nothing may be wrong in a used motorcycle's electrical system, a fuse will still fail sooner or later.) Also, do not forget to examine the fuse holder for dirt and corrosion. This condition will inhibit current flow and may cause problems, regardless of how healthy the fuse itself may be.

Remove the spark plug. Reattach its insulated lead wire. Now ground the spark plug body against the cylinder or head. With the ignition switch turned on, kick the engine's starter lever through several times (Fig. 9-3). If the spark at the plug gap is a bright blue-white, you can consider the ignition to be in basically good order (spark timing

FIGURE 9-4. Opening breaker points manually with screwdriver.

excepted, but we'll get to that later). If the spark is orange or, worse, red, a condenser is bad, perhaps on the verge of complete failure.

If there is no spark at all, the plug itself may be fouled. Remove it and inspect its sidewire and center electrode for carbon buildup, excessive wetness, or perhaps a thin carbon whisker that might have grown between sidewire and electrode. These are the more obvious causes of spark plug failure. Clean the plug, regap it, and replace its lead wire. As before, ground it against the engine and test for spark. Incidentally, the spark plug porcelain should ideally range from a light brown in most four-stroke engines to a darker chocolate in two-strokes. The steel shell encircling the porcelain should have dark, slightly sooty deposits on its surface. The sidewire, or *ground strap*, as it is sometimes called, is usually cleaner and hotter looking than the rest of the plug. The spark plug should not be dripping wet or heavily carboned.

If there is no spark at a clean, new plug, it is time to inspect the breaker points. Remove the breaker point cover. Now rotate the engine until the breaker cam totally releases the cam follower on the points. With the ignition on, snap the points open (Fig. 9-4). If no spark occurs when they are opened in this way, the problem can be: (1) a bad condenser, (2) a ground in the point wiring, or (3) burned or dirty points.

You might also ground across the points with a screwdriver blade. If you get a spark this way but not by opening them manually, the point tips are inoperative.

It is important to make sure as well that the points are actually opening. Rotate the engine until the point cam follower is on the high point of the cam. At this stage, check their adjustment and make sure they are set to factory recommended specifications. Incorrect point gap can cause the engine to misfire under load and at high rpm. Also make certain that they close fully and properly.

The coil can be checked by removing the secondary lead between the coil and ignition. With the ignition turned on, ground this lead to the engine or the frame. It should spark. If not, your coil has probably failed.

If all these investigations reveal nothing faulty or even suspicious, there is the possibility that the spark is severely out of time. Some ignitions, particularly those of some high-performance two-stroke twins and multis, are especially touchy in this area. Because roadside failures rarely leave you within access of the proper timing equipment, the best you can do under these circumstances is ensure that each plug fires just a speck before its piston peaks on its compression stroke.

Okay, suppose, after all this, that thing still refuses to fire. We have made sure that gasoline is reaching the carburetor, that the spark plug is all right; ditto, the points, coil, and condenser. We have examined in order of likelihood of failure all these bits and pieces. What to do now?

Well, at this stage, we return to the carburetor. If gasoline is reaching the carburetor and the spark plug tip is dry, remove the carburetor and inspect the needle valve controlling fuel to the float bowl. This can be stuck by rust or dirt traveling through the fuel lines. Of course, if you remove the float bowl and find it bone dry right off the bat, you've found the problem. Remove the needle and seat and blow them free of dirt. Do not use pins or wires to clean passages here. Their dimensions are critical and can drastically affect engine behavior.

Four-stroke engines can have valves hang open as a result of carbon deposits and poor adjustment. This leads to lowered compression or none at all. Additionally, two-strokes have a way of gumming up, seizing, or breaking piston rings, which also seriously compromises compression. Now, it is crucial to quick starting that the internal combustion engine has sufficient combustion chamber compression. To check compression quickly, place your finger over the open spark plug hole. Kick the engine through. If your finger is forced from the spark plug hole, there is adequate compression. If it requires little effort to keep the hole covered, however, compression is inadequate and significant trouble is indicated (Fig. 9-5).

FIGURE 9-5.   With finger covering spark plug hole, kick engine over and feel for compression. If compression is minimal or nonexistent, either piston ring is broken or valve is not sealing.

engine runs poorly after starting

The likely causes of this problem are dirty air filter, bad spark plug(s), improper carburetor adjustment, improper float level, blocked carburetor jets or fuel line, wet or defective ignition leads, water condensate in float bowl, poor valve adjustment, or defective ignition coil.

The recommended procedure goes like this: Examine the spark plug (Fig. 9-6). Is it wet, sooty, or just plain worn? If none of these, is it gapped correctly? If your machine is a two-stroke, we will repeat that it is particularly susceptible to spark plug fouling, especially if it has been allowed to idle for excessively long periods. Also, if the two-stroke is burning a gasoline-oil mixture too rich in oil, it will foul plugs and keep on fouling them until it is given a better-balanced diet.

FIGURE 9-6. Spark plug fouled by black, oily coating.

Carburetor idle mixture and float level adjustments can be seemingly just slightly off and make the engine gasp, wheeze, and run most erratically. This is because intake and exhaust velocities through the ports are low, so fuel metering and exhaust scavenging are often far from ideal. If you motorcycle's carburetor is old and weathered, it may well need a rebuild because of wear throughout its rather precise passages. Carburetor rebuild kits for most carburetors, such as Amal, Mikuni, Bing, and Keihin, are easy to come by and relatively inexpensive. Also, today's carburetors are so simple, for the most part, that first timers can do the job correctly in an hour.

When tuning for low-speed smoothness, pay particular attention to idle and pilot jet adjustment, plus float level (Fig. 9-7). Unless the machine has been modified, follow factory specifications here.

Air cleaners, especially those of dirt motorcycles, do indeed get clogged. Rarely are they clogged so badly that the engine refuses to run, but they often collect enough dirt to make a definite effect on engine performance. A dirty filter element can cause the engine to run overly rich, with consequent plug fouling, excessive smoke, and rough running (Fig. 9-8).

FIGURE 9-7. Arrows point to throttle stop screw (A) and idle mixture screws (B) on Amal carburetor.

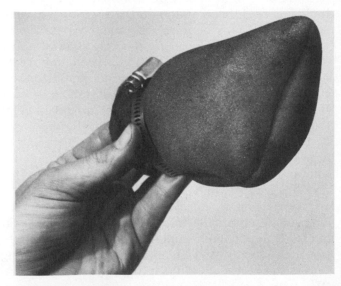

FIGURE 9-8. Soiled foam air cleaner can cause engine to run too rich.

By and large, wet ignition leads pose little challenge to the troubleshooter. After all, it is difficult to get these items wet enough to give trouble without getting the rest of the bike and yourself wet as well. Thus, when you're soaked and feeling miserable on your motorcycle, it is only logical that your sodden mount should feel the same.

Defective leads can be quite another matter, particularly in the smoggy Los Angeles basin, for example, where rubber tends to rot more quickly than it might in cleaner climes. The best medicine here, of course, is preventive maintenance and the application of rubber preservatives from time to time. If visual inspection of the leads' insulation reveals cracks or decomposition, it is time for replacement, for if they aren't causing trouble now, they probably will in the future.

Water condensate in the float bowl can mimic an ignition going sour and a host of other illnesses, so in this respect it's a real befuddler. It is very easy, however, to detect. Water will not mix with gasoline. If you have transparent fuel lines, you can sometimes see a small shot of clear fluid at the lowest point of the line, with a column of slightly darker gasoline above it. Too, upon removing the carburetor float bowl, you will find that the delineation between gasoline and water globules is apparent. Gasoline, you see, attracts water, and if you keep, say, a five-gallon can of premix in your garage, you have probably encountered this phenomenon more than once. With the lid off the can, the gasoline is bathed in moisture-bearing air. Give the air time enough to be absorbed in the confined space of the container and you'll have more than a pint or so of water in your fuel where there was none before.

Water also finds its way into float bowls when motorcycles are taken through the high-pressure spray wash booths for cleaning. The pressure is such that water is often forced up through the float bowl overflow vent of the carburetor.

Defective coils are, for the most part, rarely encountered. The things are so simple—just wire windings packed in epoxy—that barring dreadful impacts, drastic temperature changes, or manufacturing defects, they are usually troublefree.

engine runs erratically, misfiring

The causes of this ailment are much the same as those just described. Once again, it is suggested that you first examine the ignition system. Start with the spark plugs, ensuring that they are gapped correctly and reasonably clean. Inspect the spark plug cables for cracks, possible water penetration, and shortcircuiting. The breaker points, too, come under suspicion. If they are pitted, dirty, or misaligned, the engine can behave most erratically. With the methods we have described, you can also check the coil and condenser. A loose terminal or wire in the battery-ignition circuit will cause sputtering and misfiring, as will wiring chafed of its insulation (Fig 9-9). If the battery is limping along on a particularly weak charge, motorcycles with certain types of ignition systems will be adversely affected. We say "certain types" of ignition systems because there are some electrical arrangements in use today that implement the battery as more than just a storehouse for electrons. Consequently, check your battery connections for cleanliness and the battery itself for strength of charge. To do the latter, simply arc, say, a pair of uninsulated plier handles across the battery terminals. You should see a strong spark and hear a healthy "zap" (Fig 9-10). If the battery is weak, it may just sizzle weakly.

Additional causes can be water or other foreign material in the fuel, a poorly adjusted carburetor, clogged fuel tank vent, or weak or broken valve springs.

FIGURE 9-9. Make sure battery terminals are secure for good connection.

FIGURE 9-10. When battery terminals are short-circuited, strong electric arc should appear if battery is okay.

A high-speed miss can be traced to a faulty spark plug, inaccurate spark timing, a dirty air cleaner, bad gasoline, or too large a carburetor main jet. Too low a float level adjustment in the carburetor bowl will also cause a high-rpm miss, as it allows the engine to run out of fuel when it needs it most. A faulty condenser will often let an engine run smoothly at low to moderate speeds but will cause it to miss significantly at high speeds.

If the motorcycle's ignition points are adjusted to too wide a gap, its top end performance may suffer. This is because the points are open for too long throughout the engine's operating cycle and are not allowing sufficient ignition coil saturation. And, of course, the secondary ignition leads, those wires running from the coil to the spark plug, may be subject to leakage of precious voltage.

Probably one of the most vexing misses is one that occurs at a set throttle opening, regardless of engine speed. You can run yourself ragged looking for this cause. Usually, though, it can be traced to a worn, incorrect, or misadjusted carburetor needle. When inspecting this area, don't overlook the needle jet that the needle operates within. This can be clogged, scored, or worn.

If the engine misfires when it is under load but seems to run strongly and cleanly when you gear down, spark plug fouling, an over-rich air-fuel mixture, or incorrect spark timing are suspect. Visually inspect the plug. Check its gap. Is it caked with excessive carbon? Is it wet? Is it burned, with its electrode and ground strap edges rounded or deformed? Make sure as well that the spark plug is of the correct heat range. Too cold a spark plug will be prone to fouling, while too hot a plug will burn away its electrode, groundstrap, and porcelain. As a consequence, failure can come from an inordinately wide gap or short circuiting through badly eroded insulative porcelain.

The air filter should be examined for restrictive dirt buildup that will cause overrichness, particularly at wide throttle openings. If the metering needle is adjusted too high or if it is a nonstandard needle of too steep a taper, mid- to high-speed misfiring can occur.

The heavier the load placed on the engine, the more crucial is the accuracy of its spark timing. A spark occurring too soon or too late in an engine's operating cycle can wreak extensive damage in a very short time. This is because both maladies precipitate rapid and excessive heat buildup, particularly in the area of the piston crown.

Then again, make sure you're simply not lugging the engine, that is, trying to make it labor in too high a gear. Highly tuned engines, those geared for strong horsepower output at high rpm, may tend to miss or sputter if ridden incorrectly. A misfire in this case can be brought about by not allowing the engine to attain its comfortable operating speed. Although this is a problem with almost all racing motorcycles, it is not confined solely to them; some of the hotter-tempered street motorcycles around today are also susceptible. As motorcycles become more and more sophisticated, pulling more and more horsepower from relatively small displacements, such high-jinks will happen to bikes with all but the best ignition systems.

If your motorcycle's engine just refuses to attain maximum rpm in any gear, you should examine all of the areas just mentioned, plus the exhaust baffles. These items can become clogged with carbon, particularly if in a two-stroke motorcycle. A four-stroke that is well worn and uses more than a little oil during its operation may also clog its exhaust system. This malfunction can take on a couple of appearances. It may, under hard acceleration, allow the engine to rev up strongly to a point, after which it falls flat on its face. Or it may simply prevent peak revs from being attained in a more gradual manner.

Some motorcyclists enthuse over the sweet, racy smell of castor oil lubricants—and besides, it's what the racers use, isn't it? The problem is that castor-based, or "bean," oils can quickly gum up and even totally clog exhaust baffles with unburned gums and resins. Racers use the stuff because of its superb film strength and other qualities, but then racers are always tearing into their engines and gum formations have little chance to collect under such intensive maintenance. Moreover, mufflers are not items of great concern on most race tracks. Consequently, it's best to stick with the manufacturer's recommendations.

engine overheats

This can stem from several areas. A too-lean fuel-air mixture is one of the more common causes. Check that the correct carburetor jets have been installed. Inept home tuners are a machine's worst enemy, and the evidence of their bumbling handiwork is found on many a used motorcycle. The metering needle may be set a notch or two too low, thus leaning out mid-range carburetion. Also, the main jet may be too small. It is furthermore conceivable that if you have purchased a machine jetted for a higher altitude, such as that of Denver, Colorado, for example, or Albuquerque, New Mexico, its fuel-air proportions will be totally inadequate for sea level operation.

If all appears kosher in the adjustment, you should inspect the carburetor-manifold interface for air leaks as well as the intake manifold-cylinder head area. Often, an inordinately fast idle can indicate excessive leanness. If this condition comes about rather suddenly, you should make sure your intake tract is free of leaks.

Retarded ignition timing can make engine temperatures soar within a very short time. If your hitherto clean and shiny chrome exhaust pipes suddenly start bluing into discolor, the spark is likely to be excessively late. Incorrect breaker point gap, which also affects spark timing, can be at fault as well.

Of course, a new or recently rebuilt engine will have tighter metal-to-metal tolerances, so you can expect it to run somewhat hotter than a borken-in powerplant, but still, its heat output should not be excessive. Too-tight mechanical clearances, especially the piston-to-cylinder wall dimension, can ruin an engine in very short order.

If the engine has run low on oil, irreparable damage can be done from metal-to-metal contact. Oil of the wrong viscosity can also do serious harm, with overheating as an initial symptom of malaise.

Off-road motorcyclists are more likely to encounter the problem of clogging the cylinder's cooling fins with dirt. Although this is a potentially dangerous condition, it is fortunately easily detectable with just a quick visual inspection. Nonetheless, when the going is muddy, you should pay special attention that this doesn't happen.

Once again, the spark plug is also a likely culprit. If a plug has been fitted to the engine of a too-hot thermal range, overheating can result. Spark plugs, you see, are designed with an element of heat conduction in mind. Cold plugs quickly conduct heat away from the plug tip, hot plugs retain heat longer. There is a specific heat range plug for your engine, and unless your engine has been modified, you should abide by the manufacturer's specifications.

spark plugs and visual diagnosis

Much as a doctor takes your temperature, we inspect the spark plug to determine an engine's state of health. Although the examples you see in Figures 9-11 through 9-19 are extreme, these same symptoms can

FIGURE 9-11. Normal spark plug. The light tan to gray color of the porcelain in the center and the slight electrode wear indicate correct heat range.

(a)

(b)

FIGURE 9-12(a) and (b).   Gap bridging and core bridging. Particles are wedged or fused between the core nose and metal spark plug body or between the electrodes. This phenomenon is caused by excessive combustion chamber deposits striking and adhering to the spark plug's firing end. These deposits commonly originate from the cylinder head and piston surfaces. Several conditions can cause bridging: (1) excessive carbon buildup in cylinder, (2) improper oil-fuel blend (two-strokes only), (3) immediate high-speed running after prolonged low-speed running, and (4) use of nonrecommended lubricants.

FIGURE 9-13. Sustained preignition. Symptomatic of potentially serious mechanical problems, this type of spark plug has been destroyed by extremely high combustion chamber temperatures. Melted electrodes and white insulator color characterize this malady. Can be caused by (1) improper lubrication, (2) incorrect plug heat range, or (3) overadvanced ignition timing. Under no circumstances should the engine be put back into service before the problem is remedied.

FIGURE 9-14. Carbon fouled. Black, sooty deposits on plug surface inhibit good sparking. Carbon fouling is commonly caused by (1) using incorrect plug heat range, (2) improper oil-fuel blend (too much oil), (3) excessively rich fuel-air blend, or (4) worn piston rings or valve guides.

198

FIGURE 9-15. Overheating. Blistered gray or white texture of insulator indicates extremely high combustion chamber temperatures. Also, electrodes have been badly eroded. Generally caused by (1) improper spark plug heat range (too hot), (2) overadvanced ignition timing, or (3) consistent high-speed operation.

FIGURE 9-16. Wet fouled. This is characterized by a damp or wet carbon coating over the entire firing end. In some cases even sludge is formed on the unit. This is usually the result of (1) too cold spark plug heat range, (2) prolonged low-speed running, (3) excessively rich low-speed carburetor adjustment, (4) improper oil-fuel blend, or (5) worn or defective breaker points leading to insufficient spark voltage.

FIGURE 9-17. Aluminum throwoff. Aluminum deposits on electrodes and insulator core nose inhibit sparking. This is caused by preignition that melts the crown of the aluminum piston. Do not run engine until problem has been isolated and rectified.

FIGURE 9-18. Silicon fouling. Notice how the fouling deposits resemble those on the outside of the plug? This is because the engine was used without a good air cleaner in very dirty conditions. Sand was ingested by the engine and reduced to its molten state in the combustion chamber.

FIGURE 9-19. Standard spark plug, worn out. Tan to gray insulator color indicates proper heat range. Normal spark plug electrode wear is 0.001 in. per 1000 miles operation.

appear in lesser degree—with less resultant damage—if a course of routine inspection is followed.

The wise motorcyclist will not wait until his motorcycle fails to give his spark plug(s) the once-over. To someone unfamiliar with machines in general and motorcycles in particular, routine inspection is hard to get excited about. Nevertheless, it is crucial that somebody takes a peek at things regularly. This is particularly important if you have a multicylinder machine, a modified engine, or a motorcycle that spends most of its time off-road. The complexity of multicylinder motorcycles often requires more attention to details, adjustments, and so on. And even though some of these engines have proven themselves extremely reliable, no engine is so reliable that it needs no maintenance at all.

Of course, the reasons why a modified engine needs more maintenance are clear, particularly if it has been hot rodded. Often, modifying an engine means that components are called upon to do things they weren't intended to do. More intensive inspection is called for here to protect the added investment and effort.

Dirt bikes are basically toys, for recreation only. They have no real practical value. And, as a result, they are often sorely neglected. Every weekend they are used extensively, while every week they spend neglected in dark corners of the garage. Route plug inspection . . . what's that?

Troubleshooting a motorcycle does not have to be an emotional crisis for the beginning biker. It does require, however, both an understanding and an appreciation of what an engine can and cannot do. Apply this appreciation and understanding to your powerplant's three basic systems—remember? Fuel supply, ignition, and timing—and part of the battle is won already. This done, the balance of your troubleshooting success is predicated upon those other two invaluable virtues: observation and patience.

basic formulas for basic bikers

"Now, lessee . . . three tenths of a liter equals 18.3 cubic inches equals 299.88 cubic centimeters equals . . ."

Wherever motorcyclists, or any technically oriented enthusiasts, for that matter, congregate, the air is filled with specialized terminology, words and phrases that might as well be a foreign language to the layman. It can be very confusing, even frustrating, for even though you may have terrific enthusiasm for the field, you can't communicate with other enthusiasts. You can't learn what's what . . . and what isn't.

This is not to be a dissertation on motorcycle slang or a glossary; fluency in this area will come soon enough. But many beginning motorcyclists indicate that their greatest confusion comes from not understanding the basics of ratios, displacements, and other technical methods of describing mechanical things. For example, what exactly is a compression ratio? Why are some high and others low? What is meant by piston or cylinder displacement? Most of us realize that lots of cubic inches means a big engine, but just how are displacement figures arrived at?

What follows is a description of methods used to determine some of the various specifications of your motorcycle.

cylinder displacement

Basically, *cylinder displacement* is just the amount of cylinder volume. It is the total amount of air (or anything else that happens to be in the cylinder) moved in the cylinder as the piston makes one stroke in the cylinder. In other words, it is the working size of the hole that the piston reciprocates within. Figuring an engine's total displacement requires no more than the most basic high school geometry. There are two ways to do it, but the results are the same. Depending on which figures you desire—cubic inches, cubic centimeters, or liters—the arithmetic is the same. However, bear in mind the following:

One cubic inch (cu. in.) = 16.387 cubic centimeters (cc)
1000 cc = 1 liter
61.023 cu in. = 1 liter

You'll end up hopelessly confused if you neglect to make the necessary adjustments when translating back and forth from metric to our U.S. measurements.

Method 1: Cylinder diameter^2 × 0.7854 × Stroke × Number of cylinders
Example: The diameter (usually called *bore*) of an engine measures 3 inches. Its stroke is 2 inches. It is a two-cylinder engine. Thus,
$$3^2 \times 0.7854 \times 2 \times 2$$
Result: 28.2744 cu in. And if we want to translate this to cc, we multiply by 16.387 and come up with 463 cc and some change.

Method 2: This is more like textbook geometry. It goes like this:
$$Pi \times R^2 \times S \times N$$
Pi is another term for the mathematical constant 3.1416. R^2 is the radius of the bore multiplied by itself. S is the stroke and N is the number of cylinders.
Example: We have a four-cylinder engine with a 2.5-inch bore and a 2-inch stroke. Thus,
$$3.1416 \times (1.25)^2 \times 2 \times 4$$
Result: 39.27 cu in. Again, if we want the metric equivalent, we multiply by 16.387 and get 643.52 cc.

Of course, both these methods can be used to calculate displacement metrically from start to finish. Just bear in mind from the outset that while bore and stroke measurements will be given in millimeters, displacement is commonly quoted not in cubic millimeters but in cubic centimeters. This is compensated for, however, by merely moving the decimal point to the left by three positions. The Kawasaki G-31M Centurion's specifications provide a good example. It is a single-cylinder engine with a bore of 49.5 mm and a stroke of 51.8 mm. For the sake of simplicity, let's use Method 1:

$$(49.5)^2 \times 0.7854 \times 15.8 \times 1 = 99685.282 \text{ cubic millimeters (cmm)}$$
$$= 99.685282 \text{ cc}$$

(And for cu in., divide by 16.387) $= 6.08$ cu. in.

compression ratio

Compression ratio is the measurement expressing the volumetric relationship between the cylinder and the combustion chamber. Like all other such parameters in engine makeup, compression ratio is the product of deliberate design. Compression ratio affects power output, fuel consumption, piston and ring life, combustion chamber temperature, and many other elements of engine behavior. It describes in exact terms the degree to which the fresh explosive charge is compressed in the combustion chamber prior to ignition.

In mechanical terms, comparison ratio is simply this: Say we have a hypothetical engine where cylinder volume is 20 cubic inches. Its combustion chamber volume is 2 cubic inches. Let us assume that the engine is capable of 100-percent volumetric efficiency, that is, it can completely fill its cylinder with fresh charge upon intake stroke. (Because of exhaust backpressure, port design, and other factors, this is not always so, particularly with normally aspirated engines.) This means that the descending piston will draw in a full 20 cubic inches of fuel-air charge and, upon ascent to TDC, compress that charge into the 2-cubic-inch capacity of the combustion chamber. Squeezing 20 cubic inches of charge into 2 cubic inches describes an engine with a 10:1 compression ratio.

There is an important difference between this ratio as applied to two-stroke and four-stroke engines. In the four-stroke powerplant, compression ratio describes the relationship of combustion chamber volume with the piston at TDC and cylinder volume with the piston at BDC. In the two-stroke engine, however, compression ratio refers to combustion chamber volume at TDC and cylinder volume with the piston just sealing the exhaust port. (Remember, in Chapter 6 we described how the two-stroke breathes through cylinder wall ports, and among them the exhaust port is located highest.) Thus, effective charge compression does not begin to take place until the exhaust port is fully closed.

So, basically, to compute compression ratio divide the known volume of the combustion chamber with the piston at TDC into the volume of the cylinder with the piston beginning compression.

gear ratios

Grammar school multiplication is all the prowess you'll need to figure out *gear ratios*. It is important, however, that you be aware of just how many gear ratios participate in transferring power from your engine to the rear wheel. First, there is the *primary drive ratio*. Motorcycles use a geared coupling or a chain drive to transmit power from the crankshaft to the clutch, which drives the transmission. Rarely are these ratios 1:1, or *direct*, as it is sometimes called; there is a ratio reduction between crankshaft and clutch. In other words, the crankshaft is spinning faster than the transmission-mounted clutch. This is done for a variety of reasons, but primarily to slow clutch rotating speed and magnify transmission torque input. So, again hypothetically, if the crankshaft gear has 16 teeth and the clutch gear has 37 teeth, the primary drive ratio would be 2.3125:1. The same method applies to chain drives, too. It's simple arithmetic. If the drive sprocket has, for example, 19 teeth and the driven sprocket has 52 teeth, just divide the former into the latter for the reduction ratio, which is about 2.74:1.

Within the transmission, shaft speed is reduced once more to achieve a magnification of torque. In other words, power is being fed into the transmission and passes through meshing gears, with output shaft speed reduced and torque commensurately increased. Motorcycle *transmission gear ratios* vary with almost every model of motorcycle. The transmission ratios found in today's machines, however, often range from about 2.50:1 in low gear up to perhaps a 1:0.95 overdrive ratio in top gear.

The *final drive ratio* of a motorcycle occurs between the drive sprocket of the transmission and the wheel sprocket. Here torque is again, and finally, magnified. The question often arises: why? Why is all this gear reduction, torque magnification, and complication necessary? Well, to put it simply, there just isn't enough space on most motorcycles. You see, if all engine torque magnification were to take place within one gearbox, its gears would have to be large, indeed. And with big gears you encounter headaches stemming from excessive center-to-center distances of shafts, excessive weight, and other problems. As it is, engine torque is magnified a step at a time to keep components reasonably light and compact.

To determine your motorcycle's overall ratio in a given gear, you simply multiply all these ratios by one another. Let's assume our primary drive ratio (from engine to transmission) is 2.74:1. Transmission ratio—low gear in this case—is 2.50:1. Final drive ratio, with, for example, a 13-tooth drive sprocket and a 42-tooth wheel sprocket, is about 3.23:1. So, we use the formula,

$$R_o = R_p \times R_t \times R_f$$

R_o is the overall ratio, R_p is the primary ratio, and R_f is the final drive ratio. Plugging in the aforementioned figures, we come up with an overall low gear ratio of:

$$R_o = 2.74 \times 2.50 \times 3.23$$
$$= 22.1255{:}1$$

Overall ratios are calculated for all the other transmission ratios by simply using that particular value for R_t.

how to calculate top speed in any given gear

To do this requires that your motorcycle have a tachometer; most street bikes do, most dirt bikes don't. Nevertheless, the ability to perform this calculation is useful, because you can determine such things as speedometer accuracy and vehicle speed, even if you don't have a speedometer. This method is commonly used by racers to calculate the effectiveness of various gear combinations. In this way they can tailor engine power output and gear ratios to a particular race track. Three factors are required: (1) overall gear ratio, (2) tire revolutions per mile, and (3) engine rpm. You already know how to determine overall gear ratio, so next we'll explain how to ascertain tire revolutions per mile.

With the motorcycle in a vertical posture, make a chalk mark at the lowermost part of the rear tire where it contacts the ground. Roll the motorcycle straight forward; roll it to the point where the tire makes exactly three revolutions, with its chalk mark again lowermost. Mark the ground also at this point. Now measure the distance between the two chalk marks on the ground. Divide this distance by three, and you have the circumference of the tire. Why measure three tire revolutions to learn circumference and not just one full turn? Because it's more accurate. You achieve a closer-to-pinpoint figure this way. As a matter of fact, you could realize even greater accuracy by using more and more tire revolutions. But other variations creep into the picture later on that make such hairline accuracy of academic interest only.

Now that we know the circumference of the tire, we must find out how many tire revolutions will take place within 1 mile. Okay, so assume that the circumference is 6 feet, 5-3/4 inches. Just to make things easier, let's convert to decimals: 6.48 feet. This divided into a mile's 5280 feet yields 814.8 tire revolutions per mile.

Okay, so now we know the ratio of crankshaft turns to turns of the wheel. Also, we know how to calculate the overall ratio of a given gear. To calculate top speed, let's determine the overall gear ratio with the transmission in high gear. Let's assume that, as in preceding paragraphs, the primary ratio is 2.74:1 and that the final drive ratio is 3.23:1. Also, for the sake of simplicity, let's assume that the transmission high gear ratio is direct: 1:1. Thus, our overall gear ratio is 2.74 × 1 × 3.23, or 8.85:1. At this point, we multiply the overall gear ratio by the amount of tire revolutions per mile and we come up with the total amount of engine revolutions needed to travel 1 mile. In this case,

$$\text{Engine rpm/mile} = \text{(tire rev/mile) } 814.8$$
$$\times \text{ (overall ratio) } 8.85{:}1$$
$$= 7210.98$$

Bear in mind that our calculations are predicated upon engine and tire rpm . . . revolutions per minute. So, by looking at your tachometer you now have a direct correlation between miles per hour and rpm. In this case, 7200 rpm corresponds to about 60 mph. In keeping, half that—3600 rpm on the tachometer—equals 30 mph. Furthermore, 6000 rpm, 83.3 percent of 7200 rpm, equals 0.833 × 60, or about 50 mph.

Unless you're an engineering whiz, there really isn't much point in carrying these figures past one decimal point. Variables creep into the equation that must be taken into account for hairline accuracy, such as tachometer accuracy and tire expansion from centrifugal force.

To the casual or utilitarian motorcyclist, there is little value in the foregoing calculations. After all, he's concerned with getting from A to B and back with minimal fuss and bother. He's not likely to be performing tire and ratio changes in pursuit of greater performance. Racers and other competitive types, however, make mechanical changes and adjustments constantly in search of The Ideal Combination. Because of this, they see to such calculations and compensations.

how to calculate braking performance

This area can be complicated, but here we have tried to condense the necessary mathematics into their simplest form. Our formula is somewhat limited in its application however, because of this. It applies only to braking from 60 mph to 0. Of course, we could have supplied other sets of figures to allow the basic biker to calculate his bike's (and his own) decelerating performance, but unless you're proficient in such things as square roots and Newtonian physics, you're in for a fair degree of head scratching and possibly puzzlement.

Just for the record, though, we have based these figures on the following equation:

$$V^2 = V_o^2 + 2ax$$

where V = final velocity,
V_o = initial velocity,
a = acceleration,
x = distance.

The equation can also be expressed thus:

$$V = \sqrt{2ax}$$

But regardless of method, what we want to find out is, how strongly does our motorcycle decelerate? And we measure this deceleration with the same units as acceleration is measured: Gs. One G is the force of gravity. We all live at 1 G. When we jump off a diving board, we accelerate at the rate of 1 G, or 32 feet per second^2. Weightlessness is 0 G.

Have you noticed how, when the auto you're riding in accelerates abruptly, your arms and legs feel peculiarly heavy? That's a manifestation of G forces. Or, when you brake hard on your motorcycle, your wrists and forearms strain against the sudden extra load they must bear? This also is the effect of G forces. On the negative side, G forces are what crumble your bones like so many potato chips as you strike that auto making a careless turn in front of you. More succinctly, as the man shrieked as he plummeted off the tall building, "It's not the falling that scares me, it's when I hit the . . .!"

To stop an average middleweight street motorcycle at the rate of 1 G is no mean accomplishment. Indeed, most automobiles found on the highways today cannot approach the braking ability of a motorcycle. Sure, there is always some twit who'll spout, "Well, I have power brakes in my car and it can stop on a dime." Bull.

As we've said elsewhere in this book, it's easier to stop a car within its maximum abilities than a motorcycle. All the car driver must be concerned about is applying foot pressure to a pedal and maintaining a semblance of steering control. The motorcycle, however, has much greater innate stopping ability—due mostly to its light weight. To utilize this ability to its fullest, though, requires the rider to be relatively more practiced than the auto driver. The motorcyclist's physical efforts are not only confined to stepping on a single pedal, but to also squeezing a handbrake, coping with sudden forward weight transfer, and maintaining what has suddenly become a comparatively delicate balance.

Sixty mph is a good speed to use as a standard test figure. Speeds of 20 or 40 mph, for example, certainly compose the greater part of a city motorcyclist's riding spectrum. However, these speeds are still relatively slow in the overall picture when you include the freeway rider and highway tourer. Balance this at the upper end of the spectrum with the federally imposed 55-mph speed limit, which is commonly exceeded in many areas (but not necessarily by much), and our 60-mph figure becomes more representative. Also, braking from lower speeds simply does not make the brakes, suspension, and tires work hard enough. After all, during braking they're all absorbing energy at a furious rate and transforming this kinetic energy into heat.

And so we have our simple formula for calculating 60-to-0 stopping distances into decelerative G forces:

$$120.36 = G \times X$$

G is gravity force in Gs, or fractions thereof. X is braking distance from the point you first applied the brakes to the point the machine achieved complete stop. The number 120.36 is a constant. It is the mathematical shortcut, the magic number that allows us to sidestep the otherwise cumbersome physics involved.

We have excluded mention of dirt machines in relation to stopping distances because (1) tractive surfaces tend to be inconsistent at best, and (2) under most off-road conditions, 60 mph is hellishly fast.

Let's take some braking figures compiled from various magazine performance test tables. The full-dress Harley-Davidson Model FLH, although regarded as a motorcycling anachronism by many enthusiasts, still enjoys a hard core of faithful fans, even though it costs close to $4000 and weighs almost 750 pounds with fuel and oil. But to cope with its Herculean proportions, the Harley-Davidson is fitted with a double-acting disc brake at front and rear wheels. According to its test figures, the motorcycle stopped from 60 mph in 168 feet. Let's see how strong this is in terms of Gs. We solve the equation for G, so it should read:

$$G = \frac{120.36}{168} \ 0.716$$

The Moto Guzzi 850T is a well-respected heavyweight tourer, although not as heavy as the Harley-Davidson. The M-G tips the scales at 506 pounds, has a single disc brake on the front wheel and a double-leading shoe drum type of rear brake. Its 60-to-0 stopping distance was 132 feet. So, by dividing 120.36 by 132, we come up with a figure of 0.91 G, which is markedly better performance.

The Yamaha RD 400C is a highly popular machine of sporty intent. It doesn't weigh a lot (337 pounds) compared to many other machines. It has a single disc brake at its front wheel and a single disc unit at the rear. Its 60-to-0 figure is quite good: 121 feet, or 0.99 G.

Of course, the strongest stoppers in the motorcycle field are the road-racing machines. Shod with high-friction compound treadless tires (dry weather racing only!) and featuring twin disc brakes at the front wheel and a single disc at the rear, these machines are capable of stopping from 60 mph in about 86–88 feet—this, of course, with a skilled rider in the saddle. Hauling down from a mile-a-minute to 0 in, say, 87 feet yields an astonishing 1.38 G!

basic electrical stuff

Current events   The flow of electrons through a conductor is called *current*. Electrical current is measured in *amperes*. One ampere of current is achieved when 6.28 billion billion electrons pass a certain point in a conductor during 1 second. As water flow is measured in terms of gallons per minute, the rate of electron flow, current, is measured in amperes or electrons per second.

Voltage—pressure in the right places   If you have a positive charge at one end of a wire and a negative charge at the other end, current will flow through the wire. An "energy potential" exists because of these charges at the wire ends. This is because the charges have the ability to perform work by causing electrons to move through the wire. The potential energy at the wire ends is generally referred to simply as *potential*. The difference between the potentials, positive and negative, is called the *potential difference*. Another term for potential difference is *voltage* or *electromotive force*, otherwise known as *emf*. The unit of measure is the *volt*.

Thus, voltage exists between two points when you have a positive charge at one point and a negative charge at the other. And the greater the amount of electrons at the negative pole and the fewer electrons at the positive pole, the greater the resultant voltage. In other words, voltage is simply electrical pressure.

Resistance   Technically (and atomically) speaking, each atom in a *conductor* (wire) resists the removal of an electron because of the attraction exerted on the electron by the protons in the core. Also, imagine, if you will, billions upon billions of collisions between electrons and atoms as the electrons course through the conductor. What all this adds up to is electrical *resistance*. All conductors yield some measure of electrical resistance, and it is resistance that causes heat to appear in any conductor through which a current flows.

Electrical resistance is measured in *ohms*. An ohm is that amount of resistance which will allow 1 ampere to flow at an electrical pressure of 1 volt.

The ohm is named after an early pioneer in this field, Georg Simon Ohm, who lived from 1787 to 1854. He formulated what is called, logically enough, Ohm's Law. The law states that the intensity of a constant electrical current in a circuit is directly proportional to the electromotive force and inversely proportional to the resistance.

Ohm's Law can be expressed three ways:

$$\text{Amperes} = \frac{\text{Volts}}{\text{Ohms}}$$

$$\text{Volts} = \text{Amperes} \times \text{Ohms}$$

$$\text{Ohms} = \frac{\text{Volts}}{\text{Amperes}}$$

**not-essential-but-nevertheless-useful-
and-interesting department**

Horsepower and torque measurements   Metric horsepower, also called ps, is different from U.S. horsepower. The latter is a bit weaker than the former. Moreover, metric torque is predicted upon kilogram-meters as compared to the American foot-pounds. Most foreign motorcycle publications use metric measurements, as do foreign manuals, technical articles, and the like. The issue becomes particularly clear to the basic biker when he browses through specification sheets and showroom literature of some imported motorcycles. This can get confusing. . . .

As a result, the following conversion table is provided.

MULTIPLY:	BY:	TO OBTAIN:
Metric horsepower (ps)	1.014	bhp
Brake horsepower (bhp)	0.9859	ps
Foot-pounds (ft-lb)	0.1383	kg-m
Kilogram-meters (kg-m)	7.234	ft-lb

torque specifications

When working on your motorcycle, be the chores major or minor in scope, the home mechanic is often at a loss . . . and he doesn't even know it. When he is fastening mechanical components back together, the amateur mechanic's natural tendency is to reassemble the parts and then tighten up the bolts. But how tight should each nut, stud, and bolt be? There is, after all, a design limit for each type of stud on your motorcycle. Generally, these tightening limits are standard throughout the industry, unless otherwise specified. Just how much tightening torque should be applied is dependent upon the grade of metal used in the stud, its thread characteristics, and its size. The following table indicates by size of stud how much tightening torque might be safely applied to an industrially standard grade metal.

STUD SIZE	KG-M	IN-LB*
6 mm	1.0	90
7 mm	1.5	135
8 mm	2.0	180
10 mm	3.2–4.0	300–350
12 mm	4.0–4.6	350–400
14 mm	4.6–5.2	400–450
17 mm	5.87–7.0	500–600

*One-ft-lb. equals 12 in-lb

conclusion

The purpose of this chapter is to acquaint you with some of the less obvious mechanical relationships that make your motorcycle do the things it does. And in discussing such things as ratios, displacements, and such, we hope to have impressed you with the deliberation that goes into making a functional machine . . . any functional machine. Every thing, every part must work in relative harmony with every other part. Change one part of the equation and in all likelihood the whole equation will be thrown out of kilter, either overtly or subtly. As in nature, nothing happens haphazardly or without cause. There's reason in there somewhere, no matter how vexing things may appear.

11 choosing a used motorcycle

"Do you mean to tell me it's supposed to sag in the middle like that . . .?"

Buying a used motorcycle presents no small challenge to the motorcyclist. All too often, the prospective buyer has not taken the necessary steps to inform himself of such things as prevailing prices for a given model, parts and service availability for follow-up maintenance, and mechanical characteristics of that model. Under these circumstances, it is easy indeed to understand why many more motorcycle buyers than sellers end up dissatisfied with their transactions.

As a consequence, it behooves the buyer to inform himself of these and other factors. Most motorcycle salesmen are quick to point out that the majority of prospective motorcycle buyers approach the showroom woefully unprepared in several respects. First, the buyer is unclear about what type of motorcycle he wants. Furthermore, he is often equally unclear about reconciling his wants with his needs. For example, a prospective buyer may enter a showroom entertaining visions of riding away with a gloriously outfitted GL-1000 Honda four. The considerations of riding competence—after all, these things are capable of tremendous acceleration and speed and weigh about 600 pounds—and routine maintenance have been given little attention. And so the question begs, does this first-time motorcycle buyer fully realize the implications of owning such a machine? Does he realize that with a capital outlay of perhaps $3000 and the control of perhaps 80 horsepower at his throttle hand that motorcycling presents challenges of responsibility, judgment, and skill, along with the joys of boulevard cruising and wind-in-the-face exhilaration? According to many motorcycle salesmen, situations like this are not at all unusual. And it is such occurrences that put the salesman in an uncomfortable position, for he may well perceive that his customer, although smitten with a large-displacement model of perhaps somewhat specialized intent, actually requires a mount of less displacement, weight, complexity, and expense.

There are other variations on this theme. For example, the consideration of off-road riding: Many manufacturers produce a given machine in several different manners of trim. Knobby or universal-tread tires, gearing, and ground clearance are just a few of the variables in Honda's CB-, CL-, and SL-350 models. A buyer interested in a middleweight Honda twin of this genre would be well advised to appreciate the significance of these differences; that is, while the SL-350 is outfitted for dirt riding, its personality is not as well suited to extended pavement use as the more urban CB-350. Conversely, while the CB series bike may offer excellent value as a day-to-day college commuter, its taller gearing, different tires, and low-swept exhaust pipes are not very compatible with riding off the road. When you approach a dealership intent on buying a motorcycle, make sure you are clear in your own mind about what you want and what you need.

Another area in which the buyer is often ill-prepared is that of price. Of course, market value is important in all transactions. But when dealing in used motorcycles, this factor becomes doubly important. In buying a new motorcycle, the customer is confronted with fewer economic and mechanical variables. A new motorcycle on the showroom floor is assumed to be in excellent condition. It hasn't been ridden, and thus it is not worn in any way. The machine's projected longevity is at its maximum. Further, the showroom browser will find less variation in retail price from dealer to dealer; dealers generally pay the same wholesale price for a given model motorcycle.

The prospective buyer of a used motorcycle must deal with many more variables in price determination, however. Of these, his most important judgment will be to evaluate the machine's degree of wear, maintenance, and market value.

The classified advertisements in local newspapers are invaluable as a guideline in determining prevailing used motorcycle prices (Fig. 11-1). Before actually going out into the field shopping for a machine, we strongly recommend that you examine the classifieds. In doing this, you can get a fair-to-excellent appraisal of prevailing market conditions. Of course, not all models are reflected in the classifieds all the time, and if

FIGURE 11-1. The classified advertisements of local newspapers are excellent for determining the value of used motorcycles.

your heart is set upon a more exotic type of motorcycle, your gleanings may not come easily. Generally, though, if the model you desire is a major brand, perusal of the ads for several weeks may well provide you with a fairly accurate market cross section.

Another valuable aid is to have a knowledgeable friend— preferably one who is employed in the motorcycle industry—or a reliable dealer or mechanic examine the machine in question. Of course, if you are relatively foreign to the sport of motorcycling, this is easier said than done. Nonetheless, a used motorcycle can represent a sizable financial investment, not to mention the hazards posed by failure-prone machinery. So it is strongly suggested that you ask personnel at local shops for the names of competent, straight-talking technicians willing to answer your questions and perhaps examine the bike personally.

Your actual physical scrutiny of the motorcycle is of crucial importance. Consequently, we will now examine your motorcycle stem to stern, progressing from its general points to its technical aspects.

Begin the inspection with a close look at the overall finish. Is significant rust evident? If the machine has received minimal maintenance (and, of course, depending on its age), it is normal to find a modicum of rust in hard-to-get-at places. Under the fenders, the underside of the fork's triple clamp and the shock absorber and fork springs (if they are exposed) are good places to look, as well as around fender mounting bosses. If the bike has steel wheel rims, you might expect to find some slight rusting of the chrome here. Feel these surfaces if they are accessible. You see, often a telltale layer of rust can be removed, leaving a surface clean to the eye. Even though it may have been scoured from the area, however, the rusting process leaves a pitted roughness on the chrome. Of course, on easily accessible areas of the motorcycle, such as the fuel tank, fender exteriors, handlebars, headlight, and instruments, there should be nearly no rust at all. If there is, it tends to indicate that the previous owner didn't take even minimal care in maintaining its finish. The important thing here is not only to look at the motorcycle but to feel it (Fig. 11-2). Run your hand along the frame tubes, particularly in the area behind the engine near the swing arm pivot and along the swing

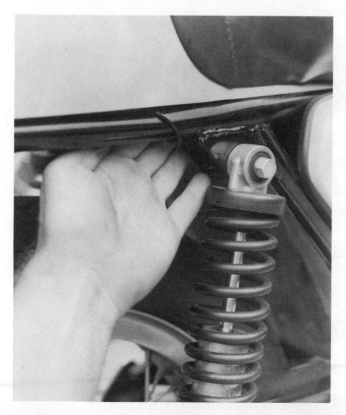

FIGURE 11-2.   Run your hand along hard-to-see frame areas, feeling for evidence of repair.

arm tubes. Feel for evidence of welds and file marks, which might indicate the bike was severely tweaked at one time and welded back together.

Next, check all electrical components, such as lights, horn, and directional signals, both with the engine off and running. The headlight should burn brightly white, of course, and not like a jaundiced jack-o-lantern, and the blinkers should blink in a reasonably sprightly rhythm. Look under the seat and closely inspect all wiring running through this area . . . there will be a lot. Most bikes mount the battery and perhaps voltage regulator here, too. Inspect for evidence of wires chafing against the frame, for this may lead to stripped insulation and shorted circuits (Fig. 11-3). Also, be sure that all electrical connections, be they soldered or of the male-female type, are soundly fastened.

FIGURE 11-3(a) and (b). Inspect for evidence of wires chafing against the frame.

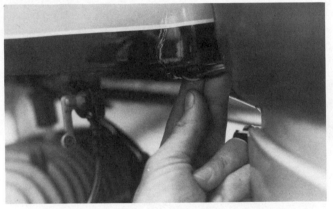

(a)

(b)

FIGURE 11-4. Examine the air cleaner element. Dirt here can indicate serious neglect and worn engine internals.

Many motorcycles have their air filters located under the seat. If
your particular bike does, by all means pop open the filter housing and
look at the element. The air filter is an oft-neglected component of
motorcycles, and a dirty one is a sure tipoff of a lazy owner (Fig. 11-4). If
the bike you're inspecting is powered by a two-stroke engine, this point
becomes doubly important. (As you may know, the two-stroke engine in
its operating cycle ingests its intake charge directly into the crankcase.
Feed a little dirt in here and the bearings may suffer irreparable damage.)

Most fuel tanks are easily removed for quick access to wiring and
throttle cables (Fig. 11-5). Tell the salesman you want a look-see. He may
very well balk at this suggestion, particularly if the tank is not easily
removable, but if hc does, he will hopefully feel that much more defen-
sive, too. If you do have such an opportunity, however, examine cable
sheaths for chafing and kinking. A stuck throttle or a frayed clutch cable
can stem from inordinate wear in this area, with potentially tragic
results.

FIGURE 11-5. Clutch, throttle, and oil pump control cables are commonly routed under the fuel tank. Remove the tank and examine these for fraying.

Other things to do: Most batteries today are made of transparent plastic, making it easy to check fluid level; otherwise, just unscrew the battery caps and inspect as you normally would (Fig. 11-6). A battery that has been run dry too often or too long, or one that has been recharged too many times, has a severely limited lifespan. Look at the metal areas surrounding or near wire connections. Sometimes you will encounter scorched paint or a rusted spot where the paint has been burned away from a loose connector shorting against the metal. Generally, the most trouble this causes at the time is a zapped-out fuse. Occasionally, though, it will result in burnt wires and melted insulation, or worse. Take your time and look around.

The most highly stressed area of the motorcycle frame is the steering head. Examine this area carefully for cracks or any other irregularities. The constant acceleration and deceleration of the motorcycle try to bend the steering head one way, while left and right turns try to twist it laterally. This is why the steering head is so stoutly braced in motorcycles; the stresses here are enormous. Study this section of the frame with eyes and fingers. Hot tip: Look for new paint here. Cracks arising from metal fatigue can be quite small and concealable with a coat of paint. Once again, look for nonstock welds, irregularities, file marks, and the like.

Your next big move is to put the bike up on a stand where both wheels will be off the ground. If the salesman says he has nothing like this in his service department, then go to your car, pop the trunk open, and get out your sturdy milk crate. Center the bike up on this and prepare to give the running gear an in-depth examination.

First, point the front wheel straight ahead. Now carefully look at the machine from head-on. Be especially picky that the front and rear wheels line up visually. They should be parallel in all respects. Study the machine front and rear. Get down on your knees. Check that neither wheel is cocked even the slightest bit in relation to the other. If you perceive the slightest deviation here, be extremely wary and prepare to call it quits then and there. The reason for this is that frame work is almost always a great hassle, usually involving lots and lots of work. Only if your continuing investigation reveals the misalignment to be rooted in something relatively minor, like an out-of-round rim or even an improperly seated tire on a straight rim, should you go ahead with the deal. Very often, however, you will encounter bent forks, axle, rear shock absorber, or swing arm that cause wheels to wander creatively. These items can be replaced *at a cost* without too much trouble, and if the frame is okay, you will have to make the decision about whether to pursue this further or go away.

If the salesman suggests that he'll knock a few dollars off the price in light of this, make sure he knocks off enough to pay for *new*, straight components. Additionally, the dealership should make the repairs, no matter what financial adjustments are made and before any money changes hands.

FIGURE 11-6. Batteries often have transparent cases. Look for varying cell fluid levels, corrosion, and deposits.

Provided nothing severely untoward has been discovered by this point, you can now check the health of each individual wheel. Start with the front; spin it fast. Look for oscillation. If some wobble is detected, keep the wheel spinning and determine if it is the rim or a poorly seated tire. Around the beads of most tires there are enough marks, moldings, and symbols to use as guidepoints in determining tire seating. No more than 1/16 inch variance should be tolerated on a street bike, and maybe 3/16 inch eccentricity on a dirt machine. If this is the cause, the tire can be seated correctly by removing the wheel from the bike, deflating it totally, breaking the bead and lathering the bead-rim interface with rubber lube. Now reinflate the tire to about twice, maybe three times, its medium suggested pressure. It should pop into place quickly.

Spin the wheel again, this time slower, while gently holding a light metal tool or perhaps a hard plastic screwdriver handle against the spokes as they go past. Listen to the sound—the tink, tink, tink. At this point we'll warn you that not all wheel designs result in the same spoke notes. Wheels with conical hubs, for example, where the spokes of one side are appreciably shorter than the other, will yield varying notes. Nonetheless, spokes of the same length should ring with pretty much the same tone. A flat-sounding clack indicates a broken or loose spoke. Of course, you should do this with front and rear wheels.

Another wheel-spinning check to perform is for wheel bearing wear. While the wheel is spinning, listen very closely for a light rattling or clicking. this would indicate that the ball bearings are loose in their races and thus sorely worn.

Also, grasp the wheel with your hands 180 degrees apart. Try to rock the wheel, alternately pushing with one hand and pulling with the other. You should feel no appreciable slack if the bearings are in good condition.

Doing this same operation on the rear wheel requires that you be more perceptive. Rocking slack can come either from wheel bearings or from worn swing arm bushings. So what you need here is a third hand. Have the owner of the third hand place his fingers at the area where the swing arm pivots at the frame (Fig. 11-7). Now, start rocking the wheel again. Does the third hand sense movement here? This is particularly important on high-speed bikes. If bushings are okay, there should be no perceptible play.

Back at the front end, it is now time to check for steering head bearing wear (Fig. 11-8). Some motorcycles use tapered Timken roller-type bearings, which are superb, at the fork pivot. Uncaged ball bearings are more the rule, however, because they do their job very well at a fraction of the cost of tapered rollers. In any event, what you do is squat in front of the bike, grasping a fork leg in each hand, and shake the fork

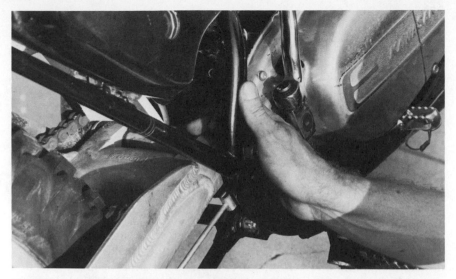

FIGURE 11-7. Place your hand on the swing arm pivot, then try to move the swing arm from side to side, feeling for play or wear.

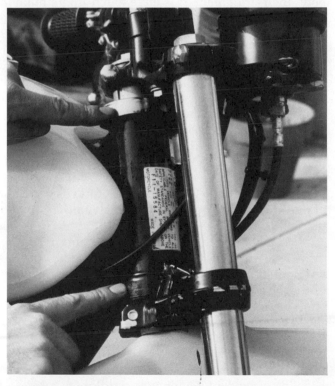

FIGURE 11-8. Steering head bearings are located here in most motorcycles.

firmly back and forth. Once again, you're feeling for play or slack where there should be none.

With the wheel still propped up, gently move the handlebars from lock to lock. Do you feel any inconsistency, any binding? Do this slowly several times. If the fork crown center nut were overtightened at one time, the bearing races could be dimpled by the balls pressing into them. This could cause tacky steering response and rapid bearing wear.

Be wary of brand new handlebar grips and footpeg rubbers. In the event of a spill, it is these parts of a bike that are commonly ground away on the road. Remove the handlebar rubber grips and look at the handlebar itself. Are the handlebar ends coarsely scraped or gouged? If they are, the bike has probably bitten the dust sometime in its past.

Exhaust pipes, too, often take a beating when the bike is dropped, so carefully inspect the flanks and undersides of exhaust pipes and mufflers. Look for areas where the chrome plating has been scraped off.

Another oft-overlooked area of the used motorcycle is the license plate. Is it bent? Or better, does it show evidence of having once been bent, then straightened? Is there touch-up paint on the plate's letters or numerals? Commonly, if a motorcycle sustains any damage at all in an accident, it will be a bent license plate. In trying to refurbish a crashed machine, a dealer can be expected to go to the extent of replacing the obviously damaged and severely tweaked components. Replacing a license plate, however, is somewhat of a different matter, for it involves dealing with the motor vehicles department of your state, which can be a troublesome, time-consuming affair. As a consequence, scrutiny in this area may well be revealing.

Also, directional signals, particularly the rear ones, are wont to break off on impact. And if, for example, a bike has both front and rear directional blinkers seemingly intact, take another closer look. This time, sight down the length of the motorcycle with an eye for the signals of one side being cocked suspiciously, either upward or downward in relation to the other.

Another possible tipoff that at one time or another the bike has been thrown down the pavement is at the rear axle. Look to the area where the nut tightens at the axle end. Often after an accident the axle nut and part of the axle itself are beveled away from scraping along the street. In a effort to make things serviceable again, the owner will often just replace the severely gnarled axle nut while retaining the axle, which may be beveled somewhat but still usable.

If the machine you are inspecting is fitted with a saddle conspicuously newer than the bike itself, there is yet another chance that it has been in an accident. Motorcycle saddles have a way of being ripped and gouged in a spill, and they are easy to replace. This is not to say, of course, that if its upholstery isn't pristinely new you shouldn't purchase the bike. Not at all. What we are saying is that you as a prospective buyer should take into consideration the saddle, the axle nuts, and all the other items we have discussed thus far in making your decision. If the bike falls short in one area alone, you shouldn't kibosh the entire deal. Instead, use the imperfections you have discovered to better your bargaining position.

Chain and sprocket wear are easy to determine. Further, maintenance of the motorcycle in this department generally serves as a fairly accurate guide in judging the bike's overall past maintenance. First of all, how is the chain's adjustment? Is it excessively loose or tight? Either way is an indicator of poor maintenance. If you're not sure just how tight or loose the chain should be, most owners' manuals typically specify somewhere between 1/2- and 3/4-inch vertical play at the chain's loosest point between the sprockets. Also, does it appear that the chain has been lubed, or is it dry, perhaps rusted? Further, chains also have tight links from time to time. This happens most often as the result of poor lubrication. However, this condition develops occasionally in well-cared-for chains, too.

As a rule of thumb, if you can pull the chain away from the wheel sprocket to where more than one half the underlying tooth is revealed, the chain should be replaced (Fig. 11-9).

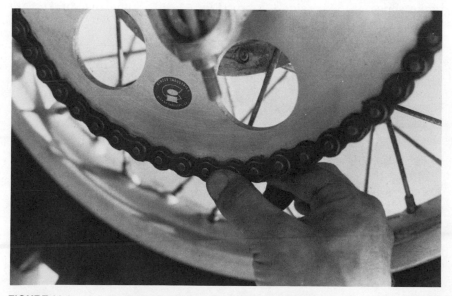

FIGURE 11-9.   A chain in good condition and adjustment should not be able to be pulled more than halfway up the sprocket tooth.

If the motorcycle you are scrutinizing is one of the superbike genre (such as Kawasaki 1000 or 750; Honda 750; Ducati Sport or SS), be particularly picky in this area. These big bores, especially those of Japanese manufacture, can munch chains and sprockets with regularity if the owners don't maintain them properly. On the other hand, if you encounter such a bike fitted with one of the aftermarket superchains or, better yet, dual-row chain and sprocket assemblies, it can definitely be a step in your favor.

Look to the sprocket teeth for deformation and side wear. A poorly adjusted or ill-lubed chain can recontour sprocket teeth in surprisingly short order, for chains are made of extremely hard metal, much harder than that of the sprocket. And, unfortunately, chances are that if you have to replace one, you'll also have to replace the other, too.

While you're in this area of the motorcycle, inspect the chain adjusters at the swing arm ends. Are the adjusting screws relatively even on each side of the axle? If not, why not? If one adjuster nut differs appreciably in setting from its counterpart on the other side of the wheel, it may indicate that the misadjustment is purposeful to compensate for a bent frame, swing arm, or shock absorber.

Other items to check are brake and clutch adjustments. Is there room left in the linkage for further adjustment? For example, if you find that the front brake has little authority without its adjusters extended to their limits, the brake cable is either sorely stretched or, more likely, the brake shoes are excessively worn (Fig. 11-10). Some rear brakes are

FIGURE 11-10. Examine control cable adjustments for signs of cable stretch and wear.

operated by rods instead of cables, but there are still adjusters in the linkage to inspect, and the principle is the same. Also examine the clutch linkage in this manner. Must all its adjustment be taken up before the clutch releases completely? Even then, does it slip? If so, the clutch plates are likely badly worn and in need of replacement.

By now, of course, the seller of the motorcycle should be convinced of your sincerity. After all, the type of examination you've just given the machine is hardly typical of the casual browser. Consequently, he should not seriously object if you request a trial ride. You see, it is at this point in the regimen, now that you are more than a little familiar with the motorcycle, that its operational traits are checked. It's time for a test ride. This part of the examination is crucial, for not only do we determine here if the thing starts, goes in a reasonably straight line, and stops on command, but we also probe the bike for less obvious shortcomings. And while before you used your eyes and hands to examine the bike, this part of the check-out requires your sense of hearing.

It goes without saying that motorcycles make noise. As a machine—a conglomeration of whirring, threshing, reciprocating, spinning pieces of metal—it has to make noise, at least certain types of noise. What we're going to do at this stage is try to discriminate between noises normal and acceptable in the machine's operation and those abnormal and symptomatic of incipient mechanical headaches.

So, on this your test ride, be especially sensitive. When the engine is kick-started cold, you may expect it to be somewhat noisier than it will be after it has warmed up. This is because the clearances between moving parts in the engine are generally larger when the powerplant is cold. As it reaches normal operating temperature, the metal parts within expand and take up mechanical slack. Also, as temperature rises from cold to normal, engine oil thins slightly and circulates with greater freedom. (Incidentally, it is for this reason that, as a rule, about 95 percent of an internal combustion engine's wear during its life occurs when it is cold!) In any event, however, due to this initial coldness, you will be likely to encounter piston *slap*. This noise is usually a gentle clatter occurring as the engine idles and when the throttle is blipped under a no-load condition. Piston slap is characteristic of almost all two-stroke engines. Sometimes it can be subtle, as in the case of a GT750 Suzuki, or it can be quite loud, as in the Kawasaki 750 Triple. The slap is due to the piston rocking on its wrist pin in a bore where clearances are overgenerous. After a few minutes of warm-up, the slapping sound should subside significantly. Other engines, predominantly four-strokes, are assembled to much closer tolerances and thus should exhibit no piston slap at all. The Harley-Davidson V-Twins and the Moto Guzzi 750 and 850 motorcycles, for example, are assembled to very exacting specifications; ditto, the fabled BMW motorcycles. Hearing piston slap in these precision mounts may bode ill, indeed.

Overhead camshaft engines, such as the Hondas, Yamaha 500 and 650 Twins, and Kawasaki 1000, exhibit very little noise from the valve train, with the exception of some possible cam chain whir. You should hear just a very gentle, evenly spaced whirring and clicking from the cylinder head area. If there is a tap, tap, tap that is predominantly stronger than the others emanating from the engine's top end, it may well be a poorly adjusted valve. Incidentally, for isolating an engine's various sounds you can use a screwdriver as a stethoscope. Simply place the point of the tool on the engine and place its handle against your forehead or temple. Sure, it may look funny, but you'll be amazed at how accurately mechanical sounds can be defined. Of course, better yet is the kind of stethoscope made specifically for mechanics. It is carried in precious few motorcycle shops but most larger auto supply houses sell them for $8 to $12.

Many British Twins will display an easily detectable double knock at idling speeds. It can best be described as a tick-tock, tick-tock. Such a noise may indicate a worn piston pin. British Twins are also famous for leaving drops of this and that wherever they are parked, like an errant terrier. For the most part, this is normal, unless, of course, the puddles form as quickly as oil is poured into the machine.

A roller bearing on the verge of failure emits a whine or screech. This sound will probably be most evident with the engine under load, usually accelerating. This noise will be coming from the lower end, or crankcase, rather than farther up in the powerplant.

Engines using pushrod-actuated valves are usually noisier in normal operation than overhead cam types. Thus, the aforementioned Moto Guzzi and BMW, while both are extremely well muffled, may display what seems to be an inordinate amount of valve noise. Actually, though, it is due to the contrasting ticking of the tappets and the superbly muted exhausts.

Upon acceleration, does the engine ping? This may mean poor fuel mixture, inaccurate timing, or cruddy gasoline. Whatever the cause, pinging, an extremely destructive phenomenon, must not be tolerated in an engine. Excessive carbon buildup in the combustion chamber will also cause pinging, as will an incorrectly sized or misadjusted carburetor metering needle.

If, upon acceleration, you encounter a more regular, deeper knocking or clunking, it may be worn insert-type bearings. This symptom is encountered mostly on four-strokes because plain bearings are generally impracticable in two-strokes. Once again, the British Twins are more susceptible to this malady than our more contemporary multicylinder mounts from the Orient. In all fairness, we should say that such machines as BSA, Triumph, and Royal Enfield are not inherently faulty in their design. It is just that most service managers regard them as more demanding in terms of maintenance and less forgiving when such maintenance is not performed properly and regularly.

In checking the general valve condition of a four-stroke engine, kick the start lever through slowly or, better yet, have some one do it for you. While the engine is being squeezed up past compression, listen closely at the exhaust opening at the intake opening. A loud hiss of escaping air heard through an exhaust pipe indicates a poorly seating exhaust valve. A hiss heard through the intake tract means the same for that valve.

Hopefully, you will not encounter any misfiring during this trial run. Two-strokes often encounter the most misfiring problems, because oil is burned with the fuel and cylinder scavenging is characteristically effective only with a relatively narrow rpm band. Consequently, the spark plug gets dirty. Furthermore, the higher the engine's specific output—the hotter its state of tune—the more likely this is to happen. Road-racing motorcycles exemplify this condition clearly. (The author recollects riding a rare 50-cc Tohatsu Twin. The tachometer didn't even register below 7000 rpm, while the engine refused to run below 9000 rpm. Usable power began at 11,500 rpm and lasted up to 15,500 rpm! And this machine is woefully obsolete in comparison to today's 50-cc racers, mounts which now rev well past 20,000 rpm and produce close to 8 horsepower per cubic inch!)

If your engine misfires under load, you should first inspect the spark plug(s). If the plug is relatively clean and gapped correctly, it's time for troubleshooting, which is covered in Chapter 9. Besides, the seller should be doing the troubleshooting. Not you. Bring the bike back and tell him that the thing does indeed miss. With luck, he'll be willing to check into the matter then and there.

An invaluable tool to have along when bike shopping is a compression gauge (Fig. 11-11). This item fits into the spark plug hole and reads combustion chamber pressure as the engine is kicked through its compression stroke. Factory literature gives recommended compression pressures. If you don't have it available, use this *very general* set of figures:

IF THE CYLINDER DISPLACES:	THE GAUGE SHOULD READ:
50 cc	100 psi*
80 cc	100 psi
90 cc	100 psi
125 cc	112–130 psi
250 cc	135–155 psi
350 cc	150–175 psi

*Pounds per square inch.

FIGURE 11-11. Use a compression gauge to determine the state of health of piston rings and valves.

If you're examining an engine with two or more cylinders, the compression spread between the cylinders is possibly a better indicator of cylinder condition. If all cylinders on, say, a Honda four read within 15 psi of each other, things are probably in pretty good shape. As a matter of fact, you can apply that 15-psi figure to most bikes. If the pressure differential between combustion chambers is greater than this, a ring or valve job, or both, may well be in order.

Okay, so you've discovered a pressure discrepancy in this hypothetical Honda, how do you know if it is caused by poor rings or bad valves? Simple. All you have to do is squirt a healthy dollop of motor oil through the spark plug hole of the low-reading cylinder. Now check the compression again. If the reading remains unchanged, the engine has a valve hanging open. If, however, the compression reading goes up appreciably, it means the piston rings are worn.

As you ride the motorcycle, try to make the clutch slip. By this we don't suggest you abuse the bike, but do make full-throttle gear changes. These will often bring out latent weakness. Also, if you have access to a freeway or expressway, take the motorcycle up to fast cruising speed in high gear. Now lightly squeeze the lever until the plates begin to slip. Applying throttle, do this several times rapidly in succession, much like pulling the trigger of a semiautomatic rifle. Listen to the engine carefully, or at least as best you can under the circumstances. Does the rising and falling of engine revs coincide with your engaging and disengaging of the clutch? It should.

Bring the bike to a stop now, once your curiosity about the engine's health is sated. Clamp on the front brake and repeatedly throw your weight forward against the handlebars, compressing the front suspension. Do you notice any noises, any clunks? Only if there is a slight amount of accepted play in the brake anchoring system should any noises be heard from here. (This excepts those types of forks that are vented directly to the atmosphere, for they make a definite wheezing sound, which is normal.) Inspect the fork legs and wipers for oil seepage (Fig. 11-12). There should be no leakage. Of course, not all suspensions

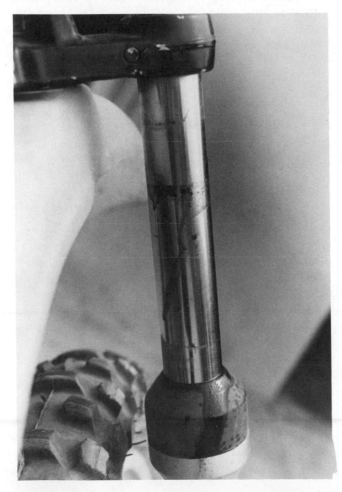

FIGURE 11-12. Oil on fork stanchions indicates leaky oil seals.

are made the same, and some characteristically leak more than others. Once again, we return to the British motorcycles, which not uncommonly leak here. The forks of the Spanish Bultaco, although an excellent high-performance component, also seem to need little provocation to leak oil.

No rear shock absorber should leak at all. If there is telltale seepage on the rear shock absorber, its days are likely to be numbered. This is not to be confused, however, with an extremely thin layer of oil sometimes appearing on a shock shaft. Depending upon the design of the wiper and seals, this may be their intended *modus operandi*. The same goes for front forks, too.

If you encounter a set of aftermarket shock absorbers of good repute on a machine of Oriental manufacture, the previous owner may have done you a real favor. Typically, Japanese original equipment shock absorbers are oversprung and underdamped, and the addition of such shocks as S&W, Koni, or Girling, for example, can account for a vast handling improvement, particularly on a used motorcycle.

Although the tenor of this chapter is based upon negotiating with a dealer, the rules of the game are much the same as when dealing with a private party. A private seller cannot offer a warranty to speak of, but such enticements are often of marginal value in used bike transactions. To boot, the dealer's price of a machine may exceed the private party's price by as much as 30 percent. The dealer, however, can offer conveniences of his own, such as parts and service.

Either way and regardless of circumstances, the decision is yours and yours alone.

index

Valve
  desmodromic, 118
  exhaust, 111, 113
  float needle, 129
    troubleshooting of, 187
  intake, 111, 113
  overhead, 115–118
    illustration of, 117
    troubleshooting of, 187
  reed, 121–123
  rotary, 121–122
Vincent motorcycle company, 13–15
Vise-Grip, 79, 150

W

Walker, Otto, 26
Water content in environment, 105
Water
  driving technique in, 90–92
Werner brothers, 2

Work, 108
Wrench
  allen, 146
  hand
    box, 152
    combination, 152
    open-end, 151
  handle of, 148
  socket
    six-point, 146–147
    twelve-point, 146–147
  torque, 153–154
    beam, 154
    dial readout, 154

Y

Yamaha motorcycle company, 21
  RD-56 model of, 21
  racing of, 28